BOOK REVIEW
Robert J. Bruss

Jay's best-selling book; "INVESTING IN FIXER-UPPERS", ruined my vacation! As I was leaving on my trip, I bought a copy at the airport bookstore. At every opportunity on my vacation I read this book, which is almost impossible to put down because it offers so many unique "how to get rich" in real estate ideas.

After working more than 20 years for the telephone company, Jay decided to quit and become his own boss. With limited savings, he elected to begin investing in lower income rental properties. Needing cash to live on, Jay concentrated on buying small multiple unit property (6-12 units).

According to Jay, lower down payments and seller financing are two key benefits acquiring rundown properties from motivated sellers. Fixing tenant problems with better management and better paying tenants often pays as much as fixing up the property; according to the author! Jay calls this tenant cycling!

Considerable emphasis is placed on the types of improvements to make, which will raise the rental income and the property value. Jay calls this his "Foo-Foo" technique, making only profitable improvements, which will add value.

Buyers of ugly properties can get the best terms, says Jay. "Sellers of older ugly problem properties are not in position to be very picky about whom they sell to. They can't play hardball with price and terms like owners of higher quality, nicer-looking properties can."

This book review by the late Robert J. Bruss, nationally syndicated real estate columnist was published as a special to the San Francisco Chronicle, August 10, 2003. Jay's book "INVESTING IN FIXER-UPPERS", was voted the no.1 real estate book for 2003.

PRAISE FOR JAY'S BOOKS

I just finished reading "Investing in Fixer-Uppers". It's by far the best real estate book I've read to date! Thank you for writing it! You've helped me take my investing to a whole new level! You're truly the king of "Fixer-Uppers" – thanks!

— *Ramone Walker*
Dannemora, NY

Most real estate books seem to sugar-coat many aspects of the business, especially financing and actual profits. Your books are optimistic but not outlandish like most! Thank you for bringing a dose of reality to the run of the mill "nothing down" genre.

— *Ryan Schmidt*
Lincoln, NE

I've been investing in the Chicago area for several years now! I've been reading books, going to seminars and taking courses for over 12 years. I've probably read 40 to 50 real estate books about investing – some old, some new, some terrible. Your books are by far the best I've ever read! Great job!

— *Joe Mueller*
Chicago, IL

As you can tell by the envelope – I am incarcerated, but trying hard to put my life back together! I spend all my free time reading about real estate investing, which I intend to pursue when I'm released. "Start Small, Profit Big in Real Estate" is the best book I have ever read. You have a special gift explaining things so everyone can understand. I'm convinced I'll do well following your advice! Sincerely

—*Roberto Sandoval*
Mercer, PA

I really enjoyed your book, "Start Small, Profit Big in Real Estate". It put me on the right path for what I'm looking to accomplish in my career.

— *Gluyomi Martins*
Haynesville, VA

Your books are excellent! They have given my husband and me the inspiration to get out there to start fixing and renting. We have just purchased our first property the way you recommend. Sincerely

— *Ken and Fran Holt*
Detroit, MI

I've been remodeling houses for 25 years – but only after reading your books have I decided to bring my 17 year old son into the business! Like you tell your readers; it's the best family business in the world for building wealth as a family team.

— *Mike Hague*
Akron, OH

We've just finished reading two of your books, "Investing in Fixer-Uppers" and "Gold Mine Houses". They are the best real estate investing books we've ever read. By the way, we've already applied several of your techniques to our own rental properties. Thanks so much!

— *Tad Lathrop Family*
Valencia, CA

Your book "Start Small, Profit Big in Real Estate" came highly recommended. We consider it the best how-to guide we've ever read. Thank you very much!

— *Marilyn Harris*
Bethel Park, PA

My husband and I read your house fixer book and absolutely loved it! We will certainly recommend your books to anyone who wants to improve their investment skills! Thank you!

— *D. L. Davidson*
Danville, CA

I've been reading your books and newsletters for 18 years – your books are the best for anyone wishing to become an investor. No one can explain seller financing like you do! Also, it's obvious why your strategies work because you understand dealing with people. Thanks!

— *Les Taylor*
Batesville, MS

Just finished reading your book, "Investing in Fixer-Uppers". This is the most helpful book I've ever read for the little guy starting out. Your street sense approach is a welcome insight for investors at any level. There's great value in your wisdom, especially your strategies for making sure investments will be profitable. The last chapter on long-term wealth should be required reading for every investor. Sincerely

— *A. M. Groeger*
Pt. Pleasant, NJ

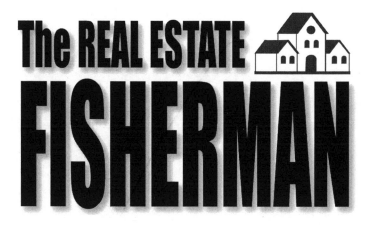

The REAL ESTATE FISHERMAN

How small time "mom & pop" investors can earn $100,000 annually - create financial security and a worry free retirement

Jay P. DeCima

KJAY Publishing Co.
P.O. Box 491779
Redding, CA 96049-1779

Published by KJay Publishing
Printed in the United States of America

ISBN 9781943290147
Library of Congress Preassigned Control Number: 2015956457

1 2 3 4 5 6 7 8 9 0 DOC/DOC 0 9 8 7 6 5 4

1. Real estate investment—United States. 2. Housing rehabilitation —United States. 3. Rental housing—United States—Maintenance and repair. 4. Financing —United States.

GIVE A MAN A FISH

AND FEED HIM FOR A DAY

TEACH HIM HOW TO FISH

FEED HIM FOR A LIFETIME

CONTENTS

INTRODUCTION

Make no mistake about it – this is a very special real estate book! Within these pages, you'll find a detailed road map that can change your financial life forever. This is not a book for people who like to read! But rather, a book for those who desire to learn! More specifically, it contains proven recipes for ordinary folks who believe that real estate investing is the path to a **better life today** and a more **secure financial future** for tomorrow!

Just like fishing, I will lead you down to the water's edge! I'll show you where all the big ones are hiding, I'll teach you which bait to use to lure them out – and I'll even show you the right way to cast your line so you don't scare the fish away. In short, I'll teach you how to become a journeyman fisherman; but in the end, it will be up to you to keep on fishin' till you're satisfied you can reel in the big ones!

This book is written and dedicated to all the *small-time*, "Mom & Pop" investors seeking **financial independence**, **a predictable source of income**, and a **worry-free retirement**. Admittedly, this sounds like a very tall order for any real estate author to fulfill, but since I'll be asking you, *the reader*, to do all the heavy lifting – my part of our educational partnership will be simply teaching you how to become a journeyman fisherman.

One of the first things I wish to do is poke a little fun at a very common, yet terribly misleading myth that says – **it takes money to make money**! Friends, this myth doesn't even qualify as a *little white lie* – it's just plain horsepucky! As you shall discover when you begin to learn more about creating wealth; many millionaires – *even billionaires*, would have never gotten past first base if having money to start was the first requirement.

Folks like the late shipping tycoon, Aristotle Onassis, who started with almost nothing and finger lickin' chicken king, Colonel Harlan Sanders who slept in his car while peddling his herbs and spices! Skin care queen, Mary Kay Ash, was close to penniless before her beauty products started catching on with the ladies. And Mr. Sam Walton, founder of Wal-Mart Inc., had to borrow money on his house so he could open his first dinky little variety store in Rogers, Arkansas.

The more you read about creating wealth, the more you'll understand that waiting around for enough money to get started is probably one of the most over-worked excuses for doing nothing. It has almost no bearing on whether you'll be successful or not! What counts the most is that personal dream buried deep inside yourself that never goes away and that teeny little voice that keeps telling you that one day, somehow, **you're gonna make it big**, even as you struggle to pay your bills today.

I wrote REAL ESTATE FISHERMAN to help make your dream come true! Obviously, **your actions** – or what you do with the knowledge I'll share will decide the issue. Just remember, it's not nearly enough to read a book that simply inspires you! That's like eating a big fish dinner which only satisfies you till you're hungry again! **With my help, you'll have the knowledge to feed yourself for life.**

Much like a live training seminar, I'll explain my best techniques and strategies several different ways in the various chapters throughout my book! This was not done because I'm senile or forgot, but rather; to make "dead-bang" certain you understand for yourself. I will promise you this much – by the time you've finished reading, you'll know how to catch the big ones while your friends are still trollin' for minnows!

<u>Winners are different because they never quit!</u> Most of those around you will – *and when they do*, you'll feel left alone and totally out of step. This is where you must rely on that personal dream and keep chargin' forward even though your closest friends will believe you've finally lost your marbles. **Persistence, determination** and yes, even **stubbornness** will provide your best defense! I think the following quote from our 30th president, Calvin Coolidge is most appropriate here:

> **Press On: Nothing in the world can take**
> **the place of persistence. Talent will not;**
> **nothing is more common than unsuccessful**

men with talent. Genius will not; unrewarded genius is almost a proverb. Even education will not; the world is full of educated derelicts. Persistence and determination alone are almighty.

Read on apprentice fishermen and let's get started! Pay particular attention to where I suggest you start fishin' and the type of properties I recommend so you can quickly catch a limit.

After you've read this book **several times** and you're satisfied you understand about how and where to fish – it's time for action! I'll end my introduction with my version of that popular ol' adage you've likely heard before: **"I can take you down to the river's edge, but I can't make you fish!"** That, my friends, **you must do for yourself.** My goal is to make you a master fisherman!

HAPPY FISHIN'

CHAPTER 1

IT'S TIME TO GO FISHIN'

*M*ake no mistake about it – you can make a ton of money investing in real estate almost anywhere, anytime and *regardless whether the economy is good or bad*. Perhaps more importantly, most people can learn the skills fairly easy, and eventually earn more money than they ever dreamed possible.

Contrary to what many folks think – it doesn't take a lot of money to get started once you learn how to invest in the **right kind of properties** to begin with. New investors, without a great deal of money to start, should concentrate on acquiring affordable rental properties, because they generate spendable cash flow much faster than other types of real estate!

In these chapters, I'll share my trade secrets and show you why **investing my way** can be your ticket to **financial freedom** and a **worry-free retirement** if you'll stay the course and follow my directions.

TWO IMPORTANT FREEDOMS

Successful investors should always be concerned with two different kinds of freedom! The first kind is the one most people generally talk about, **financial freedom** – *the end of money worries, tight budgets, and trying to save enough for a rainy day*. **Financial freedom**, for most people, means going on expensive trips, shopping wherever they please, and *never running out of money*. Simply stated: for the great majority of folks, it means living the life they've only dreamed about.

The second kind of freedom is called **personal** freedom, and it becomes extremely important after you've achieved the first kind. Money will quickly lose its insatiable appeal if there's never any time to spend it. In fact, many people will gladly give some away in exchange for more personal freedom.

CASH FLOW KEEPS YOU GREEN AND GROWING

Over the years, **investing for cash flow** (my number one priority), has paid big dividends for me. **Cash flow** is what I always advise new investors to think about first. It's the fundamental reason for investing in the first place. When you have cash flow, or **money coming in**, you are growing financially. I call this *"green and growing."* When you are green and growing, all things are possible, *investment-wise*. Without money coming in, nothing grows; except discontentment and the constant worry about pending financial disaster!

Making cash flow a *top priority* is one of the most important differences between **smart investing** – which is what most of us believe we're doing when we buy a property – and **speculating**, which most of us should definitely not be doing. I'll be the first one to admit, smart investing may not be nearly as exciting as speculating. However, it's much healthier financially. Folks who intend to stay in the real estate investing business for the long haul have no good reason to speculate until their bank account is large enough to sustain a heavy jolt – *that means taking a loss!*

TWO POWERFUL WEALTH BUILDERS

Adding value to older, rundown, multi-unit residential properties is one of the fastest, most predictable ways for new investors to achieve cash flow in the shortest amount of time. The reason for this is because these kinds of properties allow the maximum use of two powerful wealth builders – namely, **leverage** and **compounding**.

Leverage allows investors to "put up" a small amount of money (sometimes none) to purchase and control an expensive income property – for example, $30,000 to acquire a **$300,000** property. *In leverage lingo*, that's a 10 to 1 leverage ratio, which is considered very high.

For instance, let's say an investor cleans, paints, and makes inexpensive improvements to his $300,000 property, so that after one year its value has increased to $390,000. In this example, he's earned a **whopping 300% return** on the $30,000 he paid down. In just one short year, his initial down payment has grown to **$90,000** more equity or ownership! No other kind of investing I know of can earn *three times* its original amount in just one year's time! This kind of leverage, when coupled with the awesome power of *compounding*, can earn ordinary Mom and Pop investors extremely high profits. It's the magic that can turn small-time, ordinary real estate investors into **wealthy tycoons**.

Compounding can create extraordinary wealth for investors who will buy and upgrade income-producing properties. Renting them out and allowing them to grow in value is the fastest way to build long-term wealth. Allow me to explain why: *buying*, *improving*, and *keeping* your property works something like an interest bearing savings account, where both **the principal and interest** are allowed to accumulate and keep growing bigger and bigger. The results will simply blow you away!

Let's say for example that I convince you to put $1000 per month in a bank account that pays you 12% annual compound interest. You must promise me you'll never withdraw or borrow any money, including interest or the principal for 20 years. Can you guess how much you'll have earned at the end of 20 years? Would you ever imagine you'd be a **millionaire**? Well, almost anyway! **You'd have $989,255 in your bank account.**

Wow Jay, that sure sounds like an awful lot of money – but I'm just kinda thinkin' out loud here – *20 years equals 240 months*. When I multiply $1000 per month times 240, I only come up with $240,000! That's quite a bit shy of a **million bucks**! Where on earth does the rest (**$749,255**) come from? The answer, my friends, is **compound interest earnings**. Compound earnings will make you filthy rich if you allow your profits to keep earning more profits.

You might be thinking – sure Jay, all this sounds just "peachy" – but where am I supposed to find $1000 every month for twenty years?

You'll be using your leveraged real estate, that's where! Remember the $300,000 property that we increased in value to **$390,000** in just one short year?

You'll recall, we only paid $30,000 down – but after just one year of fixing, cleaning, and selected improvements, we created **$90,000 worth of additional value**! Had we instead invested our $30,000 down payment to earn interest income – say 12%, which would be considered very good today, our total earnings at the end of one year would be a mere $3,600. Making profitable improvements, like painting and clean-up work, earned us **300%** in just one year because we forced up the value **of the entire property**, not just the down payment portion! This is the result of 10 to 1 leverage, or as it's often called, **forced appreciation**. It's the awesome power of leverage at work! There's just one small catch to this forced appreciation business: you must choose the right vehicle (**the right kind of property**). A property that allows you to quickly jump in with a minimum down payment, and begin making profitable improvements right away! Underline this next sentence and keep repeating it to yourself! Buying the right vehicle (**the right property**) is the secret to success using this strategy. You simply can't drive to the mountaintop in a regular passenger car – you need a more powerful vehicle. Properties like my Cherry Street (Chapter 2) are a perfect example of the right vehicle.

Having no money for the down payment should never stop investors who are ready and willing to substitute their personal skills, such as labor, in lieu of a cash down payment. Beginners have said to me: "Jay, I'm willing to spend everything I've got to become successful, but **here's my problem** – I just don't have any money right now." My answer to them – okay, fine! **How about let's use what you have right now?** Quite often, for beginners – what they have right now is **time** and **ambition**. Assuming they have both, I've got some wonderful news. Time and ambition, mixed with training and education, such as my home study courses, or investor training seminars, will give new investors enough knowledge to get started immediately. **The opportunity is now.** It's time to fish or cut bait!

Getting started ranks at the top of my list for becoming a wealthy investor. In fact, starting is the biggest difference between investors who become financially independent – *and those who only wish they were*. Many folks have high hopes and the best intentions, but they always seem to be waiting for something to happen. Whatever is supposed to happen **seldom does**. Waiting to save up the money for a down payment is probably the world's most overworked excuse for doing nothing. Many successful investors I know started with hardly any money at all. Instead, they use personal efforts, called **sweat equity**.

MULTI-UNIT PROPERTIES ARE BIG LEAGUE MONEY-MAKERS

A small rundown apartment – or small group (6-10) of ugly-looking houses renting for only $500 today, but located in a $700 rental area, are the kind of properties that work extremely well using my **adding value techniques**. To start with, I would likely pay about *seven times the gross annual income* for units renting at $200 below the normal market rents in my town. Let's say I find six small rundown houses, cottages, or even a mobile or two all together on a large city lot, renting for an average of $500 each. That equals $3000 per month rent, or **$36,000 annually**. Let's assume I'm able to purchase the property for seven times the annual gross rents (7 x $36,000 = $252,000). Now I'm ready to start cleaning up the property and begin making profitable improvements so I can gradually increase my rents to market rates ($700). I generally allow myself 18-24 months to accomplish this task using my rents to help with expenses. Similar units in the surrounding neighborhood are all renting for $700 per month – **why the difference**, you ask? It's because they look better and they're well maintained. Naturally, renters are willing to pay more for nicer looking and well maintained units.

On the following page, Figure 1-1, you'll see my sketch of a typical six-unit property like I'm discussing here. Please don't grade me on my artwork – remember, *I'm an investor, not an artist*! The fastest profits you'll ever make can be yours if you'll jump right in and clean up these unsightly houses, both inside and out.

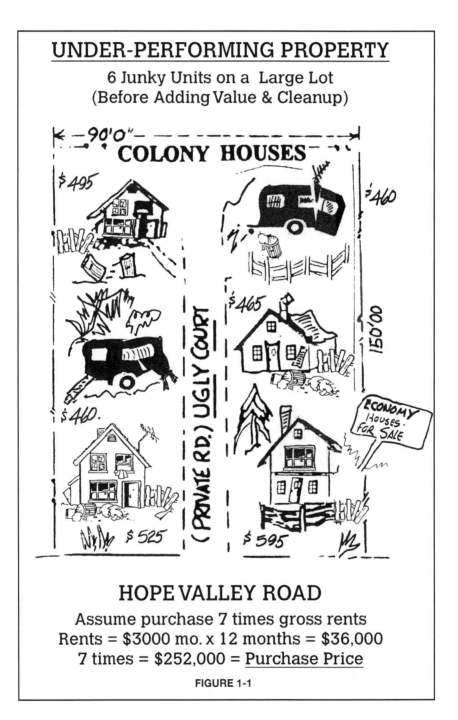

FIGURE 1-1

CREATING VALUE IS THE MAGIC

After clean-up and selected improvements, rents can gradually be increased to current market rates of $700 per month. **More income equates to a higher property value**, because investors are willing to pay more for a bigger income stream. In addition, clean, attractive properties with current market rents will sell for a higher **rent multiplier**, because the demand for attractive properties is much greater. Competition always drives up the price investors are willing to pay for cleaner-looking properties with more income.

Attractive properties that show well, are properly managed, and earn top market rents will always command a much higher price when it's time to sell. Right now, in my town, **9 or 10 times the gross annual rents** are about the average selling price for small multiple-unit properties–or as I call them, "colony houses"!

To me, it's always amazing to watch how ordinary cleaning, a few basic improvements, and a fresh new paint job can quickly **add a significant amount of value**! Looks count for everything in the fix-up business, whether you're renting or selling. Once completed, you'll own six charming rental units that will now command top market rents of $700 rent per month. Most buyers will be more than happy to pay you **nine times** the gross annual rents (**$453,600**) – sometimes even more if you offer attractive terms, or use your increased equity to "trade up" for a bigger property.

On the following page, Figure 1-2, you'll see the **increased rents and new value** after the cleaning and rehab work are completed. Please don't stare too long at my sketch! Remember, I don't get paid very much for my artistic talent, **although I am available for hire – www.fixerjay.com.**

$201,600 FOR YOUR EFFORTS

The math don't lie – with rents of **$50,400** per year and a bright 'n shiny cleaned up property that shows well, most investors will be more than happy to pay you nine times the annual rents (9 x $50,400 = **$453,600**). That's almost double what you paid to start with. **Can ya dig it?**

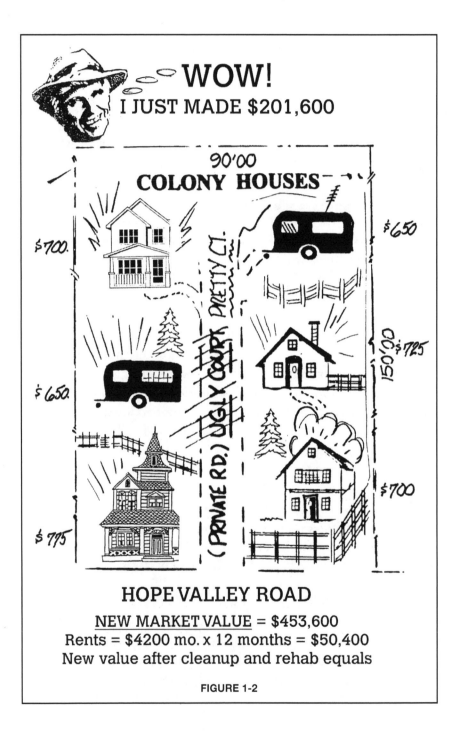

FIGURE 1-2

FOUR WAYS TO MAKE MONEY

Alright, let's cut to the chase here – it's time for me to explain where all the money comes from, so you can clearly understand what forces are at work! There are four major money sources that will make you richer – **and a lot faster** than you might think!

APPRECIATION (Natural or **Forced**)

When you pay only 10% down for a $300,000 property, you have a 90% leverage factor. That is to say – *for 90% of the property you haven't yet paid one thin dime toward the ownership* – **still, the full 100% transaction** has your name on the deed! You are indeed the owner and you benefit from the **whole property**!

Now, let's assume the property appreciates 10% during your first year of ownership. That's "peanuts" where I live (California) – but just the same, the property is now worth $330,000 (a mere 10% gain in value). But hold on just a second – the 10% increase in the value doesn't mean you made 10%. Actually, you made a whole lot more! The reason is because you only paid $30,000 down to start with! The 10% increase in the property value means you've earned back your total down payment in the first year of ownership. **That, my friend, is a "whopping" 100% return!**

CASH FLOW

Investing in rundown properties, and fixing them up the way I suggest, allows you to start earning cash flow much more quickly – you're not simply waiting around for piddly little rent increases once every year or so! **My cash flow comes from forcing up the value!** Force means I quickly jump in and start **cleaning** and **fixing** to make the property a better place to live. When I've done my job, tenants will gladly pay me higher rents to live there.

My method–**forcing up the value** allows me to create a more productive property quicker. My goal is to increase my rents by 50% or more in two years' time. Using my example (the six-unit property), you'll recall that my rents averaged $500 per month when I acquired the property.

In approximately 24 months' time, I increased them to **$700 per unit** by cleaning up the property and making attractive improvements. This means that I increased the property income by **$1200 per month**. This is how you can turn a mediocre property into a **cash flow** winner!

EQUITY BUILD-UP

Equity build-up comes from paying down the principal portion of your mortgage payment. The more you pay on the principal, the larger your equity becomes, but that's only one way and it's far too slow for me!

Most equity build-up comes from *inflation* or *appreciation*, especially **forced appreciation**! Property value grows quickly when the appreciation starts **compounding annually**. For example, let's say your $300,000 property doubles in value over the next seven years! That means you've earned **$43,000** for each year of your ownership, simply because you were smart enough to acquire the right property and employ the forces of leverage and compounding.

TAX BENEFITS

The government says that your real estate and all the various components start wearing out and begin losing value from the very first day you acquire the property. **In reality, we know the real value will be going up!** How can these two situations exist together, you ask? Because the government says so, that's why! *They call it depreciation!* For income-producing real estate like the six houses or apartments in my example, Uncle Sam says you must deduct the depreciation (wearing out expense) and reduce the book value on your 1040 TAX RETURN every year, whether you like it or not.

The government informs us that residential apartments will wear out at the rate of 3.64% each year. Carpets wear out in five years, and the asphalt driveway and parking areas will completely wear out and depreciate to zero book value in just 15 years. The IRS has all these numbers figured out in their tax codebook. Of course, we know that in 15 years, the property value will have likely doubled or even tripled – *especially if you own property in my state.*

What this means is that your real estate can be earning positive cash flow all year long, but when you file your income taxes (Form 1040), the property will actually show a loss. I call this **adult pretending** – visualize owners wandering around on the street corner, screaming at everyone who'll listen that they're losing their shirt with real estate, when the truth is they've got cash jingling in their pockets. The CASH FLOW—TAX FLOW chart below (Fig. 1-3) shows shows you exactly what I'm talkin' about! **Depreciation** (the phantom expense you don't pay) wipes out the total tax liability as you can see (taxable income).

Cash Flow - Tax Flow

"BRIGHTSIDE APARTMENTS"

2030 Lazy Street

ANNUAL INCOME		CASH FLOW	TAX FLOW
Annual Expenses		$25,000	$25,000
Taxes	$2,000		
Insurance	1,200		
Utilities	1,400		
Maint./Repairs	2,100		
Management	3,000		
Advertising	300		
TOTAL EXPENSES		$10,000	$10,000
Net Operating Income		$15,000	$15,000
Depreciation			**$6,000**
Mortgage Payment		$13,000	$13,000
CASH FLOW		$2,000	
TAXABLE INCOME			($4,000)

FIGURE 1-3

SUMMARY OF ANNUAL RETURNS
(Four Different Kinds)
For colony-type properties
(Six rundown rental houses or apartments)

	% Range of Returns
Appreciation (forced, fix-up)	20% to 130%
Cash Flow	05% to 40%
Equity Build-Up	10% to 30%
Tax Benefits	05% to 50%
	40% to 250%

This wide variation of percentages is obviously dependent on many different factors, as you might guess! However, I can assure you that many investors have achieved high returns like these. Some, I'm sure, have even exceeded the highest numbers. I have personally reached well over **200% returns** with **colony-type properties** during the first couple years of ownership.

It's these extraordinary investment returns that allow you to soar with the eagles. **Earning high returns is the secret to building personal wealth very quickly.** Take a quick peek at the COMPOUND RESULTS on Page 13. It shows the power of earning compound interest over a specific period of time, at various percentage rates. You'll notice that $10,000 compounding at 50% annually will grow to **$576,635** in just 10 years. **Compounding at 50% or greater** is very achievable with colony houses like we've been discussing here.

FIVE IMPORTANT REASONS TO INVEST IN INCOME-PRODUCING REAL ESTATE

Investing the way I teach is **guaranteed employment** for you and your family if they choose. But most important of all – you can become your own employer – and kiss your other boss goodbye.

Investing the way I teach works the same in a good economy or bad! It doesn't run hot and cold, because housing is needed by all of us. When you acquire affordable rental properties like I suggest, you'll be setting yourself up with **a guaranteed income for life**.

One of the best features about becoming **a housing provider** is you can *earn while you learn*. Investing requires a variety of new skills. Beginners are wise to learn a few basics before buying their first investment property. Also, be extra careful about who you select as your teacher. **My advice** – check 'em out good.

You don't need to be a top student or have a college degree! High school dropouts can succeed the same as anyone else who has **discipline, determination,** and **willingness to learn**. Street-smart always trumps classroom smarts in this business.

Income properties can set you up for life! They can provide a sizable monthly income of your choosing, *build a large net worth* for you and your family, and provide a very comfortable retirement you can depend on. **Financial freedom will be the reward for all your efforts.**

Whether your goal is to earn **additional income** on a part-time basis, or you've decided to fully commit yourself to **FULL-TIME INVESTING** like I did, the knowledge you'll need is exactly the same. Opportunities to profit from *the right kind of real estate* have never been better. The **Adding Value Strategies** I teach are safe, predictable, and they're not dependent on regular appreciation, bank loans, or the economy – **only on you!**

Compounding is an equal partner with **leverage** when it comes to building wealth. As I explained earlier, the magic happens when you allow your assets to stay in place and continue to earn from their earnings. Real estate equities grow exactly the same way your savings account grows when you don't touch the balance. The following graph shows how a **$10,000 savings account** will grow at various rates of interest over a **10-year period**.

05%	compounding for 10 years equals	$16,288
15%	compounding for 10 years equals	$ 40,455
25%	compounding for 10 years equals	$ 93,132
30%	compounding for 10 years equals	$ 137,858
50%	compounding for 10 years equals	**$ 576,635**
100%	compounding for 10 years equals	$10,240,000

Acquiring the right kind of properties and allowing the equities to grow is an essential ingredient for becoming **financially free** in a reasonable period of time. **Colony houses**, like we've been discussing, are the **right vehicle** to get the job done.

You'll always receive the highest returns during the early years as you initially force up the value. However, an average **compounding rate** between 40 and 50% is very achievable for investors who continue to acquire multi-unit properties! It's also the fastest way for investors to build **substantial cash flow**.

INVESTING VERSUS SPECULATING

People invest in real estate for many different reasons, but most are in hopes of making a profit. When I say *in hopes*, it's because when you ask them how they intend to profit, a great majority can't tell you how. The biggest reason for this is because many folks, who honestly believe they are investing, are actually not. They're **speculating** instead, and there's a huge difference between the two!

Webster's Dictionary defines speculating as: *buying and selling with the expectation of profiting from market fluctuations – or assuming a business risk in hope of a gain*! Folks – **let me be crystal clear about this**! Speculating is not what I do – nor is it what I teach others to do! I am a pure investor, and as you shall learn, my profits have very little to do with *market fluctuations*, or as they're more often called, *real estate cycles*.

When you learn to invest my way, there's no need to hope for financial gain. It's almost certain! *Speculation*, on the other hand, is a lot like fishing from the riverbank with a beat-up ol' casting rod hoping to land a big one. Investing my way is more akin to fishing in a rain barrel with an AK-47. **Can you picture the difference here?** Obviously, being able to count on your profits instead of guessing they'll come is a big part of that *huge difference* I mentioned above. Naturally, when you invest the way I'm suggesting, you must think like a business person; meaning, **the bottom line is always first consideration**.

On a positive note, nearly everyone has an equal opportunity to succeed with my kind of investing. Background or education have very little to do with "making it big"! As I told you already, Harvard Law students and high school dropouts are pretty much equal starting out! The reason for this is because a great deal of your investor education will come from **on-the-job training**. Obviously, you'll need what I call "book learning" or formal training, such as seminars to help you learn the basic how-to skills and where to start. But by far your greatest educational advances will come from putting your book knowledge and classroom training into actual practice. Your on-the-job training or street education will "beef up" up your confidence and provide proof-positive that you've finally arrived! There's no greater thrill for any real estate investor than to create a good deal – and then watch it perform! That means making money!

As you read about my dollar numbers and special formulas, keep in mind that it's the **relationship** or **percentages** that are most important. Dollar numbers and mortgage interest rates are always changing, but my techniques and strategies will always remain the same. They've already worked for 100 years or so – and I'll guarantee they'll keep working for another hundred if you need that much time.

Speaking of time, I have always been a stickler for the quickest payback – as in, *how long before I'm gonna be rich*? That's a fair question, don't you think? Call me a bit selfish if you wish, but I don't get much satisfaction from scrimping and saving today, *during my present life*, working on some "nowhere" plan that might make me rich long after I'm dead and gone! Naturally, age will always be a consideration for everyone; however, my investment strategies are geared in such a way so that most folks can earn their pot of gold while they're still on the right side of the grass!

Waiting for 30 years for my mortgages to pay off is far too slow for me! After all, simply investing $10,000 in a compound interest account at 25% would make me a millionaire in less than 21 years, just sittin' on my toosh, watchin' Donald Trump lose his casinos.

Although my math works just fine, some might wonder how in the world could I earn 25% interest without selling drugs. As I write today, 25% interest is more than 10 times higher than most banks are willing to pay. Fair enough, I'll accept that – however, I wasn't thinking about earning interest from the bank! **Real estate profits** can far exceed 25% returns when you invest my way. For example, let's say my $200,000 property appreciates just 10% during my first full year of ownership. I now have a property worth $220,000 – but the return on my **$20,000 cash** down payment has earned me **100%**. Obviously, it gets increasingly difficult to repeat my first year performance – but by acquiring new properties, it's fairly easy to maintain returns many times higher than bank rates. **40 to 50% annual returns** are not the least bit uncommon once you learn the ropes. There is one catch, like I told you already! **You must select the right kind of real estate in order to make this happen**. I even showed you a couple of my "high tech" sketches so you'll know exactly what the properties look like!

COMBINING THE MAGIC INGREDIENTS

I call it "hamburger helper." It's a mixture of **leverage** and **compounding**. By combining these two magic ingredients, you can truly create extraordinary investment returns. As you read through the various chapters, you'll discover many of my trade secrets for yourself. **You'll learn how the biggest profits are made** – and, of course, how long should it take to earn them. Many of the examples you'll read about are my own personal transactions, with only the street names changed to protect the innocent! Pay particular attention to the small down payments I paid in order to set up some "eye popping" returns. By learning how to synchronize **leverage** and **compounding**, you'll soon discover as I did – it's like owning your own personal ATM machine.

Referring to my compounding results on page 13, you'll observe that $10,000 compounding at 25% for 10 years would put **$93,132** in your purse. If you could somehow waive a magic wand and switch the rate to 50%, you'd have nearly **$600,000** for the same amount of time invested.

Hypothetical, you say! Playing "what if" with dollars and percentages seldom works the same way in real life! True enough, but it's not the mathematics you should blame. The fault more likely lies with investors who fail to take the necessary steps to get in the game! All the education in the world is worthless without **action**. You must find the right properties and create **workable transactions**. If you take my advice–*become a specialist*, and acquire the kind of properties I'm suggesting – it won't be long before you'll be a lot richer than all your friends on the block! That's when this stuff really gets to be fun. Regarding those **40-50% investment returns** that seem almost impossible right now! With a little experience under your belt, you'll soon discover that I've told you the absolute truth! Want more proof? Join me at a future INVESTOR TRAINING SEMINAR – I'll seat you next to a **millionaire fisherman**; this stuff tends to rubs off!

In the next chapter, I want you to close your eyes and visualize owning the property I call Cherry Street. Think about how different your life might have been if you had bought Cherry Street instead of me. Check out my dollar numbers and dream about how the income might change your financial picture!

CHAPTER 2

REELIN' IN A BIG ONE

*R*ich people earn up to 20, 30, and even 40 times more money than you do – and I can guarantee you they're not 20 or 30 times smarter than you, nor do they work twenty times harder! The rich folks have learned to use the powerful laws of leverage, and they know it's nearly impossible to get rich working for wages. Instead, they own income-producing assets that earn money 24 hours around the clock, day in and day out. The rich understand the wealth formula.

Owning income-producing real estate creates a winning formula. When you acquire the right kind of income properties, you'll soon begin making money even while you sleep. That's what this book is all about. I'll show you how I earned nearly $2.5 million by purchasing one small six-unit property, and collecting the rent for 26 years before I sold out.

When I teach you about the **right kind of properties,** I'll explain why multiple units work best for most investors; this is because they generate cash flow much faster than buying single houses when you first start out. I'll explain why the numbers and percentages clearly work to your advantage with multi-unit properties. Quite often, critics will claim that single-family houses are easier to manage for beginners – and perhaps that's true! In this book, however, I'll assume that **getting rich faster** and **quicker cash flow** trumps *easy-to-manage* if there's a choice to be made! With respect to single-family houses – I love 'em and they're a great investment – but take my advice, and establish cash flow first!

For just a moment, think about the average blue-collar worker today; he earns around $48,000 annually, working eight hours a day for the next 25 years. His total gross wages will be somewhere around $1.2 million, if he makes it until the end. By comparison, my six little houses have earned me twice that much, and my work on the property averaged just two hours a week! Creating wealth for you and your family is about **multiplying a small amount of money into a very large amount.** You won't find a better example than my six little Cherry Street houses. See Figure 2-1.

MY MILLION-DOLLAR VEHICLE

Cherry Street (not real name) was not any different than hundreds of other *small multi-unit rental properties* you'll find in almost every decent-sized town or city in my state (California). In fact, you can find Cherry Street properties in just about every state in communities with populations of 4500 or more. Many "newbies," or *start-out investors*, claim they have great difficulty finding these small multi-unit properties. However, I've found that the main reason is because their sights are generally set on finding single-family bargains, rather than small multiple-unit properties like Cherry Street. If your goals as an investor are anything like mine – that is, you'd like to "speed up" your cash flow earnings and start making profits in a much shorter period of time – pay very close attention to what I'm about to tell you next. It's what I call my **millionaire strategy** for Mom and Pop investors!

My first real up-close look sorta reminded me of an old Norman Rockwell panting with the paint all smeared together: six older houses all snuggled together on an oversized city lot, with a skinny little driveway running right through the middle. About sixty years old I'm guessing – each house had two small bedrooms and a single bath. They were pretty much typical of the smaller homes built during the late '50's and early '60's. Small "cottage style" houses, like Cherry Street, are an excellent find for investors like myself because they are extremely easy to rent – and they're affordable for most of my customers (tenants). Purchased at the right price, I can easily afford to spend a few bucks to spiffy 'em up, making them very attractive for my rental customers! **Best of all, I can still make a decent profit for myself.**

Before moving on, I want you to underline those last two sentences and never-ever forget them! They contain 38 words that are the essence of **making a million dollars** in the income property business. Let me say this one more time so it's perfectly clear! Investors who are willing to step outside the box, and *learn a few new investment skills*, can acquire these properties, rent them at affordable rates, and earn very respectable profits while the tenants are paying off the mortgages and all the expenses along the way. When you compare my results to investing in single-family homes or *flipping properties*, you'll be absolutely blown away by my **huge profit advantage**. Naturally, you must keep the properties and manage them, but in the end they'll make you a very wealthy investor. If becoming a **financially self-made millionaire** is your goal – stay tuned! I'm about to show you exactly how it's done.

My Cherry Street story began a long time ago. In the sequence of time and events, I'm currently living off the payments from my promissory note after 26 years of collecting rents from my tenants. In case you might be trying to figure out my age, I will tell you this much – I acquired Cherry Street back when I didn't mind having my picture taken! As it turns out, however, who could have ever guessed how handsome I would look with wrinkles and a beard.

CULTIVATING SIX LITTLE HOUSES

Beating down the seller to a $145,000 purchase price seemed like a shallow victory at the time. My biggest problem was trying to find the $20,000 down payment the seller wouldn't budge on! A truck driver by day, and part-time landlord when he wasn't hauling stuff, he was just ring-wise enough to see that I wanted his houses about as bad as he wanted to sell them! Back then, I was still training myself not to fall in love with investment properties! Finally, he agreed to carry back the financing for **$125,000** and would give me **15 years to pay**–but the down payment, he said, would have to be cash on the barrelhead!

I remember thinking to myself, where will I ever find $20,000? I even wondered if there was that much cash in the whole world. Eventually, I robbed Peter to pay Paul, and got the deal closed. That would be the last out-of-pocket money I'd ever have to spend on Cherry Street. My tenants would eventually pay my mortgage payments, the operating costs, and everything else. Indirectly, they're still paying me today. We'll talk about how you can make this happen in other chapters; it will absolutely guarantee your retirement! Take a good peek at my basic purchase transaction on the next page, Figure 2-1.

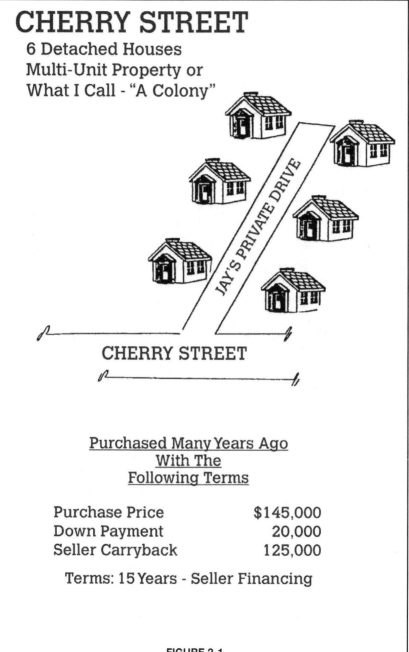

CHERRY STREET
6 Detached Houses
Multi-Unit Property or
What I Call - "A Colony"

JAY'S PRIVATE DRIVE

CHERRY STREET

Purchased Many Years Ago
With The
Following Terms

Purchase Price	$145,000
Down Payment	20,000
Seller Carryback	125,000

Terms: 15 Years - Seller Financing

FIGURE 2-1

FINANCIAL ARRANGER FOR LIFE

Cherry Street is about **making money for life**. It's about being a capitalist and living off the earnings of my assets. I like to call this "womb to tomb" investing! My basic strategy is to acquire the right kind of properties, hang onto them, and harvest the benefits as I go along. My plan is to pay a small down payment (10-15%) and come up with whatever funds are needed for fix-up. After that, all the money starts flowing in one direction – back to me! My tenants will pick up the tab for everything else. As time goes along, generally five to six years, I'll eventually be completely mortgaged out! That means every nickel I've spent will have been paid back to me from the rents. I often characterized my job as the **arranger**. I arrange to acquire the right property, I arrange the financing, and finally, I arrange to do whatever upgrading or fix-up is necessary to maximize the rental income.

As I write about Cherry Street today, many wanta-be investors are worried about lower real estate values, and they wonder if traditional appreciation is still working! These concerns are even older than I am! My good friend and investor buddy, the late William Nickerson, began investing in properties just like Cherry Street during the country's worst depression – and he did just fine. When Bill passed away, his estate was valued in the $16 million range. Pretty good I'd say, for an ex-telephone man who switched to full-time investor. In his now famous real estate book, *How I Turned $1000 into Five Million in Real Estate*, Bill writes: "*The opportunity to make a fortune is with us every day. Under the free enterprise system, opportunity knocks not just for the favored few, but for everyone who aspires to better himself. And, opportunity knocks not just once, but many times. Obviously, it's up to you to open the door.*"

Properties like Cherry Street are exactly the kind of *door opening opportunities* Nickerson writes about. They are not scarce or hard to find once you learn where to look, and how to adjust your thinking to search for older multiple-unit properties, as opposed to looking for single-family houses. Single houses are not really income properties in the truest sense! Don't misunderstand me and think that I don't like the idea of owning single-family houses! I do, I own them myself, and they make excellent investments. The problem I have is about timing – when should you buy them? Mortgaged houses rarely provide much cash flow, and that's what most beginners need first. Buying multiple units like Cherry Street provides cash flow a lot faster, and eliminates much of the risk of going broke! *It's basic mathematics* – six tenants paying rents is much safer than depending on just one. If there's a pecking order – **it's cash flow first**, buy single-family houses later.

COLLECTING RENTS BUILDS STRONG BANK ACCOUNTS

Cherry Street grossed $10,800 during my first year of ownership. When I sold the property 26 years later, my gross rents had reached $57,240 annually. Some years passed without any rent increases, but during boom times – they jumped higher than puffed rice krispies. On the day I sold Cherry Street, the books showed I had taken in **$999,010** in rent during my ownership. You might be thinking to yourself – sure, that's a lot of money Jay, but how much did you get to keep for yourself? I'll tell you a bit later on – but right now I will tell you, the rents doubled during my first three years as the owner. They went from $10,800 to $20,560. By then, the green foldin' money was starting to flow my way. Thirteen years down the line, my average rents at Cherry Street had reached $540 a month. When you do the math, you'll quickly see that my annual income had reached nearly $40,000 – *or roughly four times higher than when I started.*

People often ask me – do you think rents will keep going up? My answer is – *yes I do!* Rents are like pork-n-beans; they're a product of the marketplace. In fact, rental houses are a good hedge against inflation, because rents are just like groceries: they adjust with the times. When you finance your property sales and carry paper like I generally do, you must always consider the long-term effects of *fixed interest rates.* They are not sensitive to inflation like rental house income. A question that always seems to pop up – is it hard to manage your rentals and collect all the rents? You could say it's like learning to ride a bicycle! When you first start out, you'll likely crash a few times – but once you get some education under your belt and practice a bit, you'll find it gets much easier. Finally one day, you'll begin to realize – **your tenants are making you rich**! By then, you probably won't mind the management at all!

NEVER GAMBLE ON INFLATION OR THE FLUFF

To start with, I'm an investor; I'm not a speculator! Don't get me wrong here – when properties appreciate from natural causes or inflation, I'll certainly be the first one to stand in line to take my bows and accept a pat on the back – but inflation profits are what I call "fluff," or unearned profits. All property owners get them automatically without doing anything. It's the same for every investor whose name shows up on the deed! Investors should never count on regular appreciation or inflation to make a deal work. The deal should be structured to work without depending on appreciation to happen. Forced appreciation, on the other hand, is different! **Forced appreciation** is what I get when I intentionally make improvements to my property, which in turn, increases its value.

I paid $20,000 down for Cherry Street and I expected to earn a very good return on my money. I also expect to have all my down payment cash, plus my fix-up expenses, back in my pocket by the end of six years or so. My newsletter subscribers, and the folks who've attended my *three-day investor seminars*, already know that my average fix-up costs run about 10% of the purchase price for properties I call *light fixer-uppers,* and about 20% for *heavy fixers.* My Cherry Street fix-up costs were nearly $18,000, or roughly 12% of the purchase price. You mustn't forget, however, that 70% of those expenses ($12,600) were my estimated labor costs. Back then, I was doing all the labor myself. The only cash money I needed was $5400 for supplies and fix-up materials, which of course, maxed out my overloaded Visa cards.

THE IDEAL FAMILY INVESTMENT

Properties like Cherry Street are where every do-it-yourself investor should begin, in my opinion! It's much less than a full-time job, yet big enough to give you all the practical experiences you'll need to decide if you're cut out to be a capitalist. Six junky-looking houses are about the right size to cause you lots of grief if you attempt to finance them through your normally friendly banker. Five or more units will put you in the commercial borrowing category. When your bank officer explains why he won't give you a mortgage, you should immediately jump up out of your chair and kiss him; he's just done you a tremendous favor! You've now experienced one of the most valuable lessons you'll ever learn in this business! **It's called rejection!** Now you have no choice but to begin looking for sellers who are willing to finance their property sales. There ain't no shortage, but most folks don't try very hard unless they're forced to do it!

Six units are about the right size for a total family learning experience! Sure they'll scream and holler, but the kids will enjoy a boatload of benefits helpin' Mom and Pop with the family rental business. Several families I've known for years have actually paid for the kids' college with rent money from their houses. With just a little accounting know-how, Billy Bob's new 4x4 truck can be purchased with operating expenses – *completely tax deductible*. One benefit that doesn't get talked about nearly enough is the family involvement part – kids working with their parents learn more about responsibility. Sadly, this lesson has been lost in the dot.com shuffle in recent years. On a more positive note, what healthy young teenage boy would pass up a chance to cut grass at the family rental project in between playing video games? Don't forget to tell junior about the 10-15% maintenance allowance. That just might be the right carrot to dangle!

You needn't lose any sleep worryin' about your fix-up skills! At least 80% of all the work required is what I call "grunt work." Even if you can't grunt, almost everybody can paint, haul trash, hang curtains, fix the fence, or spruce up the front yard. Skilled work, the stuff that needs a contractor or someone who actually knows what they're doing, is only a small percentage of the total fix-up expense! *Keep in mind* – I'm not talking about remodeling houses, like moving walls around or ripping out the old plumbing system! That's not the business I'm in! My job is to upgrade the property and do my best to preserve what's already there. Rental houses must be *clean*, *attractive*, and *functional* to compete in the marketplace – **but that's it, ya got it**!

THE MAGICAL POWER OF LEVERAGE

I can think of no other business that offers so much reward for such a small upfront investment! The $20,000 down payment I needed to acquire Cherry Street was roughly 14% of the total purchase price. That means 86% of the property wasn't even mine yet – but still, the deed entitled me to 100% of all the income. When you divide six houses into the purchase price ($145,000 divided by 6 = $24,166), you can see that my down payment was still $4,166 short of paying for just one house, *let alone all six of them*. **This is how safe leveraging can turn small-time investors into rich tycoons.**

Even when you play Monopoly, you must pay for all of your little green houses before you start collecting money from the other players who land on your property. At Cherry Street, my down payment gave me full rights to begin collecting rents from all six houses, long before I'd have them paid for. Safe leverage allows you to make phenomenal returns with a relatively small sum of money. In this case, my $20,000 down payment returned $10,800 in rents during my first year of ownership. That's a 54% return without considering appreciation, tax write-offs, and the additional value I created fixing up the property.

Folks who have attended my investor seminars, or purchased home study courses, already know my feelings about selling good income properties. Just in case you don't, let me shout it loud and clear so there's no misunderstanding! **I do not recommend selling good income-producing properties!** If you buy properties right, and they begin producing *net spendable income* in a reasonable period of time, there can be very little justification for selling them! You're actually killing the goose that lays the golden eggs! The exception, of course, is when you reach the retirement mode and it's time to kick back and smell the roses. Naturally, this begins a whole new phase of profit making with your seller carryback notes. We'll discuss this amazing benefit in another chapter! I call it "pajama money!"

As I already told you, *womb to tomb* investing is my own characterization of planning a continuous and predictable income from start to finish – or as my probate attorney puts it – *until my case matures*! **Continuous income** has always been one of my most cherished benefits – you may call it my old age retirement fund if you wish! With seller carryback financing, the **money flow** never shuts off with the passing of ownership. After 26 years of collecting rents at Cherry Street, I finally succumbed to the fragrance of sweet smelling roses in full bloom! I sold my six little moneymaker houses for the going rate at the time–**$650,000,** or roughly 11.5 times the gross rents. The following pages, Figures 2-2, 2-3, 2-4, and 2-5, show you the power of multiplying a small amount of money into a very substantial amount.

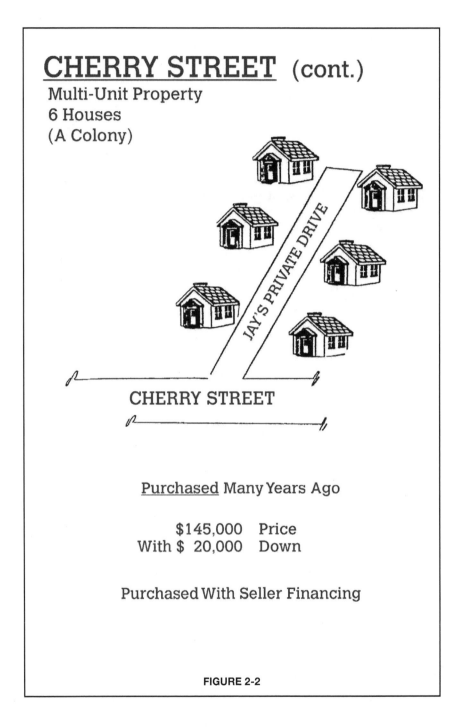

CHERRY STREET (cont.)

Multi-Unit Property
6 Houses
(A Colony)

CHERRY STREET

Purchased Many Years Ago

$145,000   Price
With $ 20,000   Down

Purchased With Seller Financing

FIGURE 2-2

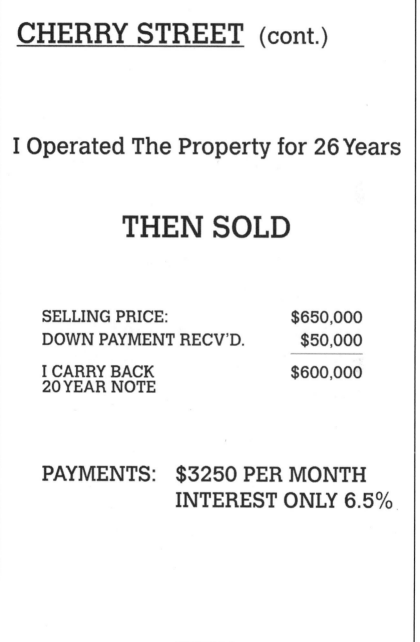

CHERRY STREET (cont.)

I Operated The Property for 26 Years

THEN SOLD

SELLING PRICE:	$650,000
DOWN PAYMENT RECV'D.	$50,000
I CARRY BACK 20 YEAR NOTE	$600,000

PAYMENTS: $3250 PER MONTH
INTEREST ONLY 6.5%

FIGURE 2-3

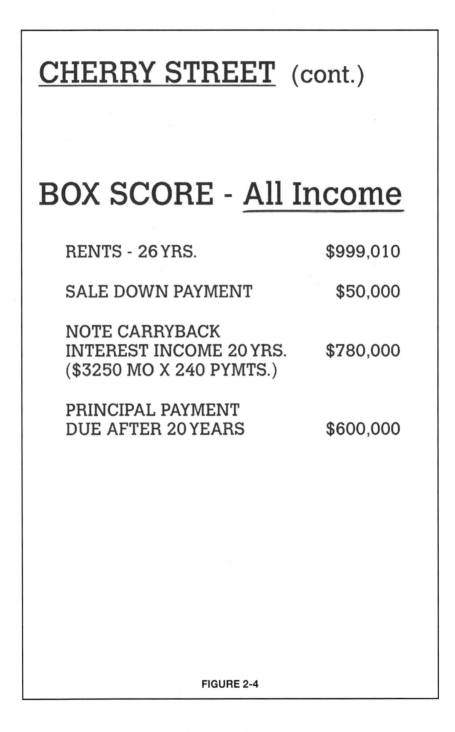

CHERRY STREET (cont.)

BOX SCORE - All Income

RENTS - 26 YRS.	$999,010
SALE DOWN PAYMENT	$50,000
NOTE CARRYBACK INTEREST INCOME 20 YRS. ($3250 MO X 240 PYMTS.)	$780,000
PRINCIPAL PAYMENT DUE AFTER 20 YEARS	$600,000

FIGURE 2-4

CHERRY STREET (cont.)

FINAL BOX SCORE
FROM START TO FINISH

TOTAL MONEY
I'VE RECEIVED: **$2,429,010**

FOR EVERY YEAR
I OWNED & FINANCED
MY AVERAGE INCOME
$53,000 ANNUALLY

From beginning till the end, Cherry Street will have earned
121.5 times the amount of my initial down payment.

FIGURE 2-5

PAJAMA MONEY

After collecting almost a million dollars of rent money, I sold Cherry Street and received a $50,000 cash down payment. I provided seller carryback financing for the $600,000 balance. The buyer agreed to pay me $3250 in monthly payments (interest only) for 20 years. After 20 years, the total principal balance of $600,000 would become due and payable. This transaction worked quite well for both sides. It allowed the buyer to take over the property and immediately begin earning cash flow income. For me, my net income stayed about the same, but as the late Dr. King so eloquently put it – **"I'm free at last!"**

CHAPTER 3

THE CREATIVE FISHERMAN

You don't need a bunch of complex formulas or mind-boggling mathematics to make a lot of money as a real estate investor. The greatest results in this business are usually attained by reasonably simple means and the exercise of ordinary *"plain vanilla"* qualities. There's really nothing I can think of to stop the average person from becoming successful except himself! I'm talking, of course, about the millions of regular hard-working folks who dream about financial independence, and have the discipline to commit themselves to a plan of action using ordinary common sense and perseverance! **Motivation, desire**, and **personal drive** are enough to overcome almost any handicap or roadblock, providing that a beginner is willing to educate himself well enough to get started in the **right direction**!

One of the major roadblocks for newcomers today is their willingness to be enticed by the endless stream of "too good to be true" fairytales, which are passed along faster than a dirty joke! The idea that average working folks can end up rich by purchasing a couple of "no money down" houses is as big a hoax today as it was when a book by the same name was published more than thirty years ago! New investors or *wanta-bees* are well advised to memorize this next sentence. **There's a price to pay and a cost for everything!** I can assure you, this applies to real estate investing! You must never forget what I told you earlier – promise me, but most of all yourself, that you'll always use **common sense** if you're serious about success and financial independence!

INVESTING BEFORE EDUCATION OFTEN FATAL

Alright, now I've said it – I've told you exactly what you need! You need **a plan of action**, common sense, and perseverance! I've also cautioned you about not falling for those "ridiculous" get rich fairy tales! When you hear one that sounds suspicious, simply back off and say to yourself: I'm from Missouri, you're gonna have to show me some proof! As an author who writes about investing, I receive my share of telephone calls and e-mails from folks who say, "Jay, I just finished reading your latest book and I'm rarin' to get started right away! What do you recommend I do first?" Some callers even tell me they've been looking at an empty house down the street! "Do you think I should buy it?" they'll ask. Calls like this conjure up the image of a second-year medical student asking the doctor, "Which of these round things are the kidneys? Do you think I should go ahead and take both of 'em out?" As a rule, most book readers are not anywhere near ready for the operating room just yet!

Unless you're lucky enough to have an experienced real estate investor for a trainer, the best and easiest way to learn the basics is to attend a seminar or two, taught by a teacher you've thoroughly checked out! **Not only checked out**, but you should also find an instructor who invests about the same way you'd like to start investing yourself. Going to seminars of a general nature might be okay, but they're not very cost effective. Besides, jumping around trying to learn a variety of different plans or ideas can be very confusing for most start-out investors! Too many plans or too many strategies can overload your mind, and will often produce conflicting information for beginners! Once again – **use common sense** and keep your education focused on the way you'd like to invest.

THE CHICKEN OR THE EGG IS FIRST

Most new investors just starting out would almost unanimously vote that the biggest problem holding them back is money! Usually, they claim that the down payment money to purchase a property is the roadblock. Yet, it's proven time and time again – money is not the holdup at all – **it's education**! The no money down strategy I mentioned earlier (calling it the big hoax); *remember*, I'm directing this comment to brand new investors, not seasoned investors who've already began to figure things out! For example, no money down **with the right terms** can work just fine! However, getting the terms you need is where the education comes in. New investors often brag about acquiring houses for no money down, but because the unpaid mortgage balance requires 75-80% of the property income for monthly debt service – it's really a train wreck waiting to happen! The dummy bunch who bought overpriced houses in the Arizona desert thought they had cash flow too – that is, until they got foreclosed!

The more education you have, the better the deals will turn out! *Nothing tricky here*, again it's just **plain common sense**! I'm constantly asked about the many different ways I've purchased properties over the years. I can honestly tell you, I don't believe I've ever done two deals exactly the same way; yet, the majority of my deals are not all that different from each other. You can find many of the same ingredients in almost all of my buying transactions. When you're negotiating directly with sellers for the purchase of their income properties, no two sellers will be exactly the same. As a buyer, it's your responsibility to structure your offer from the ground up. If you fail to end up with cash flow, the blame is on you.

I often tell my students – **good deals must be created**, they are hardly ever found. As a buyer, you must mold each transaction to fit the income a property will produce; and, you must do it in a manner the seller believes is fair. Once again, this is where learning these kinds of skills from a successful investor will pay huge dividends for you. In a minute, I'll discuss several of the most common ingredients I generally negotiate in most of my offers! I won't give you a step-by-step, one-size-fits-all method because there is none! I negotiate with people (sellers) and as you might guess, they are all different. I can tell you that most sellers will hold out for what he or she truly wants from the sale. It's up to you (the buyer) to find out what that is – **can ya dig it**?

Years ago, I was told a story about a lonely young man who decided to take a crash course on 100 different ways to make love! As it turned out, his education proved totally worthless because no one bothered to teach him how to find a girlfriend! Learning lessons you can't use is a big waste of time and money – and, like I told you earlier – it's very important to check out your teacher before you begin your lessons. Humorist, Will Rogers once said, "It's not that people don't know very much! The problem is; so much of what they know just ain't so!" I tell this story because you need to make sure your instructor is what he or she claims to be, and not a spreader of fairy tales!

NEGOTIATING IS ABOUT EXPLORING POSSIBILITIES

Negotiating to me is about creating possibilities in the eyes of the other person! Forget the idea of winning and losing or using the right phrases to con your opponent! Instead, figure out ways to get what you want by giving the other party something he wants! Newbies always think this has to be money because that's what most sellers ask for. Value is always personal and subjective, and many folks value other stuff just as much as cash, even though they don't know what that other stuff might be until negotiations begin. When you think of cash as merely something to exchange just like other stuff, it helps your creative juices start flowing! Naturally, everyone asks for cash in exchange for their property; however; negotiating gives you the opportunity to find out what else they might accept instead of cash! Remember, the only value money has is that it can be used to buy you something else you want. If it couldn't do that, it would have very little value – **agreed**! People ask for money so they can pay for something else. Find out what that something else is, and determine if you can provide it to save your cash!

Common sense shows up during negotiating in mysterious ways! My basic strategy is to purchase properties that are not very pleasing to look at. To the point, some are just downright ugly! When I approach the seller of an ugly property, I feel I have a big advantage because he has a property that only a few buyers would want. Let's face it – our entire society equates **value with looks**! Pretty girls always get the biggest diamonds, wallflowers get fewer dances, and I wasn't picked by my classmates for the school's most handsome man! Mentally, the seller of an ugly property feels a little depressed in my judgment – *and because of that*, I always feel like I have the upper hand during negotiations. Remember, I'm talking about income properties (rentals) here. Houses, someone's personal residence, can often involve emotions and personalities, which I try my best to avoid.

Since I have rarely given the seller of **an income property** what he originally asked for, meaning **price** and **terms**, asking prices mean very little to me. Sometimes when the listed price is totally out of the ball-park, in my opinion, I'll start negotiations with what I call my "see how high they jump" offer. Say, for example, a $400,000 listing price – **my offer is $200,000**. If they don't jump very high, it's quite possible they might settle down and entertain a reasonable compromise! Another version with the same type of situation would be what I call my "would ya take" offer. I say, "Mr. Seller, would ya take $200,000 cash if I could get it to you by 5 p.m. Friday?" Obviously, I don't have $200,000 cash, so I'd have to keep negotiating until he accepts or walks away! Still, I believe some agreement might be reached for **substantially less** than the original $400,000 price.

PAYING SELLER'S BILLS CAN
SAVE DOWN PAYMENT CASH

For the beginning investor *especially*, down payment cash is always in short supply. Once you get rolling along and begin to increase your earnings from cash flow properties, it may become a little easier to accumulate a down payment. Still, conserving your cash is always a worthwhile achievement. A technique I've used to avoid coming up with a hefty down payment is to offer some kind of personal debt reduction to the seller; for example, instead of coughing up $30,000 for a cash down payment! Suppose, Mr. Seller, I negotiate with your credit union to take over your $30,000 auto loan balance and relieve you from making the $600 monthly payments. If the seller agrees, this would allow me to pay my down payment with $600 installment payments over the next six years, as opposed to coming up with **the full $30,000** at closing. Chances are, I would have had to borrow the $30,000 down payment anyway; however, this way I won't need to borrow, I would simply pay off the seller's loan.

This technique is certainly not limited to car payment loans! In fact, I much prefer to pay off the seller's unsecured debt obligations like money owed to the lumberyard – perhaps the bill from his last big splurge to fix up the property. He may have a personal medical bill owed to the doctor or a hospital. These are the best bills to take over because they're marked up with high overhead charges. They're mostly personal services bills! These kinds of bills are much easier to negotiate for big discounts after you take over the debt. When I discover the seller has these kind of pressing bills, I immediately suggest the idea of me taking over these obligations **in lieu of a cash down payment**. If the seller agrees, I'll negotiate with the vendor or payee and attempt to set up a payment plan. Vendors will almost always go along with this proposal if their bills have gone unpaid for some time or they are already in collection!

The big advantage with unsecured bills as opposed to taking over an automobile payment contract is they have a lot more *built-in fluff*. They are bills for services rendered, and they generally have a large markup for overhead and profit. They are ideal candidates for negotiating a steep discount, whereas a bank-contracted car loan would probably not be! I've found that it's not the least bit uncommon to receive **25-50% discounts** for cash payoffs of unsecured service bills.

I generally wait three months or so after setting up an installment plan before I call the payee! Then I say, "Mr. Payee, I realize we've already agreed that I would pay off the seller's $25,000 obligation to you by making payments of $500 per month till it's paid. You've been more than generous to me by not charging any interest! As of today, I owe you a balance of $23,500! **Here's the deal**: my Aunt Tilly has recently passed away in Chicago and I'm about to receive about $15,000 cash. If you'd rather have **$15,000 cash** instead of waiting for payments another five and a half years, **I can get the money to you**

in 10 days! Just let me know!" *If the payee agrees*, you'll never make **$8,500** any easier! You don't have a dead Aunt Tilly, you say? Figure something else out – **OKAY**!

When you can successfully postpone or eliminate large cash payouts (down payments) until sometime in the future by paying installment payments instead, you will increase your long-term earnings. Because of inflation, today's cash is always more valuable than a string of payments in the future.

Although the government's inflation meter don't seem to be registering much these days, *I'm thinkin' the needle is stuck*! Apparently the government excludes many items most people spend their money on. They don't seem to be measuring frivolous things like food, gas, and health care. If I had to make a wild guess, I'd say 9 or 10% inflation seems like a more accurate figure! Regardless of the figure, postponing cash payments today, to be paid with cheaper dollars in the future, is a worthwhile strategy! Obviously, **$30,000 cash today** is worth **$30,000** – but four or five years from now it might only be worth $18,000 or so. The idea here is to hang on to your cash as long as you can, and pay with cheaper dollars in the future!

LEMONADE DOWN PAYMENTS SAVE CASH

Lemonade is made from sugar and lemons! We'll call sugar our **cash** and the lemons can be something else (*other stuff*)! Remember what I told you about an ugly house seller – he has a weak property because it's rundown and doesn't look very nice! He knows it! I always feel like this gives me a big advantage when making offers! Conversely, if his property was bright 'n shiny, **my creative offer** would probably not work!

"Mr. Seller, I feel the $40,000 down payment you've requested is reasonable – and I'm willing to pay that amount – *but just not all cash*! I propose to pay you **$15,000 cash** – plus, I'll give you my Ram Charger, super-x model truck (driven mostly by a widowed Sunday school teacher) for **$15,000 credit**. As a bonus, I'll even toss in my camper at no extra charge since its custom fitted for the truck. I'll also give you my deluxe ski boat, which tows two skiers with six passengers on board! It's only nine years old, but it hasn't been used much over the past four years! It cost me $21,000 brand new – but it's yours for just **$10,000**. That, Mr. Seller, will be my total down payment!" Obviously, this offer might go down a bit easier if the seller lives near a lake *during the summer months* and has teenagers who love to water ski. You'll learn these things about the seller during your negotiations if you're a good listener! **Can ya dig it?**

GIVING DEAD EQUITY NEW LIFE

The general idea here is to save your cash and use what you already have to acquire more properties! **Dead equity** refers to *equity in real estate you own which is not being used.* To me, the biggest "no brainer" is to put the dead equity in your personal residence to work, assuming you own a home! This is one of the best starting plans if you wish to acquire the kind of properties I'm recommending! This is also a "self-contained" plan, meaning you can do everything yourself at home using your own typewriter or printer. You'll need a blank **promissory note** (secured type) and **a deed of trust** and you're all set to conduct business!

For exactly the same reason weak sellers will agree to accept my pickup truck and ski boat (lemonade offer), they're just as likely to accept an **income-producing note** as well! Let me clarify my strategy here. No seller would likely ever consider the type of offers we're discussing here except for one fact – **he has a weak product** (a rundown unsightly property). Ugliness greatly reduces the number of potential buyers, which hurts the seller's chances of making a sale. This situation creates an excellent opportunity for investors to "dream up" uncommon solutions!

Drawing up your **promissory note** and **deed of trust** (the terms) will largely depend on your negotiations with the seller. Here's what I generally say: "Mr. Seller; I'm just a bit light on the down payment here! **Would ya consider** taking a well secured **$30,000 note** on my house? It will pay you $250 each month for 15 years." Remember, the terms can be whatever you and the seller agree to; however, you as the buyer must consider not only the payments on this down payment note ($250), but also the other payments you negotiate on the property you're buying. These include new seller financing and any other mortgages you assume or take over on the sale. When you add up all the monthly payments required to service the debt, make sure the property can generate enough income to pay the mortgages. Here is my magic income amount so I feel safe: **all monthly mortgage payments should not exceed 50% of the total monthly income.** If rents can be raised quickly, I might allow 60%, but never higher!

EVERY PLAN NEEDS A SECOND OPINION

For many years now, I've advised husbands and wives, girlfriends and boyfriends, and even good buddies to exchange their financial thoughts and ideas with each other in order to provide a **final checkpoint** before shelling out their heard-earned dollars for what's likely to become a co-owner investment. I know from my own personal experiences that one spouse or partner will almost always be a bit more "gung ho" about investing than the other! In my own case, starting ou*t*, I showed very little interest in the opinions of others once I made up my mind to buy my next property. When my ex-wife chimed in with comments like "**I can't see where the profits will come from,**" I always countered with, "The reason you can't is because you don't have any vision for the future!" Need I explain why she's my ex-wife? Regardless of my marital relations, I eventually learned to value her opinion, and what made matters even worse was that she was right most of the time!

Should you ever visit my home office, today you won't find those third grade "stick-um" notes tattooed on my refrigerator door in big bold print showing my five-year plan or long-term goals, *but lest you be fooled* – **I've got 'em**! You simply won't be very successful without a plan or road map! After all, without a destination and a plan to get there – *how would you ever know when you finally arrived?* I've been counseling and coaching new investors for many years now, and one of the first recommendations I make to every student is: think ahead to 15 or 20 years down the road and decide where you'd like to be financially. It's like taking a snap shot of the future so you have a target to work towards! This will help you zero in or formulate your start-out plan.

Obviously, it would be impossible to predict everything that might happen. Still, looking forward to some future date and knowing where you'd like to be will give you a better sense about the journey you must take. It should also cause you to think real hard about **the kind of properties you buy** with respect to **profits, income**, and the **benefits** they can provide for you! This will help narrow down your searching activities to looking only for those properties that fit your plan. Searching for properties can cost you many hours of extra time if you don't establish a **clear vision** of the properties you're looking for! For example, I will only look at multiple-unit properties where sellers will agree to finance a major part of the mortgage debt, or at least their equity portion! If that's not something they wish to do, then I see no need to waste my time looking at their property.

THE ONE-SIZE-FITS-ALL NOT NECESSARY

First let me say – I do not believe that every investor must wear a medium-size suit! Investors come in all different shapes and sizes; therefore, my medium-size suit will probably not fit every investor very well. I want you to apply this same kind of thinking to real estate benefits – **every investor don't need the same kind of benefits**! You might differ with what I'm saying here by telling me – Jay, I'll just bet ya all investors need cash flow and extra income every month. You're wrong, they don't – *and just for the record*, I don't! Of course I'm talkin' about now! For most of my early years, you'd be absolutely right!

The fact that you need to have a certain amount of cash flow five years from now don't mean "diddlysquat" if you have no plan to provide for it! Many investors stand about the same chance of being flat broke in five years, as opposed to having any cash flow! The difference, my friends, has a whole lot to do **with the property you buy and the way**

you acquire it – meaning, the type of property and how well you've negotiated the purchase terms.

For example, I know investors who have purchased real estate with low interest "teaser type" mortgages! I don't mind being teased a little, but these mortgages are variable interest rate loans and they are generally written with caps many times higher than the initial starting interest rates! Just think about trying to rent your properties to keep up with interest rates that are jumping like grasshoppers! To echo that old presidential campaign slogan from a few years back: "Where's the beef"? My friends, I'm afraid to tell you, there ain't none! Also, with variable rate mortgages, you might begin hearing that *big sucking sound* that ex-presidential candidate Ross Perot warned voters about – he was referring to American jobs going to Mexico, *but believe me*, variable rate mortgages can send investors there too!

A PLAIN AND SIMPLE FORMULA

I once heard a real estate speaker friend of mine explain to his audience that he'd made a serious investment decision a few years back – he'd lost a $100,000 overpaying for a property! A few people in the audience looked somewhat puzzled! $100,000 don't seem like very much, they whispered – but as my speaker friend went on to explain, **it is when that's all you've got**! For most Mom and Pop investors, who represent the majority of my students, losing $100,000 would be a very big deal indeed! If it happens in the early stage of an investor's career, it would almost always be fatal. Even "well healed" folks who lose that much money trying something new will probably never do it again. The reason this happened was because my friend fell in love with a property too expensive for his experience level at that particular stage of his career. **There's a real lesson here** – don't shop at Niemen Marcus when you belong in the Dollar Store. Always be aware of your **financial capacity** and the risks involved while you're learning the trade!

A good friend of mine and an excellent teacher, the late Jack Miller, would always tell us, "It's far too risky trying to hit home runs – play it safe, go for singles or base hits. Just get on base," he would tell us, using baseball jargon. "It may take you a bit longer to reach home plate, but your career will suffer far fewer setbacks and you'll stay in the game (investment business) to play another day!" I whole-heartedly agree, **Amen Jack**!

To "frame" your plan or *investment goals* so you'll be able to track your progress, I suggest you write down **how long** (the time frame) and **how much income** you expect to earn from your investments. Let's say, for example, that you choose a 10-year period for your plan to perform, and your plan calls for **earning $5000 *net income each month*** from your real estate investments. You now have some hard numbers you can monitor. Do not design your plan where events must occur that are not within your control; for example, refinancing or forecasting overly generous appreciation.

You can't control or even guess about available mortgages in the future – and *appreciation*, who knows? If you acquire *underperforming* rental units and because of your own efforts, you're able to create a better property where your tenants will reward you by paying higher monthly rents – **this is a proven method to increase your cash flow**. Rents are pretty much indexed to inflation like beans and toilet paper at the supermarket. In my area, rents are going up by modest bumps (two to five percent) annually, in spite of many foreclosed houses still sittin' around. Percentage-wise, ownership is down and there are more renters today.

Buying properties where you can control *both the upside and the long-term mortgage debt* goes a long ways toward creating a profitable long-term investment plan, as well as greatly reducing the risk. Over the years, I've learned that removing appreciation from my profit calculations is a much safer method for developing my long-term plan. My good friend who invests in Sarasota, Florida, recently told me that half the value in his single-family houses simply disappeared into thin air during the last financial meltdown. Houses that grew from $60,000 to $160,000 during the last 25 years are now back to where they started. My friend is okay financially because his houses are mostly paid for. You wanta know why my friend is still wealthy? **His tenants paid his houses off!** That's the kind of plan I'm talkin' about!

THE TRUTH ABOUT FORECASTING THE FUTURE

I'm certain my friend would have never guessed in a thousand years that this kind of a value decline could ever happen! I would have never thought so either six or seven years ago! The 2008 crash surprised everyone I think! Suppose you started investing ten years ago, and you were counting on refinancing about now! Your appraisals could easily be less than your mortgage balances! If your houses are leveraged and you've been counting on refinancing to free up a little cash, but now you discover there's no equity for borrowing, **what's your next move**? Unless you live near the Golden Gate Bridge – jumping may not even be an option!

I buy properties I can acquire using high leverage that will produce respectable cash flow within a year or two after I become the new owner. **Small multi-unit properties** – poorly managed, rundown, and even a bit ugly are my personal favorites. Generally, these kinds of properties will be *under-rented* because of their appearance and shoddy condition. Quite often, a "quick swish" paint job and hauling away the junk will be enough to begin increasing rents with my next round of tenants.

When these properties are financed by their sellers, as opposed to banks, my risk is reduced to almost nothing. The reason is because most sellers ridding themselves of poorly managed, rundown properties are crossing their fingers and praying they'll never see their ugly property again – **EVER**! Why is this so important, you ask? Early on in my investing career, I owned a property like I'm describing here. For some oddball reason I just couldn't keep the property fully rented. With a total of seven units, it seemed like three were always vacant or about to be. My $1400 mortgage payments, plus the operating expenses, were sinking my bank account very quickly!

For several months, $1400 was all the rent I took in! After waiting a little too long for my cash flow to improve, I finally decided to call the seller who had carried back the mortgage. I told him my sad tale of woe! Mr. Seller, I said, you may or may not know how much I'm struggling with the property, so I'm calling to ask you to reduce the mortgage payments until my occupancy improves. It's either that or I'll mail you the keys. I can only pay you $900 per month for the next year or so – or, I'll have to let you try your luck again; meaning, I'm ready to give the property back! Naturally, he wasn't very tickled about my phone call. Still, he agreed to take $900. Just try this technique on Bank of America and you'll quickly learn why seller financing is always the best game in town!

MAKE SURE IMPROVEMENTS
GENERATE MORE INCOME

When part of your plan is to make improvements on the property, you need to understand that your risk or exposure will be more than just the down payment. My estimated fix-up and cleaning costs for what I call light fixers is roughly 10% of the purchase price. For example, let's say you purchased a $300,000 property paying a 10% cash down payment. Then, you spend another 10% to fix up the property. Should you lose the property after fix-up, you'd be out roughly $60,000! Small-time Mom and Pop investors often can't recover if they lose that much. For this reason, I insist that students always fill out my PROPERTY ANALYSIS FORM (see Chapter 9) before making any offer. A **line by line set of instructions** for completing my Property Analysis Form is available in Appendix C-2 & C3. If you'll fill out my form using these instructions as your guide, you can avoid the heartache that comes from paying too much – fill out a *property analysis form* for every potential purchase, **are we clear**?

I know investors who struggle for years and never seem to improve themselves financially. Some will never see improvements until they pay off their mortgages, and far too many will give up along the way. Real estate investing is not much fun when month after month goes by without any signs of cash flow or profits. As I write today, with the lowest interest rates (mortgages) in the past 20 years, it's still difficult to generate much cash flow owning leveraged single-family houses. **Multiple-unit properties** provide lots more cash flow and they do it much faster.

INVESTING MUST BE COMPATIBLE
WITH YOUR LIFESTYLE

I wish I didn't have to be quite so old in order to tell you what I'm about to say; *but since I am*, I believe **my observation** will be more credible and hopefully, more acceptable! I most certainly have a huge advantage looking back over 50 years as an investor who's done almost everything in the rental housing business. I've made my mistakes, done stuff over, made unsound predictions (especially about the future), and through it all, I've ended up financially independent – *free as a bird to do as I please*. Frankly, it's been a great ride, immensely enjoyable and obviously, very profitable. Like many investors who start with a dream – I've worked hard, continued my education, and most important of all, I've stayed the course. Right now it's my opinion that anyone reading this book has a splendid opportunity to do the same things I've done if you'll set your mind to it and stay the course!

Most investor *wanta-bees* fall into two different categories. First, there's the group who have decent jobs, but are completely sold on the idea that real estate is the best and safest investment in the country! I believe they are correct. This group has hopes of retiring from their current jobs – but still, they also wish to invest along the way using their skills and whatever time they have available. These folks do not really need more cash flow to live on; but, like everyone else, they could certainly find a use for it!

Today's short sales and foreclosed properties provide a window of opportunity – so long as "newbies" don't short-cut the educational process! This includes learning to **negotiate well** and **buying right**! Also, and equally important, new investors need to learn "street-smart" landlording! This is not the same thing as a fee manager or "hired guns." Most property managers don't take much action until the horse is already outta the barn. Street-smart landlords (owners) learn how to keep the barn doors shut to begin with! For do-it-yourselfers, buying rundown houses can be done part-time as a *moonlighting job*. This is very practical for those who have a limited time schedule – **once**

again, do not short cut the education process before launching your investment plan! If you feel you need help, check out my one-on-one counseling service **www.fixjay.com/oneonone**.

JOB INSECURITY AND CAREER CHANGERS

My life-long goal, even though I had a good job, was always to become my own boss one day! That dream was there when I dug holes for telephone poles, and it was still there after I was promoted to manager! With a full-time strategy in mind, my goal was to eventually replace my telephone paycheck with rent checks from my tenants. Lookin' back to the time I finally left my telephone job, it's quite clear to me now, I jumped on a slow moving freight train when I thought I was boarding the high speed express. Since I didn't know any different, I immediately began buying cheap rundown houses– **but only one at a time**. As it turns out, I was dancing the two-step at a rock-n-roll concert! Old timers and folks who've read my books already know what I'm about to tell ya here – but let's give new guys a special insider tip! Besides, even the most experienced investors can stand a *re-boot* now and then!

The right investment for Mom and Pop investors who know they'll be needing income in the immediate future is **multiple-unit properties** – the same goes for those seeking a career change like I was! Houses are simply too slow, and they don't have **multiple profit opportunities** like units! Billionaire Aristotle Onassis once advised his investor minded crew members: "If you wanta be a profitable sea captain one day, you'll need a boat large enough to haul the biggest pay load!" That same advice goes for real estate investors! The vehicle makes all the difference in the world. I didn't know this 50 years ago, and no one in my circle informed me about Aristotle's advice!

You've probably heard this already, but let me say it once again anyway! **Creating real estate wealth is about numbers and rules!** Numbers like *rent-to-value ratios* and *compounding dollars*. Rules like the principles of leverage and strategies that limit restrictions and reduce risk! For example, bank mortgages are much higher risk.

They're also very restrictive with rules like due-on-sale clauses, etc. **Seller financing** is far less restrictive, as I've told you earlier. Also, purchasing with the use of leverage works like buying bananas by the bunch. Acquiring multiple-unit houses in bunches can greatly reduce the price for each rental unit.

Many of my multiple-unit properties were purchased for *almost the same down payment amount* as it would have cost me to acquire *just one single house.* **Think about that** – it cost about the same down payment ($20,000) to **purchase six units**, versus $20,000 down to purchase a $150,000 house. The house will rent for $1100 per month; however, my six units rent for $795 each **($4770 total)**. Certainly, it doesn't take a rocket scientist to see which income is best. Quite a few questions arise when I discuss buying one single house versus six units. The most common of these is; shouldn't I be starting out with just one house first? *Perhaps you should* – but if your goal is **quicker cash flow** and **more profit opportunities** – multiple units are by far your best choice!

If there's a pecking order, I always recommend *multiple units first* so you can establish cash flow! Once that's done, single-family houses are the best long-term investment I know of. Just remember, **cash flow keeps you in the game**! Without cash flow, it's easy to throw your hands up and quit! In the beginning when this concept is brand new to you, you'll need to have a little faith! Martin Luther King, Jr. said it best: "Faith is taking that first step even though you can't see the staircase?" **Can ya dig it brother?**

FREE BONUS:

4 Free Copies
Fixer Jay's TRADE SECRETS Newsletter
How-To Secrets for Investors & Landlords

INCLUDES: Jay's "Christmas Letter"
How to Create Profitable Sales Directly with
Sellers & Avoid Outside Competition

---

1. Seller Financing By Design
   *Creative Terms Set Stage for Cash
   Flow Now - Then Future Profits*

2. Buying Debt – A High Profit Strategy
   *Fix-Up Investors Can Improve Cash
   Flow 30-50%*

3. Investing Works in Boom or Bust
   *Success Is About Investor Skills - Not
   Timing or Location*

4. How to Earn $100,000 Annually
   *Financial Security Comes from Choosing
   Right Property (Vehicle)*

Go to: www.fixerjay.com/bonus

CHAPTER 4

USING THE RIGHT BAIT

*E*very time I start talking about making profits at my seminars, someone will remind me that all one needs to do is buy properties wholesale and sell them at retail! You can't help but admire the genius of such advice, but it makes you wonder – doesn't the asker realize that's what we're all trying to do? The problem, of course, is that buying low and selling high is not always easy to do. In fact, you'll first need some sound profit engineering to develop a solid moneymaking strategy. A good plan must have several common ingredients, such as *proper timing, equity creation, good financing,* and a *reasonable method to extract the profits.* None of these can be left to chance if you intend to make any serious money as an investor.

Many beginners buy houses without the slightest idea about how they intend to make a profit! Others buy real estate and they somehow figure that when it's time to sell, profits will automatically be there for them. Investing in this manner is an easy way to fail. There's simply too much speculation or guessing rather than ol' fashion investing with a carefully thought-out plan.

When you have limited funds, like about 95% of all my readers – you must make a thorough analysis or projection of future profits before you close escrow on every purchase! You need to understand exactly how each investment will pay you back for owning it. An excellent method is to explain it thoroughly to an unsympathetic spouse who would rather use the down payment for a trip to Disneyland. If you can pass this test, chances are you've already given considerable thought to the deal – which is exactly my point here!

SIT DOWN AND SKETCH OUT YOUR PROFITS

My method is a very simple one, which has served me well for a good many years. My tools consist of a yellow legal pad and a couple of pencils! I sketch out sort of a credit-debit schematic or cash flow chart showing all the dollars I expect to spend in each year of my ownership. I also estimate my income or profits for every year. These income figures represent all the monies I expect the property to pay me during my term of ownership! See Cash Flow Chart, Chapter 9 (Figure 9-4).

Lastly, I estimate my future selling price and develop a realistic plan for making the sale. By going through this exercise, I'm forced to take a hard look at the various factors that contribute to a profitable investment – and of course, that's the main purpose of the exercise! Take it from me, if you can't show someone, including yourself, **on paper** how you intend to make your profits – chances are you won't!

Looking back over my own investment career, I can tell you without any reservations, my most important wealth-building tools have always been my uncompromising desire to be successful – along with enough good sense to "shake off" my dumb ideas and failures. Equally important for me, I have always sought out advice and education from the right people. **The right people** are those with proven experience who are already successful doing the same things I would like to accomplish. I might add that most of my serious "flops" have come from my lack of research, trying to move too quickly, and from overpaying for income properties. In the beginning I didn't possess enough patience to thoroughly analyze and plan before leaping headfirst into several highly speculative transactions. Those early deals cost me, but I eventually learned from my mistakes.

DON'T BUY PROPERTIES WITHOUT A PLAN

Investing in real estate requires a lot more than simply buying the property! I often use the term **positioning** – putting yourself and your investment in the right place for the future! If you fail to concern yourself with positioning, you'll be exposing yourself to a great deal more risk than you should! Let me try and explain what I mean.

When you purchase real estate without first preparing a reasonable plan as to what you're going to do with it, you can easily be in big trouble without realizing it. My telephone mentor service has taught me dozens of different ways investors can screw themselves up in more ways than I ever imagined existed. Talking on the telephone with my customers has provided me with a long list of things investors should not be doing, but let me tell you some things most investors should be doing.

Before I discuss several **profit-making ingredients**, let me first say that one of the biggest reasons I've kept my flocks of rental houses over the years is because they provide me **a guaranteed income**! Having a reliable income allows me time to operate my properties without being under the gun (short of cash). There's a tremendous disadvantage having to sell properties when you need the money to live on, as opposed to having the time you need to select the right buyer. Waiting for Mr. Right can often be worth 20 to 40% more profit when you're negotiating with a full stomach! Therefore, it's always my standing advice – *buy a few good rental properties to start with.* Get your monthly income established so you never look hungry if you're planning to sell. Buyers can always spot a *starving seller* miles away.

PROPER TIMING SETS STAGE FOR EXTRA PROFITS

To maximize profits, you must buy properties when it seems like the wrong thing to do! Buying during a buyer's market (that's when lots of properties are available with only a few interested buyers) is generally worth at least a **20% discount** to those who have the guts to go against the flow! For example, a $100,000 property might sell for $80,000 without much haggling. Conversely, during a seller's market (opposite from a buyer's market), the same $100,000 house will likely fetch $120,000 (20% more).

As you can see, being synchronized with the "topsy-turvy" up and down cycles can be worth up to $40,000 more when you understand –

there's a right time to buy and a right time to sell! If you follow the crowd, you'll likely end up doing almost the opposite of what I'm suggesting here. To prove my point, try and find someone you know who follows the crowd and is rich! I'll bet you can't find a single soul! When major newspapers and financial reporters begin recommending real estate investing to the public, shrewd owners immediately slow down their buying and start "polishing up" their properties to sell for maximum profits to the crowd of dummies who will happily pay whatever the market will bear. Remember, *the $40,000 price difference* I'm discussing here has nothing to do with adding value or appreciation. *You earn the extra money by simply buying and selling at the right time.* When you can synchronize your buying and selling along with adding value (forced equity), you'll be at the top of your game in terms of squeezing out maximum profits on all your transactions. Takes a bit of practice at first, but it works!

EQUITY CREATION

When you purchase average properties in average condition, you can expect to pay *average prices and terms.* Equity creation or *buildup* is somewhat difficult when you purchase average properties. Equity buildup comes from two main sources. The first is rather insignificant; it's the principal payment portion of each mortgage payment you make. With each principal payment reduction you have a little less debt, and therefore, more equity!

The second kind is what I do. It's called **adding value.** It comes from fixing up the property or smoothing out people problems by initiating better management. This kind of equity is called **forced equity.** That's because the owner makes it happen. *It has nothing to do with real estate cycles or the economy!*

One of the best ways to create equity is to **improve the financial performance** (raising rents) of a property! For example, if I'm able to fix up a rundown property and increase rents from $20,000 annually to $30,000 annually, that's **forced equity creation.** If the property is worth **10 times the gross rents,** I've increased its value by **$100,000**. 10 times the $10,000 annual rent increase = **equity creation**. It has nothing to do with normal appreciation. I forced up the value with my fix-up skills. If the $400,000 property appreciates 05% next year, that will add another $20,000 equity to the $100,000 I've already created.

GOOD FINANCING

Unless you're a cash buyer, **good financing** is absolutely essential to earning big profits. If you can't offer decent financing when you decide to sell, you'll end up making concessions to the buyer, which will greatly reduce your potential profits. My suggestion for you is to mentally sell your property at the same time you are negotiating to buy it! In other words, think ahead to when and how you plan to market the property someday – think specifically about the kind of financing you'll be able to offer your buyer in the future.

If you have mortgages that can't be assumed (due-on-sale clauses), you'll restrict any future sales to a buyer who will need to qualify for new financing! If you agree to short-term notes or mortgages when you acquire the property, most buyers will balk at assuming them. Having to assume or take over high mortgage payments is very restrictive, because buyers will be concerned about cash flow.

The best kind of financing you can have on the property when it comes time for a future sale is a long-term (20-30 years) *seller carryback financing without a due-on-sale provision*. Also, mortgage payments that are substantially less than half of the total rental income at the time of sale are attractive to most buyers. This type of mortgage can easily be wrapped (wrap-around) by a new *all-inclusive mortgage* allowing the seller to earn extra profits on the interest spread, and avoid paying big income taxes by using installment reporting.

LOCATION COUNTS – BUT NOT FOR EVERYTHING

When I look at potential investment properties, I am always concerned about location. I want a good location for the specific plan I have in mind for the property. However, all my plans are not the same. They all have the same objective, which is to make a profit – but the way I plan to do it can vary with different properties. For example, some houses are excellent long-term investments. At least that's the way I view them. But, you must be very cautious when trying to out-guess the future. Don't bet the entire ranch and all the chickens on your long-term (over five years) predictions. Remember, it's still just a guess. With long-term investments in good locations, you can expect to pay a bit more to acquire them. The reason is because sellers can demand and get higher prices even if the property looks a bit rundown – the competition will keep the price higher because of its location. You can expect to pay a little more for a top location, *but of course*, if your prediction about the future turns out correct, you might just be a big winner someday!

On the negative side, higher acquisition costs and bigger mortgage payments can cost lots of extra money! Also, it can take considerably longer before you ever realize any profits or cash flow. Don't forget this part, because it can be the difference between going broke and surviving! Mom and Pop investors need **cash flow first** – and long-term profits later on. If you get these two reversed, there might not be any later on. My files are full of sad stories about broke speculators, in case you need a little more convincing. But for now, let's move on to more positive stuff that can help you make more money.

I like to think about locations as A, B and C. A locations are the best. B will be the local average, and C is just a stone's throw from away the county dump. With a little study work and some driving around, you can easily determine these locations in your own investment area. Investing in A locations is fine, but it generally takes more cash to buy properties. I've already told you the reason why. My choice is B locations, but I always look at a C to make sure I don't miss anything exciting. I stay away from HUD projects, high crime areas, and places where I don't feel safe being there! Regardless of how cheap the prices may be, both renters and buyers do not want to wear bulletproof vests or flak jackets under their pajamas. **Don't invest in the slums.**

NO CASH DOWN OFTEN
TRANSLATES TO NO PROFITS

Many neophyte investors have made the mistake of buying marked up houses for no money down. They automatically assumed they could earn a profit because no cash was invested! With high mortgage payments and short-term balloon notes, their dreams of becoming rich tycoons quickly turned into nightmares instead. The "free lunch strategy" may work well for selling slick-covered CD's on the midnight cable channel, but in the real world – you can't buy much value for nothing!

An important thing to remember–you can purchase properties **with dollars** or pay with **your personal skills** – *but you must always pay*! When you are negotiating to buy a property, stop and think about the deal as if you were the seller. Would you sell your real estate for nothing down if you thought someone would pay a normal down payment? I don't think I need to ask what your answer is – *but neither would I*. In most cases, acquiring properties for no money down means you're paying too much to start with! That's the wrong way to make profits in this business.

INFLATION OR APPRECIATION

Inflation or appreciation comes in two different flavors! First, there's the kind that comes from natural causes. Everyone gets it automatically if they happen to own properties in areas where it's happening. Sometimes it's 2% a year, but I've seen inflation jump to 25% for a short period of time. I've also watched properties nearly double in price within a two-year period of time. The problem with natural inflation is – *there's no guarantee it will happen*! And of course, that's why I recommend investors treat it like a bonus or the extra gravy. Don't build your investment plan on the basis of automatic appreciation – just clap your hands when it comes and pretend you knew all along!

Forced appreciation is my specialty and you can bet the ranch on it. The reason is **because you, the investor, can control it 100%.** When

I buy rundown houses and fix them up, I force them to appreciate in value. Much of the higher value comes from being able to attract better tenants who will pay me higher rents! I can achieve this because I intentionally upgrade rundown properties soon after I acquire them. It's simply a matter of being able to offer my customers (tenants) a nicer rental unit. On several occasions, I've increased property values by 50% in just eighteen months of ownership. When a 50% increase starts compounding, it won't be long before you can add a couple extra zeros to your net worth. **Compounding comes from leaving your investment alone.** In other words, it's like money in your interest bearing account that you never touch! If you keep your property earning rents, as opposed to selling, I will assure you–the *sales profits* will never be enough to make up what you'll lose when you interfere with compounding profits.

CASH FLOW KEEPS YOU GREEN AND GROWING

Regardless of whether your plan is to acquire single-family houses, duplexes, or multiple-unit properties (which I recommend) – **cash flow should always be your immediate goal**! Naturally, I'm assuming you're an investor with limited funds who can ill afford to pay out additional money every month to keep your property operating. That certainly describes me in my earlier investing years! That's why I've always favored fixer-uppers or properties I could immediately improve (add value) shortly after I closed escrow.

KNOWING WHAT TO FIX – WHAT ADDS VALUE IS KEY

Sweat equity can be an excellent cash saver if you fully understand values and what fixing up stuff costs! You must also understand that all fix-up work doesn't add the same value. For example, replacing the roof is costly, but don't add much value for the amount of money spent! Yet it's necessary, because you can't rent or sell a house with a roof that leaks. On the other end of the spending scale, those cutesy little three foot high picket fences I like to build around the front yard of my houses often return *ten dollars* for every dollar I spend to build them. By comparison, my long-time friend Mr. Nickerson was happy when his fix-up improvements returned *two dollars* for every dollar he spent.

FIXIN' FOR HIGHEST RETURNS

When you have the knowledge about "**fix-up $ returns**," and what various improvements will cost, you'll have a pretty good direction as to where you should spend your fix-up dollars. Another example of excellent fix-up returns comes from installing **window coverings**! Curtains, blinds, and sometimes a drape or two consistently earn me $30 to $35 more rent per month than houses with naked windows! Especially in my lower priced older units. **How do I know this, you ask?** By showing tenants my houses and talkin' with them *face-to-face* while doing my own rent-ups! Tenants will tell you exactly what they want or what they think is missing from your property. The expense for window coverings, figuring eight windows per house is $50 each–or an average of $400 per house. With inexpensive items like new Formica countertops and shower kits, you can easily earn your total cost back in less than three years – that's a good return! My window covering expenses get paid back from additional rents in 12 to 15 months! **That's an excellent return for me – and my renters are pleased as punch!**

New investors, especially fix-up investors, often start out paying too much for fixer properties. Next, they make their second mistake by **over-spending** on fix-up! Can you see why the suicide rate is so high among freshman fix-up investors? Every investor, rich or poor, should complete at least one "hands on" fix-up job in my opinion. With first-hand experience, he or she will quickly learn how tricky fixers can be! It's hard to get exactly the right feel reading a book! It's like the old Best Foods TV commercial used to say – "Ya gotta crack some eggs to make real mayonnaise." Likewise, ya gotta fix a house or two before you can become a **real fix-up investor**!

AVOID HIGH PRICE IMPROVEMENTS

Many new fix-up investors have a tendency to *over-improve*; much like homeowners do to the houses they live in. They add all sorts of whistles and bells and things that don't add much value – *worse yet*, they spend money on things that most tenants won't pay extra rent for. Things like fancy kitchen gadgets, add-on rooms, finished garage interiors, costly back yard improvements, and even "in-ground" swimming pools are just a few that come to mind. There's an old saying in real estate circles that says: you can spend all the money you want on a $100,000 tract house – but in the end you'll still have a $100,000 tract house when it's done. Sure, you might be able to sell for a few more dollars than your neighbors, but rarely are you likely to ever get your total investment back. This is called **over improving**, and thousands of amateur investors do it every single day.

REMODELING – A BRIDGE TOO FAR

Many so-called "fix-up investors" haven't quite figured out the difference between *renovating*, *fixing*, and *remodeling*. Perhaps renovating and fixing are somewhat similar, say like distant cousins. However, investors who remodel inexpensive fixer-type properties can easily end up working their tails off for very little profits, and often huge losses. The problem is, remodelers change too many things that should be kept like they are! For some reason, remodelers seem to have a fierce passion to make improvements based on their own personal likes or dislikes with almost total disregard for costs! They often rationalize their actions, thinking, "Since I'm working here anyway, I might just as well go ahead and do this or that because eventually it will likely need doing anyway!" That's like saying, "I might just as well spend my whole paycheck in the bar tonight so I don't have to worry about spending any money later on." **That's both dumb and dumber!**

AVOID PLAYING HOUSE WITH INVESTMENTS

In order to be a successful fix-up investor **(that means making money doing it)**, *you must fix only those things that need fixing.* It's important to separate your "pet ideas" from the proven **"money-maker"** fix-up work! I'm not talking about repairs here. Obviously, things that don't work must be fixed. I am talking about things like moving walls around, adding rooms, making bigger windows, ripping out kitchen cabinets and installing new ones. Remodelers often do these things, and it's generally not cost effective in the fixer-upper business. The important thing to remember here is that almost everything fixers do should **add value to the property** – *either for buyers or the renters.* Room sizes and newer cabinets will seldom matter much when it comes to adding more value to rental property.

My general *rule of thumb* estimating the costs for fixing properties is roughly about 10% of what I pay for the property. For example, if I purchase a house for $75,000, I'm thinking roughly $7500 for fix-up. My maximum fix-up estimate jumps to 20% of the purchase price for what I call heavy fixers. As you can probably guess, there's also a correct sequence for doing fix-up work. I consider this extremely important. **Fixer properties should always be fixed outside before inside**. The reason: Potential customers (tenants and/or buyers) will always judge a property based on what they see driving by 15 or 20 miles an hour! Doing fix-up work when the property is located on a main thoroughfare or a heavily traveled road **makes this strategy even more important**. Always remember, the world judges almost everything by how it looks – by the first impression! **Most ugly properties tend to look worthless!**

FIXIN' WHAT SHOWS SHOULD BE FIRST

Exterior painting changes the appearance of a property and makes it look more valuable quickly. **Therefore, it's important to do exterior painting first.** Use off-white, cream, or any light color on the main body of the house or apartment. For the trim color, eave boards, window trim, and borders around doorframes – use darker colors like brown, maroon, or charcoal for a pleasing contrast! Use medium-grade exterior latex after scrapping (wire brush) any peeling paint. A latex primer coat may be needed on older wooden surfaces that tend to suck up the paint!

Don't forget landscaping! Both tenants and buyers like green lawns and flowering plants. I've found that even watered weeds, *mowed and trimmed*, look close enough to pass the test! You might even toss out some lawn seed to thicken the stuff! If there is no lawn, plant one and water several times each day while you're working inside the house or around the property. Also, consider planting several fast growing trees where none exist. Fruitless Mulberry or Modesto Ash are cheap and will definitely improve the looks. *Shrubs* and *bushes* can add a great deal of appeal. Pyracanthas and flowering oleanders are fast growing and almost *childproof*. Even repeated relief visits by the neighborhood dogs hardly hinder their growth. Pyracanthas have thorny stickers, which stops most kids from plucking them up. They also stay green and sprout colorful red berries in the fall and spring. Oleanders make good dividers and are excellent for privacy. They grow faster than baby Dobermans and can survive with hardly any water or care, which is what most renters provide.

As I mentioned earlier, picket fences add a boatload of **street appeal** and instant charm to almost any property. **Street appeal easily adds value and a higher selling price.** Both renters and buyers will be totally impressed! White picket fences create a cozy feeling – what I call *hominess*. I build them 36" high, with pointed pickets! Sharp points discourage "jumping over" for all but the most daring kids. I use 4' posts buried 12" and cemented – 8' apart! Use metal joist hangers to secure parallel 2 x 4's – 12" and 30" off the ground. Lastly, nail on 1" x 4" cedar pickets, spaced 4" apart – paint white. Gates are optional.

CREATING MAXIMUM STREET APPEAL

Shutters and window trim add tons of charm! Think of those old Hollywood movie sets, "what people see is how they will judge your property." Both renters and buyers are looking for attractive places to live! They're either impressed – **or they're not,** as they slowly drive by observing your property! **The first 15 seconds** is all it takes to form **that all-important first impression!** I'll repeat, your house must present a good first impression – and much like those old "propped up" Hollywood movie sets, your property must show well to viewers driving by! It's that street-side view where you'll win or lose the battle for customers!

I'll repeat, customers (renters or buyers) generally say yes or no based on their very first impression! Shutters around the windows, even those imitation plastic kinds, will add lots of *sizzle and spice* to the street side view of your property; particularly when all the windows are the same size. If they're not, use window surround (trim) like 1" x 6" cedar boards installed around the windows. You can paint them using your trim color to achieve a very attractive look for hardly any extra cost. Wide fascia boards covering weather exposed rafter ends provide a nice finished look to most older houses. Again, paint them using your trim color. Partially enclosing a front entrance porch or stoop will also add a great deal of charm and looks to most older houses. Extending the roof over an uncovered front porch and enclosing the sides with ready-made 4 x 8 lattice panels, painted white or the trim color, will "spruce up" the appearance very nicely. Lattice panels can be used to cover open spaces on porches, steps, and even on top of board fencing. **I call this my "foo-foo" treatment** and it will "spruce up" any property suffering from the blahs!

IMPROVEMENTS BASED ON CUSTOMER WANTS

Ugly roofs will distract from any property! If the street side, *or the side you see driving by*, is worn and ugly, it will seriously distract from "drive-by" curb appeal! **If my budget can stand it**, I will likely have the street side of a pitched roof replaced. Leave the back side for later and just keep patching any leaks till your budget improves! Hardly anyone will ever notice an ugly roof on the back side! When it's out of sight, it's generally out of mind, and likely won't hurt that

all-important first impression! Keep the back side from leaking by applying more GOOP!

Another "biggie" for me is fencing! **I like fences!** But even more important, both **tenants and buyers like fences**! You can generally rent most houses for about 10 to 15% more money if they have rear yard fences that will keep the barking kids and screaming dogs incarcerated. Mothers are quick to pick up on this child protection feature when they visit your property and observe back yard fencing. They totally understand the value of child safety – or *kiddy corrals,* as I call them. The biggest problem is cost – **6' high board fences are not cheap**. If you don't have the budget to do back yard fencing initially, then wait for another day. **Fencing in front should always come first** because it adds immediate value to any property – it's that first impression again!

The big difference between "successful fixers" and the guys who always overspend, is learning **how** and **when** to end a fixer-upper project! Fixing older houses can cost you all the money you have in your wallet – plus, all the extra you can borrow! But it doesn't have to be that way, nor should it! *You must never forget*, it's not much fun fixing up junky houses and baby-sitting' lazy tenants if you don't get paid for your efforts! **Over-fixing** and **over-spending** are the most serious problems you must guard against. Perfection is okay for a hobby, but it has absolutely no standing when you're fixing up houses for profit.

OVER-FIXING IS OFTEN FATAL MISTAKE

Please don't misunderstand me here! I'm not advising anyone to do shoddy or crappy work. What I'm suggesting is that your work be creative and that it fits within your budget. *It can be done, believe me*! One of the best examples of what I'm trying to explain here happens nearly every day with the state highway construction builders! These guys are out building six lane freeways when every single motorist passing by can plainly see that 10 or 12 lanes are needed. However, what these workers are building is the number of lanes they have budgeted! When more tax dollars become available (at some future date), they will then add more lanes. That's exactly the way house fixers must think when planning their fix-up work! It's very important to stay within your budget if you intend to make a profit!

STARTING SMALL WITH INEXPENSIVE HOUSES

Starting with small rundown houses generally works best for most Mom and Pop investors, whether they're handy or not! Being a bit handy will certainly help – *but even if you're not*, it's still much cheaper to make your early mistakes on *smaller properties* rather than bigger more expensive ones. Cheaper houses are less costly to repair; plus, they're also much easier to rent because the largest percentage of renters can afford them. *Why smaller houses*, you ask? It's simply mathematics! **They're much more affordable to lots more people!** For example, 80% of the renters in my town can pay no more than $750 rent per month. It's a fact, there's lots more poor renters than rich ones! On the bright side – poor renters generally won't be nearly as sensitive about your crude-lookin' sheetrock repairs while you're in the learning stage!

Inexpensive houses are most often the older properties built many years ago. Some are desperately in need of rehabilitation and tons of cleanup. About 85% of the work needed is what I call *grunt work* or *non-skilled labor*. New investors or beginners generally have a lot more *grunt power* than *financial power*. Obviously, doing everything you can to save money should be a big part of your early learning experience. Fixing up or **adding value** to older properties will take some special skills – but at the same time, these older properties will provide a wide range of practical fix-up stuff that almost anyone can do, even if it takes a couple do-overs! In my opinion, operating **inexpensive fix-up properties** is the fastest way to learn the real estate investment business for the least amount of expense. **But even more importantly** – fixing rundown properties provides the quickest path to **profits** and **cash flow**. Profits and cash flow are always the highest priority for most beginners who are typically scratchin' for every dollar they can find!

WHAT DOES ALL THIS STUFF COST?

Fix-up work breaks down into **two parts that cost money**! First and most expensive is the **cost of labor**. On average, labor will cost approximately 70 cents of every fix-up dollar you'll spend. Supplies and material will average about 30 cents. Obviously these numbers can vary a bit for different type jobs, such as overlaying expensive exterior siding where the materials (4 x8 sheets) are very costly, but the labor involved is relatively quick and cheap. **My 70/30 split** is well within the ballpark for anyone estimating most fix-up jobs!

In profit-making terms, this means if you can purchase a fixer property for 30% less than its estimated "fixed up" value – say for example, a **$70,000** house you can purchase for **$49,000**. Let's say you've estimated your fix-up costs will run about $6,000, which means you'll likely spend about $2,000 for materials and supplies. Assuming you provide all the labor yourself, you can expect to have approximately **$19,000 equity** when you're done. If you find you can do this consistently, and stay on budget – **just keep doing it**! It really gets exciting when your next purchase has another zero added ($700,000). **Wouldn't you agree?**

CHAPTER 5

THE COPYCAT FISHERMAN

Many moons ago when I was still toiling at the phone company during daylight hours, *and fixin' up dumpy little houses evenings and weekends*, I met a young man named Dave. Dave would drop by my house-fixin' projects whenever he spotted my old Chevy pickup with the wooden ladders hangin' off the side. He was always full of questions about why I did this or that, and more often than not, he would jot down several notes if he liked something he saw me doing! Needless to say, this was quite flattering to me, given the fact that I'm basically a self-taught "do-it-yourself carpenter" with a general philosophy of – **Pound to fit, paint to match**!

THE STRANGER IN MY HOUSE

There's no question, my skills improved a great deal over the years; still, I've never worked around a professional carpenter or plumber! I'm self-taught with lots of reliance on those "how to" pictures you'll find on the back of material wrappers. I even taught myself how to use many special tools as I plugged along! I won't even attempt to explain what I thought a peter wrench was when I began learning about plumbing! After a while, Dave and I kinda drifted apart and I remember thinking to myself, he probably moved away or something. He never did tell me what he did for a living, and I don't recall ever asking. Many months passed, and I soon forgot about Dave!

It was about four years later, and suddenly one day – there he was!

We ran into each other in the local hardware store where I bought most of my fix-up supplies. "Long time no see," I said. "I sorta figured you moved away or something!" We agreed to have lunch the following day and I honestly don't remember who paid! I bring this up, because back in my early days, I always practiced my negotiating skills to see if I could get a free lunch. I figured improving my skills would help me buy houses. It was during lunch that Dave told me he was in the house fix-up business, just like me – and had been for some time before we met! I now understood the purpose of his house visits – and of course, the reason Dave was taking so many notes. He was copying my fix-up ideas. I also learned that Dave owned more rental houses than I did! Needless to say, I was quite surprised when he told me about this!

COPYCAT – FASTEST WAY TO LEARN

During lunch, Dave confessed about not having very good fix-up skills when he started out. He felt somewhat embarrassed when he admitted that his real purpose for stopping by to visit was to observe my techniques, and of course, copy the ones he liked for use on his own properties. *Hold on just a minute – it's all coming back to me now*! Dave did pay for my lunch that day, so I guess my negotiating skills were working pretty well after all! But right now there's something I need to pass along from our lunch conversation – *something that would eventually be worth a million lunches to me* – even if I had to pay for everyone! **It's about an investment strategy** – a strategy that Dave had been using himself, and was more than willing to share with me over lunch, so many years ago.

Dave was just an ordinary "blue collar" kinda guy who had read and studied a great deal about real estate investing. He may have been a little behind with his fix-up skills – but I can assure you, his investment skills were right on the money. Much like I do today, Dave invested mostly in older rundown rentals – *but unlike me back then*, Dave invested in **multi-unit properties**, while I was fixing up bank foreclosures (REO's)–**one house at a time**. Dave explained to me, in a way that made absolutely perfect sense, why his way was far superior to mine. The fact that I had closed escrow on three times as many properties as Dave, yet he was collecting at least three times more rent money from his houses, gave me good reason to listen and seriously think about what Dave and I were doing so differently.

REAL ESTATE IS A NUMBERS GAME

Now it was my turn to start taking a few notes from Dave! One of the most important lessons I learned was that *successful investors should always think like business people!* For example, if I were a shoe merchant, I would need to base all my business decisions on whether or not I'd make a profit at the end of the day. The style of my shoes wouldn't mean *diddly squat* unless they earned me a profit. Take a good look at ladies footwear fashion today. If I were to purchase my shoe inventory based on my own particular taste, I'd end up eating a store full of shoes. The lesson to be learned here: you must buy the style of shoes all the ladies want and are willing to pay for. The shoes I would likely choose myself quit selling shortly after WWII.

In the rental property business, the two most commonly used words in a landlord's vocabulary are **cash flow** – whether you have any or not! And much like the shoe merchant, what investors think about building types, configuration and location must always take a back seat to **counting profits at the end of the day**. One lesson I learned from Dave (but of course you'll never find it written in any real estate books), was that *you won't work any harder operating 10 rental units than you will operating just one!* I know this to be a fact because I've done both! I worked very hard fixing up my single REO houses and I work the same way fixing up a group of 10 cottages I own. There's hardly any difference, except 10 units takes me a little longer. People simply imagine it's harder with more units. They set an imaginary boundary for themselves! It's like wading into the lake till it's up to your knees, and deciding, that's your limit – you feel safe at that level, but you're not sure why. If you'll just forget the imaginary limits you've set for yourself, and keep walking a little further till the water's above your waist, you'll quickly adjust to the difference. It's called leveraging your efforts – and it works slicker than a whistle if you'll just give it a try!

USING THE RIGHT KIND OF LEVERAGE

Leveraging works with *down payments* and *profit-making* the same way it does with your labor and skills. For example, I've acquired many older multiple-unit properties (6 to 12 units) with just a $20,000 down payment. It's very common to spend that much or more on a basic three-bedroom starter house. You'll get some leverage with the house alright – just not enough to put you in the cash flow mode. Even the most economical three-bedroom house where I live, when saddled with an 80% mortgage payment, at the lowest interest rate in the past 30 years – still won't generate enough net income to pay for *day-old bagels* at the Salvation Army!

As the late Paul Harvey used to say every evening to begin his news broadcast, "And now, for the rest of the story!" Okay, I know you're gonna scream and holler about all the deadbeat tenants hangin' from the windows at Jay's 10 junky cottages! Fair enough, we'll discuss tenant issues later on, but for right now, let's think about the shoe merchant – he must buy the right shoes in order to produce a profit. Don't forget, there ain't much sense of staying open for business if there's never anything in the till! Say you spend your $20,000 down payment to acquire a modest three-bedroom house in average condition – it's likely you'll have average maintenance expenses and a tenant who pays average market rents. And still, if you're lucky enough to generate $100 cash flow every month after paying an 80% mortgage payment – you might easily win the coveted "blue star" cash flow award! As for moving up a notch to your next purchase – unless you have another $20,000 down payment saved up, you'll be effectively shut down for business! In short, you'll be a one-house operator with no way to expand!

BIGGEST BANG FOR YOUR DOLLAR

When I suggest investing your $20,000 to acquire 10 junky cottages instead of just one house, I'm assuming that many do-it-yourself investors are about like me when I first started out! Coughing up $20,000 was a major financial event in my life, and it didn't take me a whole lot of time figuring where my next $20,000 would come from. **The fact is** – it wasn't coming at all unless my investments started earning some money back!

Fixing problems for money is the first step of my profit-making strategy. It allows me to leverage my down payment money to a much higher degree than buying properties without any problems to fix! To say this another way – if you don't have much money to begin with, you need a plan that will start generating income quickly if you intend to stay in the investment business very long. Waiting for the economy to get better, or for banks to start making easy loans, is a fool's game and it's way too much speculation. On the other hand, finding properties with problems to fix is something that can translate to higher rents within the first several months and is much more predictable. Dave explained the power of this additional rent strategy – especially when it's applied to multiple rental units.

Part of our discussion must always be about where to buy these units, because that's extremely important. However, right now, I wish to convince you with simple arithmetic, why multiple units are best–the same way Dave did with me while we both enjoyed the lunches he paid for! Let's stick with our example of 10 rundown apartments, cabins, houses, cottages, or even a couple mobiles mixed in! I'm not overly concerned about the type of rental units or their configuration, so long as they make the cash register ring! The kinds of properties I'm looking to buy are always under-rented! The reason is because they are physically rundown; they're unattractive and most likely poorly managed.

The properties I'm searching for are generally renting for at least $100 and sometimes $200 below the current market rents for comparable units in the area. Why does this happen, you might be wondering?

It's because the properties have been neglected; they're rundown and the owners are not much interested in doing repairs and maintenance. As time goes along, these properties gradually deteriorate and become less and less attractive to tenants. As this is happening, the rents must be continually adjusted downward in order to keep renters in the units. As you might suspect, the quality of the tenant population goes downhill rather quickly. These owners are called "milkers." They suck all the income from the property and never put one lousy dime back for upkeep! It's like a death sentence for the property, even though it sometimes works for a short while.

UNDERPERFORMING REAL ESTATE

Certainly there are other factors to consider besides the down payment and under-market rents – but let's just suppose you purchased 10 junky little houses (cottages) with a $20,000 down payment. The cottages are currently renting for $400 per month in an area where well-maintained units easily rent for $550. Let's assume that after fix-up and cleaning, your units will now fetch $550 rents. **That's a total rent increase of $1500 per month** – *which means*, if you acquired the property at somewhere near break-even cash flow – you're now very definitely sporting a cash flow glow! Fixing problems provides the kind of leverage that can quickly earn new investors a shiny "tycoon badge."

Seldom does the written version and the actual field operation end up quite the same – *meaning, the same $ numbers* – but even if you come close, say a $100 rent increase instead of $150, it's far from a failed effort. **$1000 a month more** than what you started with is still a lot to brag about. Can you begin to see why Dave's advice, those many years ago, was like discovering gold? Over the years, my multiple-unit properties have produced much faster earnings! Without question, they're far more efficient than my early single-house investing. When you apply the leverage of numbers, which comes from adding value (fix-up) to multiple-unit properties, you'll quickly pass up all your single-house friends in terms of **faster cash flow and more of it**. Echoing the lyric from an old "Three Dog Night" pop hit recording; *ONE is truly the* *loneliest number you'll ever do*! If faster payback and bigger profits are what you're investing for, I would suggest you seriously consider switchin' to Dave's plan – become a copycat investor just like me! **It's where the biggest fish are bitin!**

WHERE TO BUY THE RIGHT PROPERTIES

Driving through a small town near where I live – the giant roadside sign reads: BUY LOCAL. At my seminars, I try very hard to convince students to follow that same advice. Trotting around from state to state or even to another town has little to do with becoming a wealthy investor. In fact, many cases I hear about suggest that moving around is a better plan for going broke. Wealthy investors become that way because they develop the proper skills. In short, wealth has very little to do with location, or even what a property looks like! It's mostly dependent on your **knowledge, skills,** and **actions**. Cash flow properties are rarely ever found that way. As an investor, it's your responsibility to **find opportunities and create cash flow**!

Any reasonable sized town, say 10,000 population or more, will offer the small-time fix-up investor ample opportunity to stake his claim. My town is less than 100,000, and there's room for dozens of fix-up investors like me to operate on a full-time basis. Once again, let me repeat – **successful investing is about knowledge**, not the size of the town. For those just starting out, I always recommend specializing! For example, I decided to specialize in fix-up because of the extra leverage it provided. *Being a specialist*, it's much easier to become the local expert and forge ahead of your competition much faster. Investing where you live (your home turf) gives you a decided advantage because you already know something about property values. It's easier to profile the renters (are they mostly young or old?), how much rent can they afford to pay, and what parts of town do they desire to live in. You can also quickly find out where all the deadbeats hang out so you can avoid buying properties in "tweaker" neighborhoods. Out-of-town buyers fall into this trap every day because they don't spend adequate time checkin' the streets after dark. If you think that sweet little old lady realtor from C-21 will be your "snitch" (informer) – chances are, you'd be better off making an offer on the Brooklyn Bridge!

DON'T BUY RENTAL HOUSES IN THE SLUMS

Obviously, you might find a bargain **price-wise** in the slums! But then you must stop and ask yourself – **what happens next?** I won't buy properties in slum locations for two basic reasons! First, I already know I'm not gonna like any tenant who wants to rent my house. Secondly, I don't wanta end up dead! *Here's the deal gang!* If you race out and purchase a rental property in a slum location – you'll greatly restrict the number of people (tenants) you can rent to. From a business standpoint, limiting your customer base is not a wise decision! You want your rental properties to enjoy the largest market possible. You don't want any unnecessary restrictions. Another serious problem with investing in slum locations is that no matter how hard you work trying to "pump up" the value, you should always remember – the value of income property is **primarily determined by income and location.** Lower rents in a slum location are very serious roadblocks!

The best rental locations are often quite different from home-buying locations, especially for start-out renters and seniors. **Affordability** and **convenience** are the key factors in making rent decisions for young renters and retired folks. Older houses, small apartments, or combinations of these, located in or near downtown areas can be ideal rental locations. These are older buildings, many rundown, that were once choice locations surrounding retail stores near the heart of the city. Over the years as cities expanded, commercial and retail development grew past and around these properties! When freeways came, residential development (subdivisions) moved out to cow pastures, ending an era of downtown residential life, except for new high-rise condos. Obviously, my customers don't qualify for condo units. Besides, they might jump off and lose my rent money on the way down!

COMMERCIAL LOTS – RESIDENTIAL USAGE

Many older residential units in downtown locations are zoned for future commercial, office buildings or whatever – but so long as the units are maintained and kept in good repair, their residential usage is generally grandfathered till they're bought out for a higher use. In my town, I've owned rental properties in downtown locations for many years without interference from anyone. My customers enjoy locations near downtown activities, and many young families walk or ride bicycles to work and shopping. In larger cities, older housing and slums will often blend together without any bright colored yardstick to clearly divide them. *This is where knowledge about your town and the neighborhoods pays off.* Clearly you must avoid slum housing for the reasons I've discussed already. If you'll do that, investing in downtown areas can be very profitable for rental housing entrepreneurs. *Entrepreneur* sounds much classier than just plain ol' landlord, **don't ya think?**

In my town, as well as many other smaller-sized cities (95,000 population), it's easy to distinguish the original city core! It's where the town first originated over 150 years ago. Originally, there were two main commercial streets with office buildings, retail stores, and hotels covering about six city blocks. Houses, small apartments, motor lodges, warehouses, and light industrial buildings created the next layer of development surrounding the six-block city core.

Over the years, new development, both residential and commercial, expanded outward, surrounding the existing buildings, much like the growth rings you see in giant tree trunks. Early on, there were no zoning laws that prohibited houses or apartments from being built next to a sawmill or canning factory! If you owned the land, you could pretty much build what you pleased. If you drive through almost any city or town today, regardless of the size, you'll see plenty of evidence about what I'm telling you here. Not much changed until the 1940's and '50's when zoning laws and freeways began to emerge and changed land development rules forever!

LOCATION IS MOST IMPORTANT

In my training courses, I divide locations into five separate areas as follows: **snob hill, downtown commercial, older residential, dense slums**, and **suburbia**. I recommend that Mom and Pop investors look for properties in the **downtown commercial** and **older residential** neighborhoods. Often these two locations will appear to be one in the same, and in many larger cities they can be difficult to distinguish from the slum areas. It's for this reason that I use another important guideline to help me choose my locations! I call it **the isolation factor**! It means that before I make up my mind to acquire any property, I seriously consider all the ways that neighboring properties might create a negative impact on mine.

It's for this reason, I won't buy a single four-plex (four-unit building) in the middle of other four-plex buildings often built in groups, but sold individually. *My reason is simple* – I could easily lose control of my business (renting to decent customers) because of how the neighborhood landlords choose to operate their rentals. Suppose they rent to "tweakers" who continually disrupt the surrounding tenants. Before long, all the decent tenants will be frightened away and the only customers who will show up to rent will be more druggies. **Isolation** is needed for tenant control as well as privacy.

Natural barriers such as vacant land, creeks, fenced power line right-of-ways, and even clumps of mature trees will offer just enough separation to avoid excessive coziness or encourage easy bonding between neighboring residents. Renters want as much privacy as they can get. As a rental property owner, it's my goal to provide as much privacy as I can. *Isolation* might be a corner property with six-foot fences down both sides – and in some cases, retail stores on one side or both, will provide good privacy. Sometimes investors can create a small multiple-unit "Shangri-La" tucked in between commercial buildings or behind the local shopping center. Another of my favorite locations is 6 to 12 rental units (large single lot) smack dab in the middle of an older, single house, subdivision. Obviously, zoning laws would not permit these types of configurations today, but so long as they're kept in good repair and continue to be used as rental units – they're generally allowed to operate under **the grandfather rules**.

FINDING GOLDEN EGGS IN THE HUNT

In many larger cities, something called *gentrification* has been going on for many years now! The term means the rejuvenation of the older downtown buildings and often slum locations where the transients live in harmony with the ladies of the evening. Many of these neighborhoods are in an upward transition phase, and the "yuppies" think it's cool to live in older downtown buildings where the action is. Often, these urban areas are home to grand old Victorian houses, many of which have long since been converted to multiple rental units and studio apartments. If they're operating as rentals, but badly rundown in terms of upkeep – you might just find a bargain. As a rental owner, however, *I'm not looking for complete re-do's, nor do I wish to put myself under the scrutiny of the permit department*! This happens more often with two- and three-story buildings where fire danger is much greater.

Renters will pay for convenience – downtown is often a favorite location for the younger population, as well as seniors who no longer drive. Once again I'll repeat myself – stay away from slums even if the property is free! Getting rich is a lot more fun when you can avoid being shot! Several considerations are important; you should ask yourself these five basic questions about any location before you decide to pursue the deal:

1. Would I personally feel comfortable working in this part of town?
2. Do I believe this location is safe at night, in relation to the general neighborhood?
3. Does the area look like it's reasonably stable and not going downhill?
4. Are city or private services, such as buses, police protection, schools, fire departments, hospitals, and decent shopping available within a reasonable distance?
5. Does this location look like a good rental area where I can attract the kind of customers (tenants) I'm looking for?

WHAT HAPPENS WHEN IT'S TIME TO SELL

When it's time to sell multi-unit rental properties, they are mostly sold or traded to other investors who have the same goals like yourself! They are obviously not sold to homeowners looking for a nest to lay their eggs. With single-family house investing, many investors do reasonably well selling to their own tenants. I have never been overly fond of that particular strategy – however, I won't knock it either. I currently own single-family houses, *but hardly ever sell them*; I'll discuss my selling strategy at another time.

For now though, let me say this for the record – **control is a big deal to me**! I don't like appraisers and those young property inspectors with more pimples than a McDonald's fry cook! And I certainly don't like institutional lenders who want me to fit their special borrowing programs, or sign their promissory notes making me personally liable if one of my investments goes bad. Signing bank mortgages with personal liability puts everything you own at risk! Bank loans are expensive, and in my opinion, the wrong direction for building personal wealth!

The rental business – *as in my ten-cottage investment example*, offers the small-time, do-it-yourself investor, **the most control he will ever find anywhere**. I don't need appraisers, inspectors, banks, termite guys, or even real estate agents (although I use them). The reason is because my kind of investing is basically a **people business** – it's about me and the party who wishes to sell. It's about the seller's needs; and, of course, what I expect to **gain** from the deal. The late Warren Harding, a very successful real estate teacher, often told his students; "You can't dance with real estate – you have to dance with the people." **I couldn't agree any more.**

CONTROL FINANCING MAKES SELLING A SNAP

The best way to sell 10 rental cottages quickly is to make your potential buyer an offer he won't refuse! Offer reasonable terms that will allow him to start making money. In case you haven't guessed already, this strategy is not exactly rocket science! Wouldn't you buy from me if I sold you a **cash flow deal**? The reason many income property sellers fail is **plain ol' greed**! They wander too far over the "hog line!" Friends, you don't need to screw the next generation of investors because there's enough lean meat in the pot for everyone. Basically, you can profit from the growth or gain, amortization and the interest (carrying charges) – and, you can do it without visiting any bankers or calling that little old lady realtor from the Century 21 office. This is one final vestige of what it means to be **a true real estate entrepreneur**! Buyer vs. seller, people working with people – and, as I said earlier, *you have total control of all the moving parts*. Selling with wrap-around financing will keep your paydays coming long after you kiss your tenants goodbye. See Chapter 20 for all the details.

BENEFITS FAR OUTWEIGH OTHER FACTORS

Most beginners (including myself) have very limited knowledge about all the benefits available to investors when they first start out. Even after Dave convinced me that multiple units were a much better deal – I still had many rivers to cross before I would eventually get all my ducks lined up. You simply can't absorb all the knowledge by simply wishing it were so, or reading inspirational books. After 50 years of operating properties first hand and kickin' tenants' butts, I'm still not absolutely certain I'm in the *right quadrant*, like Mr. Kiyosaki recommends – *but then again*, I never had a **rich dad** either!

In much the same way TV detective Columbo meticulously checks out his homicide leads–I believe investors should always check out or investigate new ideas and concepts! Then, I suggest that they thoroughly explain new ideas to their most trusted and *knowledgeable* friend to get a totally unbiased opinion. If it passes the test, give it a try and see how it works. This was exactly what I did when Dave explained his multiple-unit investing concepts to me. Not easily convinced (perhaps even a bit stubborn), I continued to plod along buying single REO's for quite some time after hearing about Dave's formula. Still, the idea was not forgotten. My brain stayed locked in on the amount of money he was collecting every month.

Much like the same questions I'm asked today – I was curious to know just how much effort it took Dave to manage his tenants and collect the rents. I also had questions about what kind of tenants he had! Dave gave me several addresses of properties he owned and told me to drive by and check 'em out! I kept wondering if his tenants would be much of a problem. To my surprise, they looked almost identical to the people I rented to!

My good friend and a *ring-wise investor*, Jimmy Napier, writes: "All investors must develop a certain mindset to become financially successful!" To the untrained eye, this valuable little tip might not sound like much – but I can tell you, **Jimmy's advice is right on the money**. People invest in real estate for many different reasons, but basically they want to make more money and build a comfortable lifestyle and retirement for themselves. This simply won't happen if you're the type of person who is not willing to explore new ideas or different ways of doing business!

SECURITY, COMFORT, AND RISK

When Dave opened my eyes to all the benefits of **multiple-unit investing**, it was as though a *total financial awakening* came over me. He explained, that I could own 10 units – *even more*, for the same amount of money (down payment) it would cost me to purchase just one single-family house! I could hardly wait to finish my lunch. I went looking for properties that very same day. To say that I was motivated doesn't sound nearly urgent enough. The only words I needed to hear from Dave was that my down payment could easily be earning me **10 times more money every month**. Back then, my single houses were renting for $250 a month. **$2500** seemed almost beyond my wildest imagination – WOW! The whole idea seemed like easy money with less financial risk! I have never considered myself a huge risk taker! I much prefer to shoot fish in a barrel, as opposed to sitting on the riverbank, hoping one swims by! The idea of earning 10 times more money each month for the same amount of down payment seemed a whole lot safer than collecting rent from just one lonely tenant.

At my seminars and in the education business, *I learned many years ago* – never try and guess who will make it, and who won't. Every time I've tried to guess, I'm almost always wrong! However, I do feel qualified to pass along my observations to those who are desperately trying to figure out the best way they should begin investing! I'll start by saying that most of us at one time or another actually dream of becoming wealthy some day! For us real estate wanta-bees, it's a dream about owning enough income-producing properties to make us financially independent! For many folks, however, dreaming is where the idea of becoming wealthy ends! From where I sit, here's the biggest stumbling block – **people fail to take any action**. Wanta-bee investors tell me this all the time, "Jay, I'd love to quit this horrible job and start working for myself. Obviously, I'd like to become financially independent and build a solid retirement! *But, here's my problem* – I don't really want to move anywhere, and I'm scared to death to invest any money from my small savings account. Is there anything else you could recommend for me?" **There certainly is** – stay right where you are until you develop the **investor mindset** like Jimmy says you need. *In my opinion, it's not optional!*

YOU'LL NEVER GET ANYWHERE
IF YOU DON'T START

I can't really explain why some people get started, while others only procrastinate – *but here's the way it looks to me*: those who have the least amount of money to invest, the lousiest jobs and some with no savings at all, seem to have far better odds of becoming financially independent than those who are blessed with more security. It just seems to me that becoming rich for the more affluent crowd is something they would like to do, so long as they're not required to give up any part of their comfortable lifestyle. Nowhere does this show up more clearly than at real estate investment clubs. Many who attend these clubs year after year, will sit in total amazement when a former unemployed mill worker shows up as the guest speaker and explains what happened! He shares his personal story about how he

earned a million dollars painting and fixing up junky houses and duplexes. They all listen attentively; *they applaud*, say thank you and goodnight–**then do absolutely nothing else**!

Small-time investors with a dream can become successful just like the big guys if they'll follow a workable plan, **commit themselves to action**, and not give up till they reach their goal. Newbies or inexperienced investors must always serve their apprenticeship! Jumping into more advanced techniques without first building a **solid foundation** leads to discouragement, and quite often, dismal failure! **Hands-on investing** offers the best opportunity for average working folks, because they automatically get real life experience right from the start! *But Jay, I'm not the handy type,* you tell me – okay, fair enough, I suggest you find someone who is and start taking notes while you help with the grunt work! That's exactly what copycat Dave did when he used to visit me!

The kind of real estate I've been discussing here (multi-houses and cottages) does not require anywhere near perfection! It's a marvelous opportunity to be creative and figure things out as you go along! Remember what I said already about being **overly cautious**. If you have to, take a few drinks – **get loose**! You probably won't feel much better in the morning, but if it gives you the courage to start – the hangover is probably worth it! Sometimes it takes extraordinary measures! **Whether you agree or not, go ahead and say AMEN!**

KNOWLEDGE IS THE ULTIMATE WEALTH BUILDER

The reason I started fixing up rundown junky houses in the beginning was because I always found pleasure working with my hands. It gave me a real sense of accomplishment every time I turned an ugly-looking property into a beautiful swan. Like most beginners, I figured that by doing a lot of the work myself and carefully buying all my supplies and materials, I'd save myself a bundle. *I figured this plan would eventually make me rich*! I was on the right trail *of course*, but I soon discovered it would not be my hands-on skills or my frugal buying habits that would affect my bank account the most! Instead, it would be my **knowledge**.

You simply cannot work hard enough or fast enough to become rich! Granted, we all start out thinking we can, but sooner or later we begin to realize that the money's not coming in nearly as fast as we're wearing ourselves out! Somehow we must find a way to speed up bank deposits, because we're simply not making enough of them – **and they're not big enough**! This will never happen while you're crawlin' under the house bangin' on the sewer pipe. Obviously, *the answer lies elsewhere!*

LEARN ALL YOU CAN FAST AS YOU CAN

You must learn to **work smarter** if you intend to become a rich real estate tycoon! If I knew another way – I'd tell you right now, but there is none. You must expand your education while you're working on your property. **Working smarter is what builds your wealth.**

Closing out this chapter, I'd like to pass along some excellent advice given to me years ago by author Robert W. Kent. He said: "You must **determine to believe**! Doubt is ever-present in all of us and will cloud your thinking about everything you hear or read." Mr. Kent went on to say that having faith in yourself is often all that separates the winners from losers! *You cannot become successful if you don't believe you can.*

CHAPTER 6

FISHIN' FOR THE LIMIT

*B*efore we dig into good houses vs. bad houses, let me first say – we're talkin' *investment houses only* – not the kind where you sleep at night; unless of course, you're sleepin' in your rental. By way of definition, let's agree, that a good house is one that makes us money – *a bad one doesn't*. As for investors, you wouldn't think that they'd buy bad houses, but the truth is, they do it every day. Not only that, but many will actually defend their purchase and attempt to convince anyone who'll listen that they're on the road to riches!

Buying investment houses without any idea of when you will earn money is a dangerous strategy. Certainly I'm aware that in states like mine, California, there are times when appreciation runs wild; and, for a short period, flippers are in hog heaven. When it stops without warning, however, many are caught in a place quite the opposite of heaven! House flippers by my definition are not really investors – they're speculators! I have nothing against speculating, but you must understand – it's just the real estate version of gambling. Besides the risk, it does not provide the investor with most of the benefits he would enjoy with investment real estate. In my opinion, speculation should only be done by those who can afford to lose the gamble *and still be okay financially.* However, for most of us, investing is what we should be doing if we're trying to achieve financial independence and long-term security.

PLANNING IS HOW YOU GET RICH

Sorry folks; you won't get rich by accident! If you wish to be rich, you must plan for it. Planning is what rich people do so that poor folks have somebody to call lucky. In my personal life it seems like the harder I work and plan, the luckier I seem to get. Most folks with money can certainly relate to that! Let's adopt another rule of mine, which says: all houses are good for something, *but some are just made for lookin' at*. They're pretty, they cost too much, and they will only earn a fraction of their mortgage payment and upkeep costs from their rental income. Investors who have owned these kind for a while will often confess that no matter how pretty or attractive the houses look – when they're costing you outta pocket money every month, while the tenants wear them out – they can start looking ugly very quickly!

There's an age-old argument that says: It's okay to have negative cash flow so long as you have adequate income from your well-paying job to support it! As far as I'm concerned – that argument sucks! I suppose the rationale behind the argument is that the house will go up in value. *The problem is* – you could easily end up paying three or four times the original cost. You might have a free and clear house after 30 years or so, but you're not even close to being rich! I've adopted a special rule for myself, which says: I only want to own *investment houses I can keep even if I lose my job*. If you adopt this rule for yourself, it will greatly assist you in selecting the right kind of investment houses. I teach new investors, many of which have regular jobs, to be extremely careful and purchase only the kind of properties they can keep should their jobs go away! Many new investors I work with are planning to become full-time investors same as I did – but regardless of whether they do or don't, they still won't lose their properties if they'll follow my advice.

EARLY SACRIFICE PAYS OFF

A great many new investors start out completely wrong in my opinion; they believe that buying a home should always be their first investment! I'll admit that with young married couples, quite often my opinion is not worth a hill of beans when the wife gets wind of my advice. I can certainly understand this because there's a great deal of emotion when young couples contemplate buying a home. Emotion is not a good ingredient when it comes to **investing for money**; therefore, allow me to have my say, and then I'll quietly shut-up about the matter.

My good friend, *investor* John Schaub, did things just right! He and his wife Valerie agreed to rent their first home and invest whatever extra money they could into rental properties. After 10 years of scrimping and investing, they were able to afford a much nicer home because they waited. This takes oodles of discipline and a very understanding couple who can agree to make the early sacrifice in order to have it better later on. *Not surprisingly*, John and Valerie have worked very well together acquiring the wealth they enjoy today.

You might be thinking to yourself – what if my mortgage payment and the rent are almost the same amount? Wouldn't I be much better off buying rather than renting? *After all*, buying will accumulate equity, whereas renting only accumulates rent receipts. That's absolutely true as far as it goes – *the trouble is*, it don't go very far! For starters, young couples tend to buy the biggest house they can afford based on their income. In almost every situation I know of – *renting is always cheaper*. Here's why: after buying a nice shiny new home and stretching the family budget tighter than a banjo string, couples stand back and say – WOW! We need new furniture. Renters will often sit around on lumpy couches with a quilt covering up the broken springs, and quite often their other furniture would make the Salvation Army wish they hadn't sent the truck out – but if they buy a new house, it's a whole different ballgame. It's off to the furniture store with the Visa card. The only question left–will the new furniture last as long as the payments? Furniture always blows the budget big time – still, that's not all!

Renters don't need homeowner's insurance, and when the air conditioner breaks, they don't call Sears. **They call their landlord.** Guess who pays these expenses when you own your own home? Then there's the matter of creating a cozy backyard and building fences if there ain't none! All these things require tools – *lots of yard tools*. And should there be a swimming pool – *there's even more tools*, plus a monthly service fee for cleaning. It's not the same as renting a garden apartment where you simply strip down to your shorts and jump in. When you rent, someone else pays for pool cleaning and those nasty bills to heat the water. Can you begin to see how John and Valerie got such a tremendous head start with their investing plan? It takes real tough discipline, but the results can be solid gold!

There's one final tip I need to share with you about saving money when you're first starting out – *and then you've got my word* – we'll move along. It's about the use of your personal time! When I rented an apartment, I didn't jump up every morning and race out to water my backyard and feed the birds. **All my time was devoted to building my personal net worth**; I was concentrating on my rental properties and increasing their values. There was nothing to distract me from going "full speed" ahead towards my primary goal of becoming financially independent! As I've already told you, you won't get rich by accident – **you must plan for it**, and then, you must make it happen! Half measures are not nearly strong enough, if you wish to start having money left over every month!

MONEYMAKING PROPERTIES NOT SCARCE

I often tell seminar students: 95% of all the real estate for sale is not worth a hoot for investment property. Needless to say, that statement always fills my classroom with puzzled faces. I agree, it sounds a bit far-fetched, none-the-less its true! Of course, I'm speaking in the context of **do-it-yourself investors**, with a limited amount of money to invest – *and in most cases, very limited knowledge as well*. New investors starting out should keep their first several investments very simple, and above all, *they must not allow themselves to get snookered into buying any property they don't fully understand*. I've owned a variety of investment properties over my long career, and I will tell you from my own experience – buying only the kind of investments you understand and can operate is the only way you'll have a long career. Since 95% of all the properties available for sale won't "pencil out" – meaning, they don't show bottom line, cash flow earnings in a reasonable time frame (within two years), you should automatically eliminate them from your property radar screen. This will free up your time to concentrate on only those properties that have good, solid, **identifiable potential** for cash flow! Pickin' through all the losers is a tremendous waste of time and effort. You might be thinkin' to yourself – boy, it sure don't sound like there's many properties left! Let me assure you right here and now – *you'll never run out of the right kind of properties* – and the more you learn, the more properties you'll keep finding!

PROFITS ARE THE GOAL – NOT STRUCTURES

Allow me to share with you the kind of properties I've spent most of my career *finding, buying*, and *operating*. I'm sure you'll recognize many of these types in your own buying areas. First, I'll set the stage by telling you I'm mostly interested in **multiple-unit rental properties**, be they individual houses, duplexes, small apartment buildings, old motels and small older hotels, motor lodges (forerunners to motels), and occasionally a few mobiles will be in the mix. My average number of rentals at one location is 7-12 units. The configuration doesn't matter too much! "Mix 'n Match" is just fine with me if they are spaced out nicely. In other words, I'd like a little breathing room, or small yards separating the units.

The lot size for my **Viola Cottages** (11 units) is 120' x 150' lot, 18,000 sq. ft.; **Hamilton Street** (eight houses) is 222' x 140' lot, 31,080 sq. ft. I've owned several properties like **Hillcrest Cottages**, an old motor lodge (22 units) situated on almost three acres. Before I leave the subject of lot size – I'm looking for adequate separation for tenants and space for parking with a turn around, but that's about it. Extra lots or a spare acre in the rear are no good for landlords. They cost money to cut the weeds and they're a magnet for non-running cars and junk. Worse yet, they don't earn one thin dime! Extra land, as far as I'm concerned, is only good to hold the earth together – **but that's it!**

LOOKING FOR PROFIT OPPORTUNITIES

Looking at my Viola Cottages, *an old motor lodge* – there were four side-by-side apartments in the back with open carports behind each unit facing to the rear street. Down the side, there were four individual cottages backing up to the side street (corner lot). In the front, there was a two-story building with a single two-bedroom apartment upstairs and two apartments on the ground floor with lots of extra storage space. The buildings were arranged so that they surrounded a large center courtyard, with all the units facing the yard except one single apartment in the three-unit building. I felt this "center court" area could be a very valuable asset to the property, although it was naked ground and weeds covered by dozens of Harley Davidson parts and old tires when I bought it. Since most of the motorcycles were in pieces, the tenants had settled down and become regular homebodies. Their transportation was non-usable and scattered all around the center courtyard. On a positive note – they were always at home for job interviews. See sketch of Viola Gardens, Appendix B.

The Viola property was listed with a local realtor, and had been so for over a year before I began to look at it very seriously! At the time, I had my hands full – so looking at more properties was a low priority on my things-to-do list! The realtor told me that he'd received one offer seven or eight months earlier – but he told me that the walk-thru had frightened the buyer away! There's one thing you need to fully understand – *the competition for properties like Viola is pretty scarce*! That means, if you're an investor with vision who can fix up an ugly property like Viola, it won't take too long before you'll become known as **the ugly property specialist** in your area! This will automatically bring you more opportunities to acquire properties similar to Viola. These kind of properties are very "tough sells" for most agents, no matter what state or town they're in. When you learn to pay the right price *by negotiating better*, you'll discover as I did that these kinds of properties are the quickest to start producing cash flow. Once they're up and running, you've pretty much created your personal ATM machine.

SELLER PROBLEMS – BEST PROFIT MAKERS

As I look back now, I did overpay for Viola, but it didn't matter much! Rents were exceptionally low – and yet, the out-of-town owner rarely collected them all. He had a local helper, but he was part of the problem. Occasionally he fixed a few leaks, but mostly, he drank beer with the tenants during repair calls. Negotiations took me a couple months or so, but I kept driving out to the property, both day and night – mostly thinking about ways I could somehow create at attractive rental complex where decent tenants would want to live! In the mornings, I always had all kinds of brilliant new ideas; however, by nightfall **I was always down to just one** – never coming back again!

Before you even think about buying properties like Viola, you need to know what the apartments will rent for once you get them cleaned up and ready to go. That means you need to learn what the **comparable market rents** are in your area. **There's one easy method** – start calling the classified "For Rent" ads in your local newspaper – **pretend you're a renter**! After you've looked at 20 or 30 apartments, you'll have a pretty good idea of what the rents should be for your property.

A quick refresher about how the money plays out should lift your spirits and help you forget about hauling off the old Harley parts! Don't ask me about the "hard-nose" tenants right now – you'll discover when you have **cash flow** every month, they all look like "pussies!" Besides, we'll talk about landlording another time. On the day I took over Viola, the rent schedule prepared by the escrow company showed $2455 per month. I can assure you, Viola tenants spent twice that much for beer. Even in the early '80s, these rents were still quite low. As I always do, immediately after I acquire a new property, I "tip-toed" around the property asking permission to haul off all the broken bike parts, tires, and filthy-lookin' outdoor couches. The tenants stayed calm, mostly drunk I think, but of course, I was very polite! Several tenants even thanked me. This has generally been my experience with tenants when you don't act like some "smart-ass" know-it-all!

For the cost of **$182,000** ($12,000 cash and a $25,000 note) – I became the owner of an annual rental income of $29,460. When you do the math you'll see that I paid just slightly over **six times the gross rents**. I assumed (took over) two private notes on the deal and the seller carried back the remaining balance. Seven months after my take-over, the rents were up to **$3640 per month** – plus an **extra $210** from my newly created laundry room.

HAMILTON STREET – THE GOOD HOUSES

I'm told my eight detached houses on Hamilton Street initially housed the workers who built Shasta Dam, California's largest dam and electricity provider. The giant structure was completed in 1945. Each house has two bedrooms and a single bath, with approximately 700 square feet of living space. In my town, this "economy-sized" house is a very marketable dwelling because the vast majority of renters work at low paying service jobs. They're affordable; they're individual houses and they have a separate yard space for each unit. *Houses like these will rent at least ten times faster than up and down apartments with comparable prices.* Young couples especially value my small-fenced yards with grass (watered weeds) where the little baby gomers have a safe place to play! This configuration, eight houses on a big lot, offers a huge marketing advantage for landlords because tenants will stand in line to rent them! Purchased right, they're a very profitable investment all the way around.

I bought the Hamilton houses from a retiring dentist who wanted to travel and stop smelling bad breath every day! A very ring-wise operator, he had owned and managed five or six similar properties over the years. He insisted on financing the sale to make sure he had the income he needed to keep his Winnebago gassed up between national park visits.

CHASIN' DOWN ANOTHER CHERRY STREET

Small single-family houses (detached) together on a large city lot are the kind of properties I lust and crave for. They're worth all the effort and detective work I can muster up during the courting stage.

Detective work means my "behind the scenes" investigation of the property. Why the "cloak and dagger" routine, you ask? Can't you simply make an offer based on what you think the property's worth and see what happens? My answer is: sure, I can write an offer anytime, but I need to know some important stuff about the property in order to offer the right price and terms. **Here's an important tip you should underline**: if you hastily write up your offer and open escrow before you know all the expense information, and *then later on*, you discover new information that makes your price too high, you'll probably lose the deal! Sellers get hoppin' mad when you suggest a lower price, regardless of the reason. Mad sellers will most likely tell you and your agent to go stuff it!

The eight houses on Hamilton Street had been owned by the dentist for many years and were free and clear (no mortgage debt). The dentist kept his rents somewhat below market rates – a strategy often used by lazy owners who don't want many repair calls from their tenants! The idea here is that tenants tend not to call an owner when they know rents are low! Their call might just cause the landlord to think about increasing the rent to offset his service call expenses. In my view, this is a very poor strategy for several reasons! First, tenants attempt to fix things themselves rather than call for repairs. *This may sound great until you see how tenants repair things.* In many cases, by not attending to minor repairs when you should, they often become very expensive later on. Not keeping up with proper maintenance is never a wise strategy in the long run.

LOW RENTS GUARANTEE CASH FLOW

Another major reason for keeping rents closer to market rates is because the rental income stream is primarily what dictates the property value and selling price when you decide to sell or trade an income property. This is the sad predicament the dentist found himself in when I showed up to negotiate the purchase. Discovering low rents are one of the main reasons I lust and crave for properties like Hamilton. It's a textbook example of what I sometimes refer to as "shootin' fish in a rain barrel." There's almost no way I can miss having **positive cash flow** unless I drive my car in the river on the way down to the closing.

SELLER FINANCING IS THE RULE

When I speak to investment clubs and discuss the benefits of **seller provided terms** (more often referred to as seller financing), the bulk of my audience looks at me as though I just arrived on jet skis from Mars. Naturally, I forgive them; for I know from whence they came (they're typical single-house buyers without a clue). House buyers do get seller financing occasionally, but as a general rule – they don't! I've heard realtors advise their house-selling clients that *seller financing is simply not done anymore.* Can you begin to see why it took me four long years to train my real estate broker Fred about the income property business?

Smart sellers like the dentist understand the financial benefits of selling with good terms. Once again, you need to understand that seller financing, as we generally call it, is not really financing at all! *It's actually an extension of credit, or terms offered to the buyer to facilitate the sale of the property.* The seller simply says to the buyer: I would like to have all cash for my property; however, I will allow you to pay it to me over the next 30 years if you'll just add 7.0% interest to the payments." The dentist understood the value of extending credit to me and receiving payments every month. First of all, selling over a period of time allows him to stall *or put off* paying his capital gain taxes. He only pays a little dab each time he receives monthly payments from me. With a cash sale, he'd be required to pay the full amount in a single tax year! He also understands that extra earnings from interest spend just as well at gas stations and grocery stores, same as the principal amount. **Installment sale treatment** is the tax term for this transaction, and over the payback period, my $145,000 note balance will mushroom into **$347,288** worth of payments. This should help the dentist a great deal with his Winnebago expenses – plus, keep him traveling the back roads and countryside a whole lot longer.

DEALING WITH RING-SAVY SELLERS

Finding income properties without any mortgage debt is quite rare! It generally means the seller has owned the property a long time. It also means he hasn't cranked the property (taken money out via borrowing). Most free and clear properties I've purchased over the years have been acquired from elderly sellers who fully understand that *wealth comes from long-term ownership*. Finally, one day they realize–it's time to kick back and smell the roses! That was the situation at Hamilton. These types of properties owned by investors like the dentist are truly *the low hangin' fruit* when you find them, because there's absolutely no limit to the creative transaction you can structure.

Long-time owners, like the dentist, are smart enough to understand that they must leave something on the table for the next guy when they decide it's time to step aside, sell their property, and carry back the financing. The last thing any seller wants is to take the property back when they're living four states away enjoying their new life! The best way to guarantee that this doesn't happen is to make sure you structure your sale transaction so that the new buyer makes enough money every month so there's very little danger of a "come-backer." That's a property that doesn't earn its new owner any money – *and eventually*, he becomes discouraged and walks away or gives it back. Sellers who demand the highest price with unrealistic terms are prime candidates for **"come-backers."**

Investors, who own five or six of these multiple-unit properties like the dentist, are not folks who just fell off the turnip truck! They're generally the **Mom and Pop millionaires** I write about. They can't be treated like a dummy house seller because they're much more sophisticated – **that's why they're millionaires**! For new investors, *or even old ones*, this situation can work to your advantage in a number of ways. I've already told you about the huge benefit of **seller provided terms** – it's the "Cadillac" of all financing arrangements. *Why is that, you ask?* Because unlike banks or other institutional lenders who might have four or five different lending programs, *or products*, sellers can dream up hundreds of different creative ways they can allow you to pay for their property – and of course, **this is the key to engineering cash flow deals**. Remember what I said earlier about my "behind the scenes" detective work. Find out who the seller really is! Is he young, old, rich, poor, single, or married? *This is the kind of information that helps you negotiate well.*

SAFETY IS A MAJOR CONCERN

As I quickly discovered with the dentist – the size of the down payment and the monthly payment amount required to purchase his property, were not his number one priorities. Remember the low rents he was charging his tenants? He already had a high monthly income, and no doubt a pile of money in the bank after 40 years of "drilling and billing!" The top priority for the dentist was not about grabbing the last penny – **it was about his safety**! Once I discovered this, it became clear to me that I could pretty much dictate my own terms (within reason of course), so long as the dentist felt adequately protected. We had several face-to-face meetings to negotiate exactly what would be required to make him feel safe. His first concern was my "teeny-weenie" down payment proposal of $15,000, *less than 10% of the purchase price.* The dentist seemed quite concerned about having to take the property back if somehow I messed up – or became a democrat and started dating the tenants. Obviously, this issue is a very serious concern for most older sellers. After 35 or 40 years of nurse-maiding tenants, most landlords are ready to head for the Promised Land! Once his Winnebago roared past the city limit sign, the dentist had very little appetite for turning around! I eventually solved this small down payment issue with what I call my "2 Fer 1 Plan"– but first, let me tell you why the dentist was so concerned!

NOTHING TO LOSE CAN SPELL
DISASTER FOR SELLER

It's plain ol' commonsense: the more you have invested in something, the much less chance you'll ever give it back! That's why skinny down payments always invite seller skepticism. Sellers will automatically ask themselves – *or at least they should* – what happens if I should have to take my property back because the buyer quits sending my payments? Since I have experienced this terrible dilemma, let me tell you what happens – you suddenly realize you're the **"stuckee"** instead of the **beneficiary**, and it's not a pretty thought – especially with multiple rental properties and a whole bunch of unsupervised tenants hangin' out the windows.

When a failed investor-owner loses his property via a regular foreclosure action, chances are, your losses *as the grieving seller*, might be more or less limited to just the monthly payments you've been receiving. In my state, foreclosure involves a third party trustee sale and it's pretty much an automatic procedure, even though seven or eight months can easily fly by before you receive a dime's worth of relief. During the foreclosure period, while the failing owner is in a downhill spiral, it's not the least bit uncommon to see the apartments stripped of all appliances, coolers, heating, and everything else that can be carried away! What you'll finally recover after foreclosure may be just a stripped down skeleton of your once attractive apartments. Naturally, you'll be responsible for paying all the foreclosure expenses and additional legal costs to take the property back.

So far I've only told the good news – *or the best-case scenario* – if your distressed investor reads a few "do-it-yourself" legal books or happens to be dating a legal aid attorney, he or she is likely to add on another layer of misery by filing a bankruptcy. This can cost you big bucks as a beneficiary because now you're involved with the federal court system – *and of course*, the line starts behind all the other deadbeats! You won't be seeing any payments for a very long time, and there's a real good chance that if and when any payments do come in, they'll be used up by the bankruptcy trustee. Well, I think you get the picture; and of course, the dentist was very aware of all this stuff himself! If you'd like to learn a little more about defending yourself against the mean ol' federal bankruptcy judge – you need to read about my experiences at Creekside Estates: *Gold Mine Houses*, McGraw Hill, available at most bookstores or call ***1-800-722-2550***.

JAY'S 2 FER 1 PLAN SEALS THE DEAL

When you own multiple investment properties like I do, you don't need more money to grow bigger! **You need to become more creative**. Using creativity is much more fun than spending your money! Save your money for Disneyland, where you'll likely meet many of your future tenants. My "2 Fer 1 Plan" is about offering more safety using additional collateral. The dentist wanted 30% down on his Hamilton houses! As he put it, "I want the buyer to be good 'n stuck so he won't even think about giving the property back." Those were his exact words. As you might guess, a serious meeting of the minds was necessary to reconcile the dentist's $50,000 down payment requirement – and the **$15,000** I had at the time. He also reasoned, **with a larger amount down**, the payments on his carry back mortgage would be much less each month; *therefore*, easier for the new buyer to make.

I asked the dentist if $15,000 would work if I made up the difference by giving him a good solid equity as additional security, in another property I owned. He was open to the idea, so long as he could be the sole judge in deciding the value of equity I was offering! He was beginning to eat outta my hand when I offered him a choice of three properties to choose from. Folks who have attended my seminars know that one of my *basic business records* is called **Jay's Schedule of Real Estate Owned**. That schedule shows a current list of all the properties I own showing estimated values, current mortgages, who I send payments to (beneficiaries), telephone numbers, and addresses – plus the net rental income for each property. Naturally, I don't pass this information around unless I'm involved in serious negotiations with someone I'm about to do business with. This was the situation with the dentist and his Hamilton Street property, and I really wanted the houses bad because of the huge profit potential I envisioned. Usually, I'll meet with sellers at a local coffee shop or in the title company conference room to introduce the idea. There, we can both review my list of properties I'm prepared to offer as **additional collateral**.

I offered the dentist a second mortgage deed on my Willow Creek apartments in the amount of $25,000. My down payment would **still**

be $15,000 cash – but the $25,000 mortgage on my Willow Creek property would temporarily serve as additional security to make the dentist feel safer while I paid off the balance on Hamilton. Willow Creek was fully rented, very attractive seven-unit property – my estimated value was $275,000, and the first mortgage balance was $112,500. I had offered the dentist a choice of three different properties, but he picked Willow Creek. My equity at the time was $162,500 (based on the value). He apparently agreed with my estimate of value, or at least he felt well enough protected. I call this additional collateral arrangement – **my "2 Fer 1 Plan."** Here's what I tell the seller – Mr. Seller, if I don't keep my promise to you and make timely payments as agreed–and you're ever forced to foreclose; you'll be in position to take back two properties, both Hamilton and Willow Creek. I call this my 2 Fer 1 Plan because you sold me just one property, but now you get to take back two!

USING WHAT I HAVE TO GET MORE

Giving a second mortgage on Willow Creek made the dentist feel safe – and, it didn't cost me a plug nickel. It does create a $25,000 lien on my property, but so long as I perform according to the terms of our agreement, it's simply another parcel number recorded on the deed. It specifies there's a $25,000 lien for *non-performance*, but there are no additional monthly payments involved. I will generally negotiate a reconveyance clause that says – **after five years of faithful performance** (meaning a good payment record), the beneficiary will release the added collateral deed. I would also recommend that you ask for a *substitution of collateral clause* in the event you need to move the second mortgage from Willow Creek for some unpredictable reason (perhaps you wish to sell). By talking to the dentist and allowing him to see all the properties I owned, he felt very comfortable with me and gave me these two special clauses. I cannot overemphasize the importance of sitting down **one-on-one with sellers** to put these deals together. Sellers who are willing to finance their properties want to meet with you, *look you in the* eye, and talk directly with you before trusting you with their future. **Ask yourself,** isn't this what you would want, if the situation were reversed?

HAMILTON HOUSES WERE PURE GOLD

My take-over rents at Hamilton were $2045 per month and all eight houses were rented. Although the rents were slightly different between houses, they were all extremely low at the time. It's no surprise why they all stayed rented when average rents were only $256 per month – *or nearly $75 per month* under the market rates. As I mentioned above – the Hamilton houses were worth fighting for; and of course, the dentist was savvy enough to give me easy payback terms. With less than a 10% down payment, I would enjoy cash flow right from the start. *Granted, not too much* – but still, it's very rare with 90% cash leverage, to be in a positive mode on the day escrow closes. My mortgage payments of $964.69 were less than 50% of the gross monthly income, which I consider excellent. The houses looked tired and rundown on the inside, and eventually would require new floors, paint, and some rather heavy upgrading as the existing tenants moved out! Even so, it was almost a full year before anyone left. One year after closing, my rents were nearly **$1000 a month higher.**

Properties like Hamilton are the kind you should start with if *your goal is to establish a good solid income you can count on.* The two properties we've been discussing, **Viola Cottages** and **Hamilton houses**, are perfect examples of properties that will generate predictable spendable income within a couple years of ownership. You won't be rich yet, but you'll be headed down the right road. *I'm a strong advocate for creating a dependable income stream before doing anything else in the real estate investing business.* Naturally, I'm talking about folks like myself – who wish to become self-sufficient – and eventually, financially independent. To do that, it takes **monthly cash flow** you can count on! **Can ya dig it?**

CHAPTER 7

FISHIN' IN THE RIGHT POND

About 90% of all amateur investors purchase the wrong kind of property to begin with! I define *amateur investors* as those millions of hard-working people willing to take on a second job, spending what limited resources they have in an effort to make a better life for themselves and their families – folks who share my dream of becoming rich (or at least semi-wealthy) with real estate. Buying the wrong property first often ends up a nightmare because most folks simply don't know enough in the beginning to make critical evaluations about any kind of property. What mostly happens is that new investors, or *wanta-bees*, will overestimate the positive, and grossly underestimate the risk involved.

AN AMERICAN DREAM OR A GASTLY NIGHTMARE

Since I'm about to challenge some sacred territory – **The Three-Bedroom Dream House** – let me first make my confessions, least I be judged a hypocrite! It's my personal opinion that *medium-sized three-bedroom houses* with a couple of bathrooms make the finest investment in America, bar none – **but only after they're paid for**. I own them myself and I'm extremely pleased with how they pay my expenses during my sunset years. **However**, getting them paid for – well, *that's a horse of a different color*!

Buying houses just because somebody said so can make you wish you'd decided to become a rock star instead of a real estate tycoon.

Behind all the glitter can be some harsh financial discoveries that weren't very well explained during your 90-minute real estate guru lecture at the "Dew Drop Inn!"

In my hometown today, the average three-bedroom, two-bath house has a value of $275,000, down from a high of $350,000 a couple years ago. Let's say I can buy the place for 20% below appraised value ($220,000). Sounds like a steal, right? But, don't forget – **it's a rental investment property**! I have $30,000 saved for a down payment – but that's every dime I can get my hands on!

Since my credit is good, the mortgage company has agreed to a 15% down payment and a 6.00% 30-year amortized mortgage with monthly payments of $1121.17. I feel very good about the mortgage because most banks nowadays insist on some type of variable rate mortgage when it's a **non-owner occupancy** (rental house). So far – so good!

If you took the time to investigate the rental market in my town, you'd quickly discover that houses like mine would rent for $1350 tops. Talking with the four largest rental agencies, they tell me that 70% of all the renters in Redding can only afford $800 per month. Assuming the remaining 30% are split (50% can pay more, 50% less), my house will only be affordable to 15% of Redding's rental customers. Needless to say, competition for $1350 renters is fierce right now. Just a quick drive around town, you'll see the signs: FIRST MONTH FREE – and pit bulls are always welcome. *Dependable income* is what I need! Even if I find a renter, I'll just cross my fingers and pray that he doesn't qualify to purchase a new home anytime soon.

DON'T FORGET THE COST OF OPERATIONS

My amortized mortgage payments for the next 30 years include principal and interest. Thanks to California's Proposition 13, my taxes are only $200 per month! Insurance will cost another $40, so I'm already operating below zero profit. I'm hoping nothing breaks and that I've picked a decent tenant. My good friend, John Schaub, tells me it costs roughly one-third of his rental income, or about 35%, to operate his single-family houses year 'round. That's about the best anyone can expect, in my opinion! When I subtract 35% from my $1350 rent, I'm left with only $877.50 to pay my mortgage and expenses. It suddenly occurs to me, I need a cheaper mortgage payment or a lot more income!

Experienced investors know about various methods to solve a negative cash flow dilemma, *but most new investors don't.* Taking on partners and selling half the house can solve cash shortage problems, but these options are very limited to a new investor before he establishes himself. Most outsiders who are willing to cough up their money seem to take the same cautious approach that banks have been using for years! They're always more than willing to put up their money or make you a loan – **after you're already rich.**

Obviously, there are some tax benefits to consider; plus, the hope of future appreciation, but there's also hard work and additional expenses during vacancies and routine maintenance. **In my opinion, dream houses consume too much time and money without enough payback when you're first starting out!** Obviously, if you're forced to cough up additional funds to supplement the deal, it makes it that much harder to earn a decent profit. Many investors I've observed, *both new and experienced alike,* seem to completely forget about **the time factor involved.** It's almost impossible to become financially independent without establishing a deadline or time limit. **How long will it take before you arrive at the promised land?** Answering this question will help you determine the kind of real estate you'll need to take you there. In the dream house example above, how long would it take me, assuming I could afford the negative cash flow every month? *I honestly don't know* – but I can tell you–it'll take me a long time to save another $30,000 down payment to buy my second house.

If you're somewhat new to real estate investing, or if you're currently feeding too many *cash eating houses,* I think it's appropriate to back up and re-read my very first sentence. I'll save you a little time here and just write it again! **90% of all amateur investors purchase the wrong kind of properties to begin with.** It's what they're told to do by seminar gurus, golf buddies, office co-workers, the local preacher, and almost everyone else who's never done this stuff before. As I've already told you, *buying houses is easy* – it's paying for them that's difficult.

As I sit here with pen in hand, I'm very much aware that in certain locations around the country where appreciation is almost non-existent, the money ratio between rental income and the cost of the house will produce somewhat better results than where I live (California). Still, there's the matter of speed! **How long will it take to get rich, or at least financially well off?** That consideration must be a part of every investor's planning! How long will it take was certainly part of my early dream – *and today*, I'm extremely grateful it was!

FINANCIAL FREEDOM PAYS
FOR ANOTHER FREEDOM

Financial freedom can mean many things to different people, but generally speaking, it means the end of money worries, tight budgets, and saving for a rainy day. *In simple terms*, the rainstorm is over! For some folks, financial freedom is about taking expensive trips, and shopping anywhere they please without ever running out of money. *Simply stated*, for the great majority of people, it means living the kind of life they've only dreamed about. However, there's a twin sister to reckon with, and complete success will never be fully achieved without her.

Personal freedom is her name, and all the money you can ever make will quickly lose its irresistible charm if there's never any time to spend it. In fact, many folks with oodles of money will gladly give some away in exchange for more *personal freedom*. My purpose in telling you this is because whichever investment vehicle you choose to make your millions, be it houses, apartments, or racing ponies, you must always consider – **when will I be free to enjoy my wealth?** Most people I know would rather have less money and more time to spend it before they're facing the wrong side of the grass! If you agree, then you must consider **investing in the kind of real estate that can meet your timetable**.

BLUE COLLAR RENTALS IN SMALL BUNCHES

I have long held the notion that every start-out investor who dreams of becoming financially independent in the shortest amount of time, should start with **older multiple-unit properties as their first investment**. Obviously, there are countless objections to this suggestion, but bear with me a few moments while I argue my case! You mustn't forget – **I wrote the damn book**!

To begin with, a down payment of $30,000 will buy six or eight junky houses or apartments just as easily as a three-bedroom single-family house. Competition is not nearly so intense for multi-unit bargain hunters; therefore, *inexperienced investors* will likely get more for their money by investing differently than the crowd.

Investing has a lot to do with risk, and when new investors discover how to deal directly with sellers about **financing** and **customized terms,** as opposed to signing 20 pages of gobbely-goop paperwork at the bank or mortgage company – they'll suddenly begin to realize, *without banks,* there's a whole lot less risk! One argument opposing rental income property that seems to generate a lot of "hot air" from many *so-called* "real estate gurus," are warnings against becoming a landlord. Some claim this thankless task is beneath the dignity of "millionaires in the making." It's a lot cooler hangin' out at Starbucks, waiting for a text message response to your offer! I'll certainly agree that landlording is never a piece of cake, but still, it's the **tenant's rent dollars** that made a bunch of us pretty rich. **Also, you mustn't forget**, when you're the owner, you're the one who selects the tenants. If you wanta end up wealthy, pick the ones who pay – YA GOT IT? I sometimes amaze myself with such profound advice!

Unless you intend to build real estate wealth buying and selling (sensitive to the market and bank mortgages), you're going to have tenants. If you can deal with one tenant, you can certainly learn how to handle six! From a straight economic standpoint, **six rents of $750 per month** will always trump a single house renting for $1350. With just $30,000 for a down payment like I had, you need to select an investment vehicle that can pay you back in the shortest possible time. Obviously, six rents of $750 will give you a far superior return. My goal has always been to find ugly-looking under-rented properties (six units or more), that have the potential for increasing the rents by 40 or 50%, within a period of 24 months or so.

My plan is to upgrade the property and cycle in new tenants who can pay higher rents. Let's assume, starting out, that my six units are renting for $500 each! In my town, fix-up investors are willing to pay about eight times the annual income stream ($36,000) for a property that has the *potential for substantial rent increases.* Savvy investors understand that owners don't rent their property for $500 a month in a **$750** neighborhood unless there's a good reason! Usually it's because the owner has allowed his property to run down so that it will no longer attract decent tenants who can pay market rents.

Roughly 90% of all the properties I've purchased were renting substantially below the market rents because their owners had allowed them to physically run down (lack of repairs and maintenance). In addition, many of the properties had undesirable tenants who basically did whatever they pleased. Both of these conditions create a destructive cycle so that decent tenants will no longer come near the property. Rents keep slipping backward because fewer and fewer renters show up to rent, and the ones that do are mostly the same type who caused the downward spiral in the first place!

Curing these problems and turning a low-performing property around is where the big money's at! I like to call it **"fixing short-term problems in exchange for long-term wealth"** because that's exactly what fix-up investors can do. Before anyone starts thinking these types of properties are only found in the slums – *let me make myself clear about location.* **I don't buy properties in the slums and neither should you.** You'll find my kind of properties in the *older neighborhoods* and in *downtown commercial areas* of most cities. Both are excellent rental locations. Most renters don't judge locations the same way homeowners do – especially younger renters who must carefully keep a close watch on their household budget. They want convenience, near jobs in a respectable neighborhood. Obviously, you won't find these kinds of properties in the newer tracts or sprawling subdivisions.

RETURN ON YOUR INVESTMENT

I realize we've skipped over the part that makes any fix-up project successful; namely *doing the work, where to find the fix-up money,* and so forth. You can find more details on my "MOM and POP MIL-LIONAIRE BLOG," www.fixerjay.com. Right now, let's talk about the returns on your **$30,000 down payment** should you decide to spend it for multiple-unit properties like I suggest!

It's the **income stream** that multiple-unit duplexes or apartments produce that pretty much determines the property value. For homes (houses), the value is generally determined by other like properties (comparables) in the neighborhood. It's very hard to jiggle the value of houses unless the whole neighborhood goes up in value from *natural appreciation*. When you can improve a rundown property by cleaning, fixing and switching the tenants, you'll automatically be rewarded for the efforts. It's called **forced appreciation**! My goals are to **increase rents by 50%–and double the property value, or close to it within a couple years**!

Here's how the math looks when you increase rents over a 24-month period from $500 to **$750**. The property's annual income goes up to **$54,000**. Obviously, to obtain the top rents, the houses or apartments must be attractive and all the unruly tenants cycled out. This tenant cycling issue will basically solve itself, because *$500 tenants cannot afford to pay $750 rents*, even if the toilets start spewing gold nuggets. Renters, *like homeowners*, generally live at the highest amount they can afford.

Since income-producing units are primarily valued by the income stream they produce, **it's very important for you to learn these values wherever you choose to invest**. They are not the same everywhere – although in many locations they're quite similar! As an investor, you must understand values and how they are determined. Do this before you spend your money – *not afterwards*. Folks who have attended my seminars have copies of my local GROSS RENT MULTIPLIER CHARTS in their binders (see Appendix A). Obviously, these charts are for my town, so you must develop a chart for your own particular investment area. **How do you create these charts, you ask?** You look at lots of properties, you read FOR SALE ads, you talk with real estate agents, and you find out what these properties actually sell for **before fix-up** – *and after*. This takes some time, but it must be done. You shouldn't buy a property based on what someone else thinks its worth. It's your money, **you need to know values**!

Now, back to our exciting episode *starring six junky rentals*. When the dust finally settles, we have six bright 'n shiny units renting for $750 each. That equates to an annual income of $54,000 (**$18,000 higher than when we started**). Investors will always pay a higher GRM (*Gross Rent Multiplier*) for cleaned-up, well-managed units, because it's a much safer and more profitable investment. Today, in my town, buyers are willing to pay about **10 times the gross rents** for these kinds of units (**$540,000**). By offering soft terms (as in seller financing), you might even sell for $600,000. Whichever way you judge this deal, there's hardly any place on the planet you'll get more bang for your **$30,000 down payment**.

Still, selling is not what I recommend – *there's no need to sell*! You now have a monthly income of **$1500** more than when you started. I'll assume you paid about $280,000 with $30,000 down, which means your equity is at least $260,000. Even if you over-spent on your credit card in order to do the fix-up work, you've now created enough additional equity so you can easily borrow money on the property to pay off your Visa card. Also you'll notice, **with this kind of investment**, it don't matter a "hill of beans" whether there's natural appreciation or not. Obviously, property values will go up with the times, so appreciation is always in the mix, but the primary value increase is a direct result of fixing up (**adding value**) to the property – **it's all within the investor's control**, so you're not sittin' around waiting for natural appreciation to happen!

I cannot overemphasize the value of keeping your investment plan simple! Lord knows it will complicate itself as you go along without much help from anyone. **Real estate investing** is a people business and in order to do well, you must learn to deal with people in many different ways! You must learn how to clearly explain your deals to ordinary people – *because if you can't* – most folks will simply get up and walk away from your proposal. **Keep your deals simple and be prepared to explain them!**

A PLAN WITH MULTIPLE BENEFITS

Although I do many different things in my real estate business to extract the benefits I'm after, my basic strategy, or *template*, for acquiring properties has remained pretty much the same over the years. I stick with my basic plan because it keeps working over and over again! Allow me to repeat what I told you already: "*I didn't invent fixing houses or adding value* – however, I do take the job more seriously than most people I know." Fixing up rundown houses may sound simple enough, but there are a number of different ways to profit from these properties that most investors have never even heard of! By the time you've finished reading, you'll understand what I'm talkin' about – **scouts honor**!

My buying formula sounds fairly simple. *I'm looking for rundown multiple-unit properties from 6 to 15 units* – preferably, detached houses or duplexes on a single lot at one location. House-apartment combinations will work; even a couple trailers and sometimes an old hotel or motor lodge will stir my interest, depending on the configuration and where it's located! I'm searching for rundown under-rented properties – most likely with tenant problems that I can acquire for a **substantial discount**. To me, that means **40-50% less** than what I estimate the fixed up value might be.

There are several accepted methods to calculate the value of income-producing properties; however, the **gross rent multiplier formula** has always worked best for me. The calculation simply expresses the amount that buyers are willing to pay for a property based on the amount of income it generates. The purchase price can also vary somewhat based on location, age, and condition of the property.

Take for example, my fixed up, 52-year-old, six-unit property located on Liberty Street, *an average neighborhood*. The property shows well and each unit brings in $725 rent. In my town, at this particular time, investors are willing to shell out about **nine times the gross annual rents** to purchase this property. Here's how the numbers look: six units at $725 each equals $4350 per month; twelve times $4350 = $52,200 annual income (9 x $52,200 = $469,800). **Remember**, these are *my numbers for my investment area at this particular time*! They may be too high or low for your area. Also remember, these numbers are continually changing, so you will need to update your values from time to time. When I first began keeping close track of selling prices in my town, hardly any investor would ever pay more than *nine times gross rents* for the very best units.

KNOWING VALUES IS YOUR RESPONSIBILITY

Every investor must develop this information for his or her own investment area! It takes some time and effort, but it's critical for determining how much you should pay – *and ultimately*, whether or not you'll end up with cash flow and profits! Tons of worthless information concerning income properties is handed out by selling agents, which don't mean diddly squat about bottom line results. In the business of profit making, you must always focus on **two important numbers**. What will your customers pay for your product? **And** – what can you afford to pay (purchase price) to provide your product and still make a profit for yourself? *You should not move forward without these answers.*

The following chart shows you a range of rents and values for a typical six-unit property in my investment area. You'll notice the rents vary from a low of $425 for what I call a "pigsty" property – to $900 per month for Snob Hill. This chart is based on my most popular size rental unit, **two bedrooms, one bath**, with approximately **750 square feet**. It's also my most profitable rental unit!

GROSS RENT MULTIPLIER CHART – INCOME VALUE
Typical Small Income Properties, 2-Bedroom Unit
750 Sq. Ft. – Jay's Investment Area
(Example = 6 Units)

GRM	DESCRIPTION	RENT	RENTS (6)	ANNUAL	VALUE $
13 X	Snob Hill	$900	$5400	$64,800	$842,400
12 X	Premo	$875	$5250	$63,000	$756,000
11 X	Deluxe	$825	$4950	$59,400	$653,400
10 X	Nicer	$795	$4770	$57,240	$572,400
9 X	Average	$725	$4350	$52,200	$469,800
8 X	Economy	$635	$3810	$45,720	$365,760
7 X	Butt Ugly	$540	$3240	$38,880	$272,160
6 X	Pigsty	$425	$2550	$30,600	$183,600

Determining the rents and values in order to build your **gross rent multiplier chart** comes from doing some grunt work. To learn rent values, pretend you're a renter in search of housing. Call telephone numbers in the classified ads for different locations within your investment area. Drive out to see what $700 per month will buy you in a two-bedroom house or apartment. Do the same for $500, etc. Once you become familiar with different parts of your town, you'll be able to read the prices in newspaper ads and have a pretty good idea about what the property will look like and how well it's maintained.

Another important benefit that comes from actually checking out rentals and talking to people – *you'll begin to learn about locations and where tenants at various rent levels choose to live.* You'll learn about the "hood" areas – and where the "tweakers" hang out. Don't let the age or condition of a property fool you here! Dopers will often live in newer buildings – and trashy properties can often be found in the best rental locations. Sometimes, out-of-town owners will milk a decent property until it completely runs down and looks like a pigsty! You must do your research to find out!

It's important to know how much rent the majority of renters can afford to pay in your investment area. For example, in my town I can rent two-bedroom, single-bath houses to young couples with a small child or two. I also rent to senior couples. Both of these customers can afford to pay about $800 rent. Knowing what my customers can afford to pay helps me determine which properties I'd like to own. Smart investors will study the marketplace in order to deliver the right product (affordable houses) to their customers. **It's important to remember** – if the tenants can't afford to pay for my houses – **I can't afford them either**! It would be very unwise, and much too risky, to own a stable of houses that rent for $1200 per month, if you're investing in a town full of $800 renters. If the majority of renters in your investment area can easily afford your houses, it's much easier to keep them occupied and profitable. CLAP YOUR HANDS IF YOU AGREE!

PROPERTY VALUES ARE YOUR BUSINESS

Learning about property values in your investment area can be accomplished much easier with the help of a knowledgeable agent or broker. Obviously, most agents don't have much time for teaching wanta-bees and looky-loos. They need to earn commissions to buy groceries and beer for their babies. If you're not quite ready to buy a property just yet, you'll need to polish up on your acting skills and **make 'em think you are**, if you expect much help from agents.

Most real estate agents have files full of information about what properties actually sell for. They can even tell you how they were priced to begin with, and what sections of town investors like best. When you know what properties are selling for within your buying area, *along with the rents they generate*, it becomes fairly easy to develop your own GROSS RENT MULTIPLIER CHART just like mine.

As you talk with buyers and sellers – *making offers and negotiating deals*, you'll soon discover, it doesn't take very long before you develop a good working knowledge about rents and property values. Folks will sometimes ask me, "Isn't that what appraisers are supposed to do?" *Of course it is* – but you need to know values for yourself so you can respond immediately when it's time to make an offer. Like I've already told you, *investment property values are primarily based on the amount of income they produce*. If you'll take the time to learn rents and values, you'll be able to act very quickly when a good property becomes available. While your competition is still scurrying around gathering stacks of information, you'll have the deal in escrow – **and closed**.

Although there are other considerations when acquiring income properties, they're far less important than determining whether you'll end up with **cash flow and profits**. Investment properties can suffer many different problems, but most of them can be fixed if the property makes money. One warning is worth repeating here – **do not buy income property in slum areas**. You'll have great difficulty recovering your fix-up costs – also, your maintenance and repair expenses will run about double in slums. The second reason, *and equally important* – you're not going to like the rental applicants who show up to rent. Even if the purchase price is rock bottom cheap, it's extremely difficult to increase the value no matter how much fix-up you do. Just remember, the single biggest reason for failure in this business is lack of cash flow. It's for this reason – **I've always made cash flow my number one priority** – everything else begins in second place!

When I first began fixing up properties, I made the same two mistakes almost every fix-up investor makes before he or she can expect to qualify for their journeyman badge! First, I shied away from **true fixer-uppers**. I bought properties that didn't need a whole lot of fix-up work done. The only reason I painted one property, I recall, was because I didn't like the color! I also spent too much time and money adding special *customized features*, like tiled entryways, simply because I liked tile myself. My second major mistake was paying more than I should to acquire income properties. Needless to say, these early mistakes kept me from graduating with honors. **But worst of all, they kept me from making profits a lot quicker!**

IMPROVING THE GRM GUARANTEES PROFITS

To say I could do this fix-up stuff in "my sleep" might sound a bit boastful, but it's not a terrible stretch of the truth. It's an absolute fact; *people will pay a lot more money to acquire attractive real estate.* Tenants will pay higher rents when they perceive more value – **looks** and **added value** are my stock and trade. **It's where the money's at in the fix-up business.**

I purchase lower-end ugly rundown properties. Referring back to my GROSS RENT MULTIPLIER CHART (see Appendix A) – I'm always searching for properties I can purchase for **six or seven times gross rents**. The reason is because these lower-end properties can easily be cleaned and fixed up rather inexpensively, creating substantial equity. Once again (referring to my GRM chart); if I'm able to fix up a **six x gross multiplier property** – so it now becomes an **eight x gross multiplier property**, my chart shows I've added over $180,000 value to the six-unit property. *How long should this take, you ask?* My goal is to complete the task in 24 months or less. *In terms of cash flow*, I've increased my rents from $425 to $635, for a total of $1260 additional income per month, or more than **$15,000 annually**. Notice the property value almost doubles!

This cleaning and fix-up work is called **forcing up the value**, and it works almost anywhere, at any time, so long as you follow a few ground rules. For starters, don't purchase properties in the slums or near the Beirut Airport. Both investors and renters alike are afraid of troubled areas where they can see future problems. Consider locations where neighboring properties will not affect the operation of your property. For example, many investors acquire a single four-unit building (4-plex) in a project with many other four-unit buildings, all part of the same group. This, I don't recommend because you give up too much control. If the other owners rent to deadbeats and tweakers, you can't fix the problem! I much prefer houses or apartments on a corner lot location – somewhat separated from potential troublemakers. I call this **the isolation factor**. Buying a property for 50% of the asking price, only to find out it's next to a crack house, could easily be a nightmare instead of a bargain.

THE RISK FACTOR WITH FIXERS

Avoiding the greatest danger of all – **running out of money** – or going belly-up! I seldom meet many start-out investors whose finances are not stretched tighter than a banjo string. Investing for the average person is always a real strain on their pocketbook. It's for this reason that students who attend my Investor Training Seminars always pay very close attention during our discussions about finding money or borrowing!

Let's assume for the moment, you've acquired the six-unit property we've been discussing here! You bought it for **six times the gross income** – now you're cleaning and fixing, hoping to improve the value to 8 x GRM. You've spent all your personal funds – maybe you've even raided the kid's piggybanks – *your Visa card is overloaded*! You know this because they wouldn't even approve your restaurant tab for Friday night's chicken dinner! WOW – that's embarrassing! What you really need is some breathing room – *and the faster, the better*! Had you paid 20% down for an average (non-fixer) single-family house, you could forget about looking for any financial help from the property! You would still owe most of the 80% mortgage and there's no additional equity you can tap!

The good news is, *your multiple-unit fixer property is different*; once you've completed your fix-up job and increased the rents – **you've now created borrowing equity**. Your *loan to value ratio* will likely be somewhere around 50%, which means, relief is just one small loan away! Frankly, I'm not suggesting you should plan on borrowing money – but when you find yourself without any wiggle room, sometimes stronger measures are called for – say like obtaining a small "hard money" equity loan. I'm sure you'll agree, it's a lot more comforting to know that because **you bought the right kind of real estate to begin with**, the property can now come to your rescue! You might consider yourself saved by **sweat equity**, and it doesn't matter whose sweat! What matters, is **you've added extra value to the property**! You could honestly say; buying the right property comes with a **built-in safety valve**!

Other Books by JAY DECIMA

FIXIN' UGLY HOUSES FOR MONEY
How Small time Investors can Earn $1,000,000 and Lots More

INVESTING IN FIXER-UPPERS
A Complete Guide to Buying Low, Fixing Smart, Adding Value, and Selling (or Renting) High
McGraw Hill, N.Y.

START SMALL, PROFIT BIG IN REAL ESTATE
Fixer Jay's 2-Year Plan for Building Wealth - Starting from Scratch
McGraw Hill, N.Y.

INVESTING IN GOLD MINE HOUSES
How to Uncover a Fortune Fixing Small Ugly Houses and Apartments
McGraw Hill, N.Y.

Available at most books stores and online

CHAPTER 8

TROLLIN' FOR A COLONY

*R*ight now is an excellent time for self-evaluation, and perhaps a good time to modify your investment strategy to take advantage of today's opportunities. On a positive note, there are many new opportunities for do-it-yourself investors who are willing to take their best shot at the **American dream** and **financial freedom**. There are also some new challenges and a few different roadblocks to keep the game interesting. **Education** and **know-how** will continue to be the main ingredients for success with any plan, same as it's always been – *nothing new here!*

I'm always baffled by the new breed of *wanta-bees* who attempt to launch their investing careers very quickly without dedicating the necessary time to learn a few basics! These folks employ what I call "the Christopher Columbus" technique! First, they decide to set sail without the foggiest notion about where their investment boat is headed. When they actually arrive somewhere, very few can even begin to explain how they got there. And finally, most will encounter serious money problems and can only hope that someone will step in and help pay for their ill-fated voyage! Obviously, this technique is seriously flawed, since the Queen of Spain has been dead for more than 500 years.

NOT EVERYONE CHOOSES TO WEAR A BLUE SHIRT

Through my books and seminars, I've been teaching *different strokes for different folks* for many years. Not only have I taught that idea – but I'm also my own best example because that's exactly the way I invest myself. By the way, *you should never take lessons from anyone who don't use their own strategy!* That's like receiving marriage counseling from a gay priest! The best advice I can offer to anyone starting this business is to learn your lessons from a teacher whose techniques and strategies are pretty much in tune with how you'd like to invest yourself.

The general area of real estate education is about the size of an elephant. You need to break it down a bit and specialize at least in the beginning. I've been investing in one form or another for nearly 50 years, and I sometimes feel like I've barely scratched the surface. Obviously, in my particular specialty, I feel like I can hold my own with nearly anyone – still, my confidence comes from many years of practicing my trade and learning my skills from the experts before me. It's for this reason I always suggest that investors first develop their plan around the set of benefits they need, or at least the benefits they would like to have. They should do this before deciding the kind of property they need! Obviously, this basic preparation (developing a plan) will automatically eliminate a whole range of real estate that won't provide the benefits you're after. *See how simple this stuff is!* We're just starting out here, and already, you can stop lookin' at about half the properties in the marketplace!

ONLY YOU CAN DECIDE ON THE BENEFITS

Different properties provide **different benefits**, as well as a different set of challenges. For example, a single-family rental house with a *low rent-to-value ratio* won't put much jingle in your pockets until the mortgage debt is paid or the house sells for a profit. Looking at numbers in my own area; a $220,000 medium range tract house might earn $1200 per month rent. The rent to value ratio is .065 ($14,400 annual rent divided by the house value = .065). Assuming operating expenses will use up 35% of the income, I will only have $780 per month left for the mortgage payment. After 20% down ($45,000), I would still need to finance $175,000 at today's 06% investor rate, with *amortized payments* of $1049.22 for 30 more years. As you can see, it would take a lot more money down (roughly $50,000 more) just to break even – plus, hope I never have a vacancy. If my dream (benefit) is to take an exotic cruise somewhere – I'm afraid my ship will have long since rusted out and sank in the harbor before my house investment provides any spendable cash. I had best come up with another plan or perhaps take up swimming instead!

Although we all like to dream and picture ourselves on Fantasy Island – you must be very careful with your planning and never lose sight of **what's real and what's not**. Your plan must be practical and built on a solid foundation. Also, you mustn't lie to yourself about the money you have to invest. If you don't have any, fess up right from the very beginning. It'll make a big difference in the properties you must search for. For example, the average three-bedroom, two-bath tract house in my area that sells for $220,000 will require at least 20% down for non-owner occupied investors. That means you'll need $45,000 in your purse and a decent credit report to just barely own it. You'll still be upside down in terms of cash flow, but if you can't meet the $45,000 requirement – it don't matter about the rest of the deal! Right now, it's simply beyond your capacity to acquire it! *A big mistake many newer investors make is looking at properties totally out of their financial reach.* Don't waste your precious time – **I hope you're with me here**, *just nod your head anyway.*

BENEFITS ARE ALWAYS PERSONAL

I'm almost certain that I'd be looking for different benefits than you because of where I'm at financially! For example, you may need cash flow and I don't. You might possibly have *carry forward losses* from excessive expenses, so you wouldn't need a tax shelter benefit right now. If you have adequate cash flow from your job, there's not much sense of earning more regular type income that automatically gets reduced by state and federal tax authorities! A far better plan would be to sharpen up your *negotiating skills* and buy a $200,000 property for **$100,000**. Now you've earned $100,000 without any tax consequences.

Sometimes new investors can get financial relief from their mortgage payments by investing in a nice duplex to start with. Quite often, the tenant's rent will cover most of the owner's mortgage payment. This means you, *the owner*, will get very cheap housing costs by living in the second unit. You will also get the depreciation and tax deductions for expenses on the side you have rented out. As a bonus, *living right next door to your tenant* will teach you how to pick 'em right! This will help your landlording skills in the future.

One major benefit, which is often difficult for new investors to find, is **seller financing** for single-family houses. In the single-house market, everyone involved, including selling agents, owners, banks, and even the buyers, fully expect traditional bank financing will be a requirement! Seller financing is even more difficult for new investors because they haven't yet learned how to make a convincing argument to get sellers to participate! Worse yet, the same thing applies to most real estate agents who will nearly always advise their clients against it!

When your investment plan or strategy is to acquire **multiple units (five or more)** a whole different mindset can be found. A very large percentage of sellers (including me) are greatly in favor of **seller financing**. In fact, as you will soon read, *seller carryback financing* has been a very big part of my overall wealth strategy for making big profits in this business. In my opinion, do-it-yourself investors who leave financing for others to figure out will have great difficulty reaching their full profit potential! I often tell students at my seminars and investment club presentations – there is just as much profit in the *financing* as there is in the real estate transactions themselves! Naturally, I get some very puzzled looks from my listeners! Before you've finished reading this book, you'll understand why I can say that!

IT'S ABOUT THE PROFITS – NOT THE BUILDINGS

In part, Webster's Dictionary defines investing as *to make use of for future benefits or advantages – or to commit (money) in order to earn a financial return.* You'll notice there's no mention of what kind of investing you should use to accomplish this task. Real estate investing offers a wide range of profit-making choices and each investor may choose his own poison. By the way, *poison* is exactly what many naïve investors seem to choose – investments that not only fail to provide any profits, but will quite often suck the investor completely under water! It's for this reason that I suggest looking for **benefits** and **advantages** rather than properties. Almost all properties have some investor benefits, but when you can learn to pick out properties with the most benefits – along with greater profit potential, you'll be well on your way to bigger bank deposits – plus a whole lot closer to becoming what I call a Stage II investor. You'll find my description of the **Three (3) Investor Stages** in my final closing thoughts at the end.

Most of my readers are aware that multiple-unit properties (five or more units) are my specialty – *but they haven't always been*. There was a time when I purchased one house at a time and looked at almost every property presented to me. In my early years, the excitement of looking, bragging and buying heavily financed properties was enough to keep me happy. Profits on paper (not actual deposits) had me convinced that it wouldn't be long before I'd be filthy rich. Back then, so long as I could keep borrowing from Beneficial Finance, everything seemed okay!

Borrowing never failed to put a big smile on my face the day I picked up the check – but by the time I had to pay those monthly mortgage payments, much of the fun had disappeared! Using forced equity to borrow more money on a single house is seldom covered by enough additional rent! More often than not, the added mortgage payment would turn a break-even house into a cash-eating alligator. Even if your plan is to use most of the borrowed money to purchase your next investment, you've effectively created an alligator property by borrowing and adding on more debt. It also makes the property difficult to sell because of the higher monthly payments. After you've done this a few times, it's easy to end up with break-even or negative cash flow properties with hardly any equity, making them very difficult to sell or trade. Finally one day, the bank will pull the plug on any more loans – *you've reached your limit for borrowing*, they'll tell you! **Investing by banker rules will often shut you down long before you reach the Promised Land.**

PLANNING MUST BEGIN WITH YOUR GOALS

Here's the deal gang: if you don't have a plan for where you're going – how will you ever know when you get there? Wishing to become a rich and famous real estate investor is like trying to eat a whole elephant – it's simply too big to tackle and it doesn't offer the slightest hint about where to begin. Still, if you take small bites, you can eat the elephant! Likewise, designing your real estate plan can be best accomplished by reducing the task down to smaller bites. My earliest investment plan could best be called "seat of the pants investing," and it was fueled mostly by my blind faith! Faith had me absolutely convinced that owning any kind of real estate was bound to make me rich. I labored under this false belief for far too long before realizing I was using the Christopher Columbus technique I spoke of earlier. Looking back, *I bought the wrong properties, did too much borrowing, and sold properties I should have kept.* My lack of knowledge cost me thousands of dollars and many backbreaking hours doing things my way–**instead of the right way**!

Over the years I've discovered there are basically three kinds of do-it-yourself investors like me. There's the person, or family, with a good solid job who intends to keep it and invest on the side (part-time). *Next* – there's the wanta-bee investor who has less than a secure job, who can already see it may be coming to an end. He or she will remain working so long as the job holds out, *but regardless*, they've pretty much decided real estate investing will be their backup plan. *Finally*, there are the folks who are *sick 'n tired* of their current employment or maybe already laid off – this group has visions of immediately jumping in and becoming full-time investors – career changers! This group is different than the first two because they need to start generating **spendable take-home income** as fast as they can or pray for another unemployment extension. All three of these groups are most likely regular working folks with very modest savings, so money to purchase real estate is almost always an issue.

NOW – THE DOCTOR'S OPINION

When I advise people who wish to become investors, here's what I tell them: You must be very clear about what you have to contribute – both your time, as well as money. Obviously, for the investor with a good solid job he intends to keep, **time to invest** will be extremely important. In my opinion, purchasing one starter size, three-bedroom house every year to keep as a rental property is a simple and very practical plan! For leveraged purchases, there will likely be no cash flow (try for break-even), but with a decent job, cash flow is not really the immediate goal. Buying one house a year will allow the novice investor adequate time to learn how to perform routine maintenance and minor repairs, as well as becoming acquainted with the business of landlording. This plan will also provide a **great retirement supplement** and allow excellent tax write-offs within the limits of TC 469 (passive loss rules).

For the investor wanta-bee with an unpredictable employment future, I'd suggest a slightly more aggressive approach just in case the job peters out. Obviously, *spendable income* from the investment becomes more critical in this situation. Depending on the investor's blue-collar skills, acquiring cosmetic fixer-uppers or multiple-unit properties from two to four units offers a very sound strategy. With small multiple-unit properties, you'll often find the **down payment**, *or the cost to buy in*, is no more than the down payment would be to purchase a single-family house. In most cases, however, you'll find the cost per each unit is much cheaper! This translates to a higher **rent-to-value factor**. Remember, the rent-to-value equals the annual rent divided by the full value of the asset (unit). For example, suppose you acquire a three-unit building for $150,000. With rents of $500 each, the rent-to-value = $1500 monthly rent divided by $150,000 (apartment value) = **1.00 percent rent-to-value**. Any factor above 1.0 gives an investor an excellent chance of having net spendable cash left at the end of the month, assuming the debt service is reasonable (no more than 55% of gross income). Obviously, with fixer-upper properties, the investor who can fix things himself, and learns to buy at a discount, has an excellent chance of ending up with cash flow (maybe not much). **But still, it's positive!**

For those investors whose goal is to become a **full-time career changer**, and their plan is to rely on their real estate income for survival – *they first must be totally honest with themselves.* Leveraged single-family houses will be pretty much out of the question. You can earn more *spendable income* with a paper route or shaggin' beer cans in the parking lot! Being honest with yourself means standing back and looking at the big picture. Get some help or advice if you need to.

For a moment, let's assume you have $100,000 to spend for real estate (by the way, that's five times more than I started with). Ask yourself: where could I invest $100,000 and immediately begin to earn money back every month for my personal living expenses? Can you earn a 15% return today? *Would that be good?* Could you support yourself, family, etc.? The answer is **yes**, if $1250 per month is satisfactory! **And that's assuming you can find a 15% investment opportunity.** My last question is the toughest: do you actually have **$100,000** to invest? I want you to thoroughly visualize the task at hand so you understand it won't be too easy. **Changing careers** or becoming a **full-time investor** is a bit more complicated than simply racing out and buying a property. **Let's talk about why!**

Many investors like myself have always dreamed about financial freedom, job security, and the personal independence that comes from being your own boss! My first recollection of such a dream dates back many years to my days as a young paperboy delivering our local newspaper on my bicycle. With 120 customers, seven days a week, freezing cold in the winter months and baking in Redding's 100 degree summers, I still remember thinking to myself – **there must be a better way**! It would be quite a few more years, loads of hard work – plus a lengthy spell working two separate jobs before my dream would begin to take shape. Looking back today, I missed a lot of shortcuts, made a bunch of dumb mistakes (which I didn't realize were dumb), *and waited far too long to educate myself.*

A BRIDGE TOO FAR

Almost every new investor who wants to become full-time fails to adequately develop a plan to achieve the goal. Of course this is the main reason most will fail! The old adage that most folks don't plan to fail – **they simply fail to plan**, certainly applies to career changers full-time wanta-bees. As we discussed earlier, investors who have 9-5 jobs and intend to stay employed, can invest almost any way they choose. They can purchase property with negative earnings and still be okay because they have grocery money from another source! Not so for career changers and full-timers who must learn how to develop an income much quicker if they intend to survive. **Career changers don't have the luxury of merely hoping things will work out okay!** Fortunately, there is another way, but you'll need to think outside the box, *as they say*, and it's quite likely you'll need to overhaul most of your present ideas about real estate investing.

MULTIPLE UNITS – ADDING VALUE AND HOLDING ON

As you shall learn, there are many reasons for acquiring this particular kind of real estate (colony-type units), but heading up the list is the fact that you'll be able to leave about 95% of investor competition in the dust. I'm sure it comes as no big surprise that eliminating competition is a very important ingredient for getting ahead in any business! Another major ingredient is searching for *and finding* **underperforming** real estate. **This is like discovering a hidden gold mine.** *Underperforming* is a term used for income properties that are renting for $500 when all the surrounding units are producing $750 rents. Why does this happen, you ask? There are several reasons, but probably the biggest one is the owner has allowed his property to run down! **Milking the property**, they call it. He sucks out all the cash flow, putting nothing back in for upkeep and maintenance. Eventually, it runs down to a point where tenants will no longer pay the market rents. Eventually, the property will only attract inferior-type tenants and troublemakers who pay less and less rent because of the property's declining condition.

As you can probably guess, career changers and full-time wanta-bees will need a little special education before tackling these *gold mines in the rough*. For starters, you must learn and understand values, **both rents and property values**, in the neighborhoods where you plan to invest. I will always recommend that you attend a seminar or two on basic landlording techniques. It's not difficult to improve or "fine tune" your skills as you go along, but you need to have a good understanding of the basics to start! Still, these colony-type, rundown properties can move you to the front of your class very quickly. **Underperforming, multi-unit properties** provide more income and much faster than any other real estate I know of. It will take dedication, yes, but the goal is well within your reach if you'll stay focused – and don't just take my word!

In 1961, investor-author Robert W. Kent wrote a very informative book: *How to Get Rich in Real Estate*, Reward Books. Mr. Kent tells how he acquired small multiple-unit income properties, affordable to his local blue-collar tenants. He developed his landlording skills and eventually owned many of these same kinds of properties! They made him a millionaire. About these type of properties, Kent writes: "It is entirely feasible for any man or woman who is steadfast in purpose, and is free of three cardinal faults; **timidity**, **negativeness** and **laziness** to achieve great success with these kind of properties and end up rich." The cover price was $3.45 back in 1961 and Kent's book was hailed as "The Modern Gold Rush." The basic formula that made Kent a millionaire was buying affordable rental properties that earned a positive monthly income. Kent's formula is still **the same gold rush** for investors who'll adopt his strategies today.

IT'S ALWAYS THE MONEY FIRST

I will tell you from my many years of experience, investing in all different kinds of real estate – that even the most beautiful property in the world will begin to look mighty ugly when you're forced to pay out your hard earned dollars every month just so you can say you're the owner! Obviously, *career changers* and the folks who need income don't have the luxury of buying these alligator properties. Trophy buying impulses, *as we investors call it*, must be curtailed and put on hold for another time. **Right now, cash flow is all you'll ever need!**

The first thing investors need to understand is that no seller will ever reduce his selling price without **some good reason**. *Sellers with well-performing income properties don't sell at fire sale prices because they don't have to!* There are oodles of buyers who will pay retail price and many of them have a wheelbarrow full of cash to boot! How in the world can the little guy or Mom and Pop investor compete? The answer is obvious – **he can't**! What this means for investors who need income quickly – and at the same time have very little money (down payment) to purchase any kind of property – **they need a different plan**. Small *multiple-unit* underperforming properties that look rundown, tired, and ugly can be exactly what the doctor ordered. The primary reason is **lack of buyer competition** – seems that most buyers are turned off by ugliness and decline.

LEARNING TO IDENTIFY OPPORTUNITY

Colony houses I call them; although they might be small apartments or several mobile units in the mix, are ideal properties for Mom and Pop investors because they offer the fastest path to cash flow. I've found there are three main objections from rookie investors! First, they look like a big fat mess (unsightly). New investors are confused about what fix-up entails; and lastly, most rookies lack the vision to see through the dirt, grime, and unsightliness to visualize the golden nuggets once the ugliness is wiped away. It's like my Mom used to say: *ugliness is only skin deep* – just below the surface, is where real beauty can be found. **What exactly is this real beauty, you ask?** In case you've been reading too fast – *daydreaming*; or even worse, you think the author is just an "old fuddy-duddy" with a dinosaur strategy! Allow me to explain how real beauty works today!

I'll refer back to my explanation of an *underperforming property*. We'll call it a **colony property**, consisting of five detached houses and a single duplex situated on a large oversized city lot. Picture seven rental units on a single lot with a driveway down the middle. Each unit has a small fenced backyard, which affords decent privacy for the renters. The property is rundown; knee-high weeds are covering the front yard where a small patch of green lawn would make a real difference in the looks. There are several broken windows with cardboard cover-ups and the raw wood siding hasn't seen a drop of paint in years. Disassembled (junk) automobiles and a couple VW buses sitting on firewood blocks present a picture of very poor management, *it's like nobody gives a damn!* As is generally the case, the occupants (renters) look like a perfect match for the property! What they lack in appearance, however, they make up for in numbers. Makes you wonder how they all fit inside!

IT'S HARD TO VISUALIZE A GOLD RUSH

This is the reason why 95% of all the competition, **potential investors**, drive by, *but won't ever get out of the car.* There's a huge image problem with rundown properties and it's tough to visualize a gold mine in such unattractive surroundings. Still, you mustn't forget my Mama's words: "Ugliness is only skin deep!" The real beauty is the $500 rents in a **$750** neighborhood. I'll assume you memorized the values like I told you already – *and by the way,* don't dare make a move to acquire this or any other property till you know what rents should be. Assuming you do, *let's play a little "what if!"* **What if** you are capable of cleaning up this pig-stye, switchin' out these renters for a better lookin', higher paying group and hauling all the junk cars away? Suppose you can accomplish this task in a year or so and you're able to start collecting the current market rents of **$750**! Can you understand the financial feat you've just accomplished? You've increased your income **$21,000 annually** for one colony property with seven rental units.

I realize I'm not giving you lots of details about how to paint or replace the windows – or even communicate with your less than attractive occupants. *I'm going to assume you're willing to learn this stuff!* Obviously, that's an absolute must! Don't forget what Robert Kent said: You must not be *timid, negative,* or *lazy* if you wish success. That rule hasn't changed in the last hundred years. It's my objective here to get your focused on the kind of properties that can do you some good – given your circumstances! We've already established that you wanta be a *career changer* or you need *income much quicker* than someone with a steady job to rely on. This is a very worthwhile strategy that can work for almost anyone – but what makes it so much better than more popular investments (say single-family houses), is that you can use your own initiative to build a **cash flow property** without hardly any outside assistance – and you can do it with a minimum down payment cost as well!

When you acquire **small colony-type properties** like I'm suggesting, and they're mostly occupied by renters, it's quite easy to operate under the radar of local building officials, health department *do-gooder's*, or any of the other wonderful government agencies who love to dictate how you should run your business. *Grandfathering laws* and *local practices* generally provide a great deal of latitude to property owners who perform – *or at least oversee* work on their rental properties. I have found that larger cities with bigger budgets tend to pester owner-operators a bit more than in the than smaller communities. To say this another way, you must be a little more knowledgeable and perhaps a bit more sneaky (aggressive) in the wealthier neighborhoods, especially areas where you sniff the smell of salt water – *or perhaps where city officials are all democrats*. It's for this reason I much prefer investing in cities or towns with less than 100,000 population. You won't find near as many government vehicles parked around local coffee shops in my town!

On the following page you'll see a schematic of my colony properties containing six individual properties (Figure 8-1). **I call this my wheel, hub and spokes concept.** That's me, the hub in the center with spokes running out to each of my six colonies. This is my basic investment model consisting of six individual colonies containing a total of 40 individual rental units. Each colony ranges in size from five to eight units, consisting of detached houses, duplexes, several mobiles, and a small six-unit apartment. Although there are 40 rental units, each providing income, there are only six separate properties in my total operation!

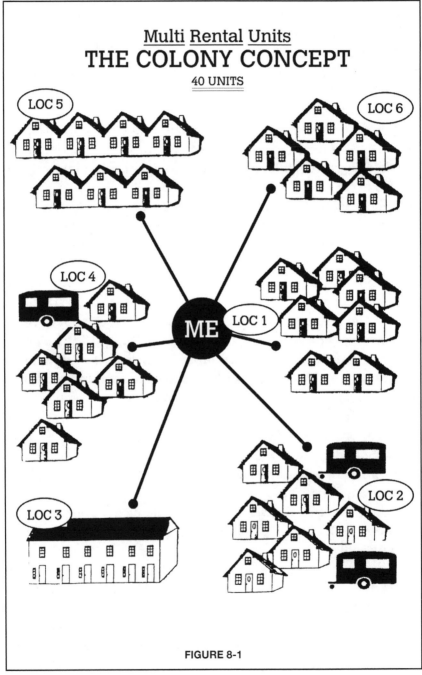

FIGURE 8-1

Having only six locations to service is very doable by almost any dedicated investor.

These six individual properties are controlled by my central management company; **which of course, is me**. This makes for an easy to operate, centrally controlled system suitable for both **full-time** and **part-time** investors alike. This strategy lends itself well for a part-time investor starting out – then converting to full-time as additional colonies are acquired. It's a great "learn as you go plan." This strategy is not about speed or how fast you can acquire these properties, but rather, **the quality of each individual colony**.

A new investor can start with just one colony and after it's up and running – move on to number two. By acquiring the kinds of properties we're discussing here, **underperforming properties**, the investor can quickly develop **a solid cash flow operation** before moving to the next. To give you an idea about the kind of income that can be generated when all six colonies are up and running – I've used average rents of $695 similar to my town. With 40 units rented, **the gross rents are just under at $334,000 annually**.

Most Mom and Pop investors I know today can survive quite nicely on this amount. Assuming **$334,000** is your annual gross income; an owner-operator or investment family could expect to keep roughly **30%** or slightly more than **$100,000 per year**. Making these earnings even more attractive, **these six colonies** will produce about **$80,000 worth of depreciation**, which means you get to keep all the money. Also, because monthly rents generally go up with the economy, same as sardines at the supermarket, they'll stay pretty much indexed for inflation. The following chart shows how I've calculated the income for my six colony properties (40 units).

LOCATION	DESCRIP. OF UNITS	NO.OF UNITS	AVE. RENTS	MO. RENTS	ANNUAL RENTS
LOC 1	Duplex+5 Detached Hses.	7		5,130	61,560
LOC 2	6 Detached Houses+2 Mobils	8		5,400	64,800
LOC 3	6 Unit Apt. Buildings	6		3,675	44,100
LOC 4	6 Detached Houses +1 Mobil	7		5,275	63,300
LOC 5	4 Unit Apt.+3 Unit Apt.	7		4,475	53,700
LOC 6	5 Detached Houses	5		3,845	46,140
TOTALS:	**APTS., MOBILS and HOUSES**	**40**	**695**	**27,800**	**333,600**

THE VALUE OF ADVANCE PLANNING

What I've just described to you is a very workable plan for any investor who needs income fast as possible – **and of course, has the time to learn about the business so he or she can make things happen.** A big part of your education will come from *on-the-job training*, but new investors should learn a few basics so they start out on the right foot! Seminars and home study courses will speed up the learning process!

As you begin to learn more about the business of real estate investing, you'll soon discover that **real wealth comes from the benefits each property will provide**. This means, the better you scrutinize each purchase for maximum benefits, the quicker you can reach your financial objectives. For example, changing the looks of a property from an ugly duckling to a beautiful swan can be a reasonably quick technique to earn higher rents – or bigger profits should you decide to sell the property. *This strategy relies strictly on the investor's ability*, as opposed to waiting for natural appreciation or a better economy. With this kind of property you can expand your business regardless of the economy because it's your personal efforts that are forcing up the value. *You alone are in control of higher rents and profits.* **Very important!**

Two of the major benefits associated with finding and acquiring *underperforming properties* are greater cooperation from sellers and far better financing and terms. Sellers who own rundown properties don't have a very strong position to bargain or negotiate from because their properties are not very attractive! **Seller financing** will most likely be their only option when they decide to sell. Both **owner financing** and **cooperative sellers** are high profit benefits for investors who learn to acquire these properties, turn 'em around, and improve their financial performance.

Negotiating seller financing with liberal terms have propelled more Mom and Pop investors to Easy Street than any other single benefit I know of. In the final analysis, **real estate investing is a people business**. Banks will always push their structured products (loans or mortgages);

whereas people who buy and sell from each other will agree to financing and terms that will strictly benefit each other. Banks have little interest in this issue! Eventually, when it comes time to sell out and smell the roses, I'll show you how all your efforts to negotiate **seller financing** really pays off! See Chapter 20; "Fishin' In Your Sunset Years."

CHAPTER 9

HOOKIN' YOUR FIRST COLONY

When asked about the inherent risks associated with his mega
shipping empire, Aristotle Onassis replied: If you expect to
make any serious money hiring out your ships for profit, you'll need
to set a course that exposes both the ships and their crews to many
unpredictable dangers on the high seas. It's impossible to earn much
money floating around in the safety of a protected harbor!

Many wanta-bee investors I talk with seem to immediately focus
on the risk factor when I attempt to explain all the benefits of investing
my way. Friends, allow me to blurt this out loud and clear – **risk comes
with the territory**. There's no way to invest in real estate without
taking risks – it's simply the nature of investing! It's also the juice that
keeps the game alive and exciting. How much fun and excitement
would there be for a tightrope walker if we stretched his rope flat on
the ground instead of forty feet high above the crowd? Not much I
suspect! Besides, he'd probably give up without any challenge!

EDUCATION BEST DEFENSE AGAINST RISK

When you dedicate the time and effort to learn what you're doing,
you automatically reduce the risk factor. Onassis learned a lot about
the business long before he ever owned his first ship. As a young
teenager, he sailed with the master seaman of his day. He learned
about the treacherous currents, about weather patterns, and how to
seek out the safest sea channels that would one day protect his fleet

from the violent typhoons and hurricanes. Onassis wasn't born with these sea-farin' skills! He learned them from the best teachers he could find, **but most importantly**, from teachers who practiced what they preached. **This is the very same recipe real estate investors can use to pursue their dreams.**

Many of the strategies I use and recommend will seem as strange as Mars when you're first starting out! However, once you learn how to use them, you'll be able to sail the investment seas with the confidence of the most capable sailors. **Education will reduce your risk so that it becomes very manageable.**

Many neophyte investors are of the opinion that multiple-unit investing, which of course I very much favor, *and mostly teach about*, is somehow much more complicated than acquiring a single house. Nothing is further from the truth – the only difference is that your investment training will be a bit more directed toward the extra benefits you'll receive.

Quite often, new investors say to me – Jay, I certainly like what you say about multiple-unit properties having more benefits; however, I'll be lucky with my available resources (money) to pay for a single house. That statement to me means you've never seriously looked into buying multiple units before – otherwise you would know that quite often *the down payment needed* to purchase multiple units could easily be about the same amount required to purchase a single house! Down payments, or what I can "buy-in" costs, often have very little to do with the number of units you're buying. The down payment amount has a lot more to do with seller motivation and the condition of the property.

I'm aware that buying a house for your home as opposed to buying a rental property often allows credit worthy buyers to purchase for very small down payments. However, for the purpose of this chapter – I'm talking about *acquiring investment properties*, not homes to be occupied by the buyer. Investment properties are much higher risk for institutional lenders and normally require larger down payments for safety! When you begin to own a string of rentals, you'll find down payments on a percentage basis will hardly be much different than buying single house investments or small multiples.

HOW TO EARN $100,000 ANNUALLY

Most of my readers already know that my specialty, and of course my primary focus, is on multiple-unit rental properties. I often call these properties **colonies**. In size, they range anywhere from 5 to 12 units, with some even larger. These are what I call my "bread-n-butter" investments, and they're the kind of properties I mostly write about in my books and newsletters. During my Book Tours I often present my ideal colony set-up with six separate properties, consisting of 40 total units to demonstrate how small-time Mom and Pop investors can set themselves up to earn **$100,000 annually**, become financially independent, and retire like a king! As a bonus, I show you how the $100,000 is completely tax sheltered so you get to keep nearly everything you earn! **Chapter 8** provides the financial details.

Obviously, you'll need to learn a few lessons and work your tail off, *but consider the possibilities*. I'm talkin' about **a guaranteed income stream**, financial security and **a worry-free retirement**, regardless whether you collect Social Security or not! After creating your own financial security and building a **substantial net worth**; I'll show you how to double your profits and live off what I call–**"pajama money."** I'll show you how to sell out without reducing your income, and live a king in much the same way Onassis developed his sea-farin' career. You'll need to learn investment skills – and you'll need to accept a little risk. But when you measure the extraordinary opportunities against splashin' around in the harbor going nowhere, your decision to move ahead should be much easier – JUST SAY AMEN!

EATING AN ELEPHANT – ONE COLONY AT A TIME

Buying your first colony is the way to get started! You can educate yourself as you go along, which is extremely important! Although your ultimate goal might be to acquire six colonies like my teaching example, it's important to break the total task down into "bite-size" acquisitions because buying one colony is doable starting now! There's also much less risk, because it gives you time to learn as you go and make your mistakes early as you work the bugs out. Trying to speed up the process can cause you to repeat the same ol' mistakes over again! I can assure, you, Onassis didn't start out with a big fleet! In fact, his very first ship was a rusted out ol' bucket that would just barely float! Can you imagine the education he got just trying to keep the thing afloat!

Take a quick peek at my SIX COLONY DIAGRAM (**#1 Location**), Chapter 8, page 132. Let's pretend this is our first acquisition. The property consists of five detached houses and a single duplex apartment (two units), all situated on a single city lot (one APN or parcel no.). The lot size is 95 feet wide by 160 feet deep, with a narrow driveway running through the middle. The units sit on both sides of the driveway and each has its own little yard, partially fenced, providing fairly decent privacy. It's my guess these houses were built in the early '50s, so I'll estimate they're about 60 years old or so! They all need some fix-up and painting, plus there's quite a lot of junk accumulated around the houses. The elderly seller admits, he simply can't keep up anymore and has known this for some time. *It's time to retire, he says.* Rents are low – and of course, that's why he's kept the units fully rented most of the time. In landlord jargon, this seller is what we often call a "milker." For the past few years, he's pocketed all the rents and hasn't spent a dime for maintenance or upkeep.

One of the very first things you must learn as a new investor is what properties are worth (values) in your town – *or buying area.* You cannot delegate knowing values to anyone! **Why's that, you ask?** It's because we're talking about **your dollars** and hopefully, **your profits**. I constantly talk with new investors who ask their real estate agents questions like: What do you think this property is worth? What should rents be in this area? *And so forth.* Please promise me you'll stop this kind of nonsense right now if I'm talkin' about you! It's your responsibility to offer the right price, **your price**, and it's up to you to know what the rents should be and what tenants can afford to pay in your investment area. Obviously, you'll know what they're paying when you purchase the property, but it's your business to know if the location is suitable for increasing the rents after cleaning and fix-up! Remember, no one gives a rat's hoot about this kind of information except a profit-motivated owner. You can't delegate profit-making decisions. They're your responsibility. **Ya got it!**

WHERE SHOULD YOU BE LOOKIN'?

I've told you this already, but it's worth repeating. There are two primary locations to begin your fishing trip. The first is in the **older residential areas of town**. You'll be looking for older houses and/or small apartments – or sometimes a combination of both, built in the 1940s and '50s. You'll often find oversized city lots with a large main house fronting the street and several smaller apartments or cottages in the rear. Sometimes you'll find the units behind the main house with an alleyway access from the back. Be **snoopy** when you're lookin'! Park the car – get out and wander up a few driveways. Watch for dogs and irritable owners. If you're caught, tell 'em you're a telephone man checking out phone wires. If there are no wires – tell 'em you're looking for Bob – *or maybe you're lost*. This will be good practice for later when you're tryin' to out-smart your tenants.

The second location I like is the downtown areas of your city where you'll find residential units mixed in with commercial buildings. Lots of young renters like living downtown where they're close to work! **But, they want decent housing**. I have owned many multiple-unit properties in my downtown district – houses and small apartment sitting on C1 lots (commercial). Don't fuss about the zoning. If the property has been a rental property for years, it can stay that way! It's what we call *grandfathered*! The use can stay the same so long as the property is kept in decent condition. Sometimes selling agents will rave on about higher values because of the future potential usage! *Commercial potential*, they call it! Basically, you should tell them to go suck rocks. We pay for residential rentals only. But do it politely! Remember, they're just trying to make a sale so they can buy milk for their babies!

Finding seven rental units tucked in behind the supermarket next to the old shoe factory or department store can make an ideal location for a colony – especially when it's fenced off and can be separated into small yards with privacy. *Let me remind you, we are looking for locations where renters want to live*! That's the goal. Renters have a completely different mindset than homebuyers. They want *convenience*, *affordability*, and *safety*, so that's where we need to be fishin'!

When I purchased six small two-bedroom rentals behind the soap factory on a large L shaped commercial lot, several of my friends thought I had *totally flipped out*! Several times each day a loud shrill whistle blew and steam shot out from two giant pipes towering 60 feet high above the plant. We planted lawns (the steam kept the grass green) and created small individually fenced yards. Young renters loved our houses. Small children had a safe place to play and were totally fascinated by the loud whistle and steam bath that followed. We rarely had vacancies for any length of time. **Remember, long-term tenants make landlords rich**!

Oliver Street (not real name), which I've written about in my book; *Start Small, Profit Big in Real Estate*, McGraw Hill Publishers, was another ideal **colony property** with a combination of duplexes and stand-alone houses. It was located somewhat by itself about a block away from a supermarket and across the street from a cabinet shop, housed in two metal buildings. Once again, this is not a homeowner property, **but for making money** – they don't come any better. It was seven rental units altogether and it came with 19 *non-running cars*. I was first told about the property by my roto-rooter man who had been there on a sewer blockage. By the way, service guys know about rentals in your area, so I want you to ask 'em!

DON'T BUY PROPERTIES
IN UNSAFE NEIGHBORHOODS

I won't buy properties in dense slum areas and neither should you! In fact, you should never agree or sign on to become the owner even if the property is free! **The risk is simply not worth all the problems.** I've had students who ignored this advice and wish they hadn't. The biggest issue is the never-ending harassment from troublemakers. One student bought a scumbag property so cheap, she simply couldn't imagine why it wouldn't be profitable! It didn't take her long to find out! She jumped in, cleaned up all the junk around the four-unit building and gave it a brand new paint job – *the trim and everything*. Next morning, the glistening white building was totally *spray can* painted on all four sides with ugly black graffiti. They even did the windows! Slum dwellers are slow to accept sudden changes in their environment! But Susan was a very stubborn gal. She repainted and installed a five-foot high chain link fences around the entire property! Much like the next move in game of chess, the neighborhood responded by stealing every inch of Susan's new fencing. They did leave the naked steel posts and repainted graffiti on the building – *this time in bright crimson red*!

Beyond the physical problems of trying to operate in the slums, there's also a serious matter of the economics! *It's almost impossible to increase the value of a slum property*, no matter how many improvements you make. Can you relate to that age old saying – "its money down a rat hole"? That's the picture I'm trying to paint here! From a pure operating standpoint, I have two primary reasons why I won't buy property in the slums. The first has to do with the *rental customers* – the other is a bit more *personal*! From a rental customer standpoint, I'm almost *dead-bang* certain I'm not going to like the people who show up to rent my property in the slums. I simply don't want customers who are willing to live in slums! The second reason is a bit personal – *yet extremely important to me*. I don't wanta end up dead! I personally don't feel comfortable working in the slums, nor do I wish to send my workers there either!

ALWAYS CONSIDER ISOLATION FACTOR

Before you consider buying any property – I want you to stand back – across the street is perfect! Now look very closely at the units! Then, I want you to ask yourself this question: *What could possibly go wrong here that might hurt my rental income*? Think about bad things that might happen where you would have very little control to fix the problem! This is what my **isolation factor is all about**! I'm looking at bad neighbors, too much traffic, too many rental units next to mine – or perhaps the units are within smelling distance of the local sewage treatment plant. I'm always happy to see fencing, which separates me from the neighbors – also, I like lots of mature trees and shrubs, which provide a natural barrier between neighboring properties. Tenants (my customers) **pay top dollar rents** when I can offer them decent privacy and seclusion.

I like my small colony properties to have adequate separation between me and the properties next to mine. I don't want tenants from the neighboring units hangin' out at my properties. I like fences and natural barriers, like thick shrubs or berry vines with big thorns! Anything that would make the next door neighbors walk around or cause them extra effort to borrow a cup of sugar from my tenants. Closeness, *tenants ganging up*, breeds landlord problems! This is one reason why my properties downtown on commercial lots work so well–there are generally no residential neighbors around them. My six small two-bedroom houses behind the soap factory I told you about earlier fits my description of a **perfect isolation factor**.

RISK HAS CHANGED OVER THE YEARS

I'm an investor who makes a living from my properties – **therefore**, I take any risk very seriously because it has everything to do with **my income** and **well-being**. Stated another way, if something should happen to my houses, making it difficult to rent them – *say for example*, a situation develops where I suddenly can't attract decent paying renters anymore! That would be a life threatening problem to me – or certainly a threat to my lifestyle! Regardless – I would take it very seriously! To guard against this risk, *my separate colony strategy provides me a reasonable level of protection*. Allow me to explain why!

Years ago, I improved my cash flow problems by switching from single-family houses to **multiple units**. As my "rag-tag" collection of small apartments, duplex units, and even an old motor lodge property grew in number, many different locations were involved. Servicing each location became rather expensive. They were somewhat better than single-house call-outs – but still, having so many locations required way too much travel! Back then my long-term goal was to one day sell off all my scattered properties and exchange them for one big 100- or 200-unit apartment. I could collect all my rents from a single location. Compared to chasing all over servicing many locations, owning one large apartment seemed like a landlord's ultimate dream! I even pictured myself in some faraway place casually sipping mint juleps without a care in the world!

SOCIETY'S RULES BEGAN TO CHANGE

Several of my investor friends shared my dream of owning just one large apartment and beat me to the punch! They accomplished the task of trading up long before I was ready to start. I was still mowing the grass at my old converted motor lodge when my buddy closed escrow on 145 units in the capital city of Sacramento. To say I was filled with both envy and jealousy would be a gross understatement! Just why I moved so slowly, I'll never quite understand!

Almost five years to the day after Kevin bought his apartment, I got an early morning call from his assistant manager. So far this morning he informed me, I've already received 51 move-out notices and we've only been open less than an hour! A drug related shooting in the parking lot had triggered this panic move-out situation! 51 renters who won't be paying rent on the first is not the kind of news apartment owners wish to hear. Before that early morning phone call, I had never even heard of such a thing! But it certainly got me to thinking! At that particular time in my career, I'm guessing I owned 130 rental units or so! If suddenly I lost 30% of my income, there's simply no way I would ever survive! Neither did my friend Kevin! Although he tried hard to attract new tenants, the damage was done. He finally lost the property in bankruptcy!

When I first began buying income properties, drugs were not such a serious problem like we see today. Once in a while I'd have an issue, but I could usually fix the problem within a few weeks, so it never put much of a strain on my income. However, things have changed – in today's environment, I'm a lot more convinced that my **separate colony**

strategy gives me far greater protection if something goes seriously wrong. Should I ever face a problem like Kevin, I may have problems at one colony, but it wouldn't wipe out my total income. Naturally, I wouldn't like it very much, but it wouldn't destroy me financially or drive me out of business. Likely in a couple months I could straighten things out! Having my separate colonies, **each at different locations**, pretty much allows me to cut off an arm to save the rest of my body. In other words, a single bomb won't knock out all my earning power.

FINANCIAL RISK MINIMIZED
WITH SELLER FINANCING

Seller financing comes almost automatically when I purchase colony houses. To begin with, my colony properties with five units or more would require a commercial mortgage if I were dealing with banks. Not only are commercial mortgages difficult to get, but most bankers don't like older properties like mine to begin with! Even if they held their nose and gave me a mortgage, it would certainly have a variable interest rate with periodic adjustments. This is the kind of mortgage I don't want. And here's another deal killer for me! Almost any bank that approved my financial statement and offered me a commercial mortgage would also insist that I sign as personally liable, in addition to pledging my property. Bankers are like men who wear belts and suspenders both, just in case one snaps. I have never had to sign personally with **seller financing**.

Occasionally, almost every investor buys a property that seems like a super deal going in, but the results turn out quite differently! Okay, I *can hear you thinking here* – Jay's probably talkin' about me! **Only if it fits!** We're all guilty of this and if you're actively in the game buying properties, sooner or later it's bound to happen! In my own case, I once owned a small five-unit group of houses (a colony) in a very nice neighborhood several blocks down the street from a junior school. In terms of looks, this property was one of my better ones. The general appearance was probably a little too good, looking back! That must have been the reason I paid too much to begin with.

I violated several of my own rules when I negotiated the purchase! To start with, **I overpaid** because I felt there would be very few expenses to "doctor up" the place, meaning my "FOO-FOO" treatment or cosmetic fix-up! Another problem was that the rents were already near the top of the market when I closed – this meant that no matter how much fix-up I did, or money I spent, there was no way I could increase the rents by much! **The main reason I buy rundown properties with below market rents is because I can always generate cash flow after fix-up!** I'm sure I knew this back then, but for some odd reason, I totally ignored it, and it cost me dearly!

Besides **overpaying** – I also agreed to mortgage payments too high for the income – *and at the same time*, I experienced a higher than normal turnover rate (move-outs). Seems like my tenants in the front houses facing the street were always in some kind of argument or conflict with young teenagers coming and going to school. They would call me to complain at first, then several months later they'd just move out! I've never really understood why. After a couple years, I finally decided to quit dumping more money in the property! I attempted to re-negotiate my mortgage payments, but the three sisters who owned the mortgage could never agree to reduce my terms, so I gave the property back.

RISKING WHAT YOU HAVE INVESTED

Obviously, no one likes to give a property back! Still, when you're an income property investor and you can't make the property produce income for whatever reason, you'll soon be facing bankruptcy if you don't make a quick change in your operation. This is yet another good reason to always stay on top of your record keeping so you can make *financial decisions quickly* when you need to. I've heard many horror stories about big companies who didn't realize they were losing money every month – until finally one day, they were broke! This is not the kind of record keeping you want. If you need help with this, call me – let's get it fixed! 1-800-722-2550.

With nearly all my **colony financing** (83%) – *it's the property sellers who carry my debt*. It's the folks I bought the property from who carried back mortgages and now receive payments from me. This is called **seller financing** and the debt is secured solely by the property they sold me – *and no other personal assets beyond the property*! Therefore, with any give-back, it's usually the keys for the deed if you've kept the lines of communication open with the seller. This was my situation when I finally gave up on my five units. Obviously, no one likes to give a property back, but it's much less expensive than a formal foreclosure initiated by the mortgage holder. As I said earlier, **seller financing** allows you to minimize the downside risk should suffer a setback you didn't anticipate!

Oliver Street, which I mentioned earlier, is an ideal model for colony investors because it had all the right ingredients – *the right benefits*! A seven-unit colony, consisting of houses and duplexes, located about a block away from a neighborhood supermarket. You can learn more details and even find a sketch of this property in my book, *Start Small, Profit Big in Real Estate*, available at most bookstores.

When I acquired the property it was **a big fat mess** – 19 junk cars, low rents, and tons of trash! But the owner was willing to jump through hoops in order to get some offer he could live with. He had tried his best to hang on, but to me, he simply wasn't cut out to be a property owner! Since I love a good joke now and then, I could have easily suggested he become a junk car trader or just a plain ol' junk dealer. I could see he didn't have much humor, so I restrained myself! He was going broke and nothing was very funny to him at the time!

In the adding value business, or fix-up trade, acquiring a multiple-unit property *with rents 30 to 50% below what the local market rents should be*, is almost an unconditional promise you've bought yourself **a money machine**! At Oliver Street, rents were only $400 per month when I acquired the property! In the part of California where I live, $400 rents are about as low as you'll find and still get four walls with a roof. The only lodging cheaper is under one of our three bridges crossing the Sacramento River. A quick peek at my GROSS RENT MULTIPLIER CHART (see Appendix A) will show you that the biggest profits in this business are always made by increasing rents on the least expensive units! It's also at the lower end where you'll find the biggest pool of renters in my town. When I first did a survey on what local renters could pay, I found that roughly 80% of all the renters in my town could pay no more than $400 per month. Today it's up to $800! **You need to know this info where you live.** For example, if you can find colony houses that rent for $600 per month in an $800 neighborhood and you have the ability (knowledge) to fix up the property for approximately 10% of the purchase price – *you're already a millionaire in the making whether you know it or not*!

THE BENEFITS ARE WHAT YOU WANT

I probably don't have to tell you – but I'm going to just the same, *acquiring the right benefits will greatly reduce the biggest risks of income property ownership*. The reason is because many benefits such as **under-market rents** can quickly be converted to **cash flow**. For example, at Oliver Street! The difference between seven units renting for $500 per month and $700 is **$1400 per month**. Let's say that you purchased the property at *break-even* cash flow–you've now earned yourself a healthy **$1400 monthly increase** after fix-up! How much time will the fix-up take, *you ask*? I allow myself up to 24 months to complete a property turn-around. However, my rents will start increasing within three to four months after I become the new owner. **It's important to remember** – most of the risk associated with income property can be greatly reduced with **CASH FLOW**!

When you're out scoutin' the neighborhood searchin' for colony-type properties – remember you're trying to find a motivated seller. Look for properties like Oliver Street! *19 rusty ol' cars* are fairly easy to spot! The Oliver Street owner dropped $50,000 from his asking price during my second visit – however, he insisted he would still need to have a $20,000 down payment. He gave me some oddball reason why, but I kept on blabbin' about how we're gonna move all these junk cars?

BUYING YOUR FIRST COLONY

On the next few pages – let's play **WHAT IF**! We'll start by making an offer on Easy Street, consisting of seven units, five separate houses and a duplex (see sketch Figure 9-1). The current rents are shown alongside each rental unit. When you add them up, you'll find the total monthly income for Easy Street is $3610.

At this time, seven-unit properties like Easy Street should sell for approximately 9 or 10 times the gross rents in my town, assuming the units are earning average rents for the area, $600-640 range. But since they're not, I intend to offer **8 x gross rents** to reflect the property's rundown condition. Total rents are $3610 per month – **or $43,320 annually**! Therefore, my offer will be 8 x $43,320 = $346,560 (rounded) to **$350,000**. My offer will be 10% down, which is typical for this type of property. See details of my offer, Figure 9-2. You'll find my INCOME PROPERTY ANALYSIS FORM showing my projection of income and expenses, as well as my proposed mortgage payment of $1400 per month for 20 years (Figure 9-3).

10-YEAR ANNUAL CASH FLOW CHART

I always prepare what I call my ANNUAL CASH FLOW CHART (see Figure 9-4), for every property I acquire. Let's pretend my offer to purchase Easy Street has been accepted by the seller for the price and terms I've offered (Figure 9-2). The **annual cash flow chart** (Figure 9-4) is my projection (estimate) of how the property will perform over the next 10 years. Please notice the first three entries showing **my estimated fix-up costs–$10,000, $20,000** and **$5,000** (line 16). These are my projections for how much and when I'll be spending $35,000, *my estimated cost for fix-up*. Lines 17 and 18 show **cash flow** and the **accumulated cash flow** as I project them during my first 10 years of ownership. This cash flow chart is my estimate of income and expenses for the next 10 years. It provides an excellent financial tool for forecasting and tracking results.

EASY STREET – 10 YEARS LATER

Continuing to play "**what if**," I'm anticipating the sale of Easy Street **after 10 years of ownership**. Notice my rents are projected to be **$76,500** (see Cash Flow Chart, Figure 9-4). I'm expecting to sell for **10 x the gross rents** at that time, (see Figure 9-5). Figure 9-6 shows you the details of my proposed seller financing, using a **wrap-around note or mortgage**. I am proposing a 20-year term with interest only payments to me of $3500 per month at 06% interest. Most buyers, including me, prefer interest only payments because it gives us better cash flow. **Cash flow** ranks higher than paying down the principal. When I receive my $3500 monthly payment, I must then send $1400 to the first mortgage holder, leaving me a net income of **$2100**.

Assuming my carryback mortgage reaches maturity, I'll have received 240 payments of $3500 each. My net earnings will have been at least *half a million dollars* (**$504,000**) even if my underlying mortgage payments continued the entire 20 years. At the end of 20 years, and after receiving **half a million dollars** – my **$700,000 principal payment** is now due and payable. Friends, I don't know about you, **but this works for me**! Seems like a decent return for my $35,000 down payment investment. **Don't you agree?**

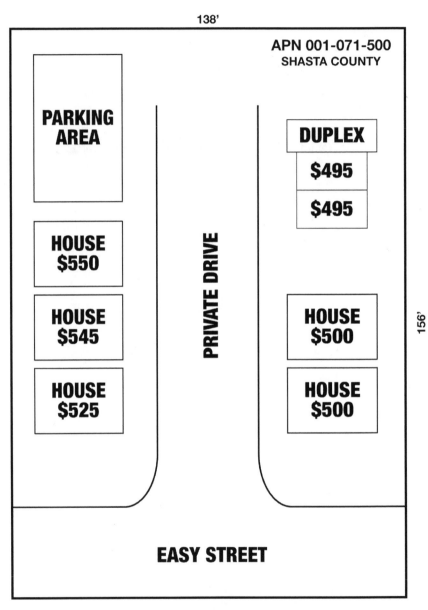

FIGURE 9-1

Offer To Purchase Easy Street

$3,610 Per Mo. X 12 Mo. = $43,320 yr.
X 8 Annual Gross Rents =
$350,000 (rounded)

Offer	**$350,000**
Down Payment	$35,000
Seller Carry	$315,000 *

*Payments = $1,400 or More Per
Month @ 5% Interest, 20 Year Term

FIGURE 9-2

INCOME PROPERTY ANALYSIS FORM

Property Name ___**EASY STREET**___ Date _____

LINE
NO.   INCOME DATA (MONTHLY)   **PER MONTH**

1	Total Gross Income (Present)	$_____3610_____	100%
2	Vacancy Allowance Min. 5% LN-1	$_____180_____	05
	Attach copy of 1040 Schedule E or provide past 12 months income statement for verification		
3	Uncollectable or Credit Losses (rents due but not collected)	$_____180_____	05
4	GROSS OPERATING INCOME	$_____3250_____	

EXPENSE DATA (MONTHLY)

5	Taxes, Real Property	$_____315_____	08	
6	Insurance	$_____250_____	06	
7	Management, Allow Min. 05%	$_____360_____	10	48%
8	Maintenance	$_____360_____	10	
9	Repairs	$_____180_____	05	
10	Utilities Paid by Owner (Monthly)	$_____350_____	09	

Elec	$ _____	
Water	$ _____240_____	
Sewer	$ _____	
Gas	$ _____	
Garbage	$ _____110_____	
Cable TV	$ _____	
Totals =	($_____350_____)	

11	Total Expenses	$_____1815_____	48%
12	NET OPERATING INCOME (LN 4 - LN 11)	$_____1435_____	

Existing Mortgage Debt		(Monthly)	Due Mo/Yr
1st Bal Due ___315000___	Payments $ ___1400___		20 Years Ask For
2nd Bal Due _____	Payments $ _____		_____
3rd Bal Due _____	Payments $ _____		_____
4th Bal Due _____	Payments $ _____		_____
5th Bal Due _____	Payments $ _____		_____

13	Totals _____ (13A) $ _____		
14	MONTHLY CASH FLOW AVAILABLE	35	
	(LN - 12 - 13A) (Pos or Neg)		

NOTE: Line 14 shows available funds to service new mortgage debt from operation of property.

REMARKS: All lines must be completed for proper analysis. Enter the actual amount on each line or 0.

FIGURE 9-3

ANNUAL CASH FLOW CHART • EASY STREET

LINE	PLAN YEARS	PARTIAL 6 MONTHS	YEAR 1	YEAR 2	YEAR 3	Under 4% YEAR 4	Apprx. 4% YEAR 5	Minimal YEAR 6	3% YEAR 7	3.5% YEAR 8	4.0% YEAR 9	3.0% YEAR 10
1	GROSS INCOME $	21,660	43,320	55,200	61,560	63,960	66,500	67,000	69,010	71,415	74,265	76,500
2	VAC. ALLOWANCE	1,080	2,160	2,760	3,060	3,300	3,325	3,350	3,450	3,570	3,715	3,825
3	CREDIT LOSES	1,080	1,080	1,400	1,000	1,000	900	1,000	700	100	1,200	1,250
4	OPERATING INCOME	19,500	40,080	51,040	57,500	596,660	62,275	62,650	64,860	66,845	69,350	71,425
5	R.E. TAXES	1,890	3,780	3,840	3,960	4,360	4,400	4,510	4,600	4,810	4,910	5,000
6	INSURANCE	1,500	3,000	3,100	3,200	3,200	3,300	3,300	3,620	3,600	3,720	3,770
7	MANAGEMENT	2,160	4,320	5,520	6,150	6,395	6,650	6,700	6,900	7,140	7,425	7,650
8	MAINTENANCE	2,160	4,320	5,420	3,100	6,300	6,550	6,700	6,550	7,100	7,320	7,500
9	REPAIRS	1,080	2,160	1,860	1,900	2,100	2,100	2,400	2,360	2,400	3,000	3,000
10	UTILITIES	2,100	4,200	4,300	4,380	4,475	4,490	4,540	4,600	4,615	4,725	4,800
11	LEGAL & ACCTG	600	1,200	1,200	1,300	1,400	1,400	1,500	1,500	1,500	1,600	1,600
12	ADVERTISING	—	—	300	460	460	300	650	400	500	600	500
13	NET OPERATING INCOME	8,010	17,100	25,500	30,050	30,970	33,085	32,350	34,330	35,180	36,050	37,605
14	DEPT SERVICE $	8,400	16,800	16,800	16,800	16,800	16,800	16,800	16,800	16,800	16,800	16,800
15	NET RENTS	<390>	300	8,700	13,250	14,170	16,285	1,550	17,530	18,380	19,250	20,805
16	FIX-UP COSTS	10,000	20,000	5,000	—	—	—	—	—	—	—	—
17	CASH FLOW	<10,390>	<19,700>	3,700	13,250	14,170	16,285	15,550	17,530	18,380	19,250	20,805
18	ACCUM CASH FLOW	—	<30,090>	<26,390>	<13,140>	1,030	17,315	32,865	50,395	68,775	88,025	108,830

FIGURE 9-4

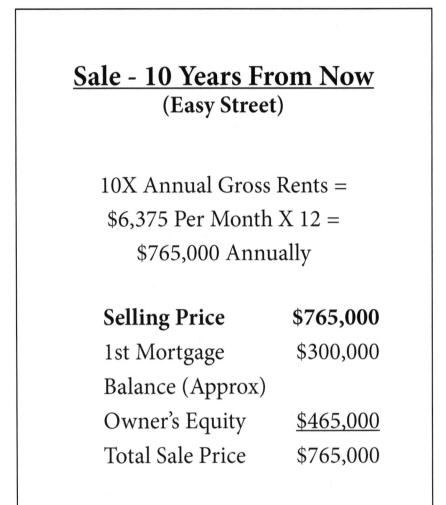

Sale - 10 Years From Now
(Easy Street)

10X Annual Gross Rents =
$6,375 Per Month X 12 =
$765,000 Annually

Selling Price	**$765,000**
1st Mortgage Balance (Approx)	$300,000
Owner's Equity	$465,000
Total Sale Price	$765,000

FIGURE 9-5

Seller Financing
10 Years from Now
(Easy Street)

Selling Price (10 X Rents)	$765,000
Down Payment	$65,000
Seller Financing	$700,000

Using Wrap-Around Financing
Terms = 20 Years (Interest Only 6%)

Payment Receivable	$3,500
Underlying Mortgage Payment	($1,400)

Seller Receives	$3,500 per mo.
Seller Pays Out	$1,400 per mo.
Seller Keeps	$2,100 per mo.

FIGURE 9-6

Buying colony houses like I recommend is one of the safest and most profitable long-term investment strategies I know of. It's also an excellent business opportunity because colony houses will generate spendable cash flow quicker than most leveraged real estate investments. This means that ordinary "Mom and Pop" investors who don't have a ton of money to spend can still enjoy a positive income with only a minimal upfront investment. It is indeed very possible to acquire six or seven income-producing houses for about the same down payment required to purchase a single-family home. The big difference of course, is that **one provides a decent income** – the other doesn't!

PEOPLE MAKE PEOPLE RICH – NOT BANKS

Real estate investing is all about the benefits – and they don't come any bigger than **seller financing**. With older colony houses (five or more units), 90% of all the sales will include seller financing for at least part of the deal. *Sellers are the key to negotiating terms that will ultimately determine cash flow at the property.* Obviously, depending on their motivational level, sellers can provide terms that institutional lenders wouldn't dream of offering in a thousand years. This one benefit alone can make you rich!

CHAPTER 10

DISCOVER WHERE THEY'RE BITE'N

The most difficult task for greenhorn investors is finding their first golden pond with the right kind of fish! The good news is, it gets lots easier once you break the ice – that means acquire your first income property. Even students who attend my seminars and workshops often return home and stray from the fundamentals they learned in the classroom. Hey – keep your chin up, *I didn't promise you a rose garden* – starting from scratch is the difficult part for everyone, *so cheer up*!

The process begins by first selecting your investment pond or a decent fishing location – that will be the area in your town or community where you decide to invest. I always advise beginners to keep their investment area as small as possible. Obviously, in smaller towns or cities, the investment area must be large enough to contain a good selection of target properties. **Target properties** for the purpose of these instructions will be small multiple-unit properties – *or, as I like to call them*, **colony houses**! Five to eight unit properties are the ideal size and it doesn't matter whether they are houses, duplexes, small apartments, an old motor lodge (cottages), or even a couple of mobile homes on the same parcel or a lot with the stick-built units. If five to eight units sounds a bit scary for your first investment, please take my advice and at least shoot for a duplex or three units! C'mon you guys, let's look for multiple rents – **keep reading, I'll hold your hand**!

SEEKING ODD-BALL PROPERTIES
IN THE NEIGHBORHOOD

For the most part, you should be searching for older properties in residential areas or in downtown commercial locations. These older colony-type properties were mostly built 60 to 70 years ago, beginning in the 1940s. No need to worry about current zoning ordinances, because so long as these properties are still being used as residential rentals, they're allowed to keep operating under the grandfather rules. Notice I said **keep operating**! That means they've pretty much been used as residential rentals during the past few years. Once they become vacant for any length of time – *its buyer beware*! The *grandfather rules* may no longer apply. It's for this reason I always recommend acquiring properties with live breathing occupants living there, even though some may appear like they don't have a pulse!

Many new students, who begin searching for multiple-unit properties with my help, using my TELEPHONE MENTORING PROGRAM, will call me shortly after their initial search and tell me – **there ain't none**! I've learned to expect these phone calls! I've found my typical student's initial search is much like a tourist's sightseeing venture in the hills of San Francisco on a dense foggy morning! *They simply don't see nothin'!* But I've found, with the passage of a little more time and some aimless wandering – the fog finally lifts and **eureka**! Suddenly things that weren't so visible in the early morning fog begin to take shape in the bright afternoon sun!

Like senior citizens (including me), there's no shortage of *older*, multiple-unit properties – obviously, they are not as common as single-family houses and they're often hidden behind commercial buildings in downtown locations or in older residential neighborhoods. Sometimes you'll find them tucked in behind overgrown trees and bushes behind the main house facing the street. It's for this reason I suggest walking tours in the older neighborhoods where you have decided to invest. Don't bother looking in subdivisions or in the modern tract developments. You won't find many 1950s houses still around. You'll have much better results near the downtown center. They can also be found in the older rural areas that sprung up before freeways and modern-day subdivisions. Many grand old houses in the city have additional rental units snuggled in behind them on deep tree covered lots. Look for multiple *mailboxes* and *extra telephone wires* going to the property. These are generally clues that more units exist on the same property.

One question always seems to pop up: are there enough of these older multiple-unit properties around for all the starry-eyed wanta-be investors? **The answer is yes**, there are more than enough for all the investors who will actually take serious steps to acquire them. The great majority of new investors are chasing single-family houses – and of course, the bigger, more sophisticated investors are likely more interested in larger and newer buildings. Small multiple-unit investments, like I'm suggesting here are often thought to be *too big for little guys – and too small for the big guys!* As a result, the competition is greatly reduced for these kinds of properties, *which turns out to be* another major advantage for **colony house investors**.

LOCAL RENTAL KNOWLEDGE IS A MUST

It doesn't matter how you learn – **so long as you do**! *You must know the rent prices where you plan to invest.* I've said this already, but one way to learn prices is to pretend to be a renter and dedicate several Sundays to calling the rental ads in your local newspaper. Next, drive out to the neighborhoods to see what a typical two-bedroom unit rents for where you plan to acquire properties. Do this same thing with one-bedrooms and the larger threes. By the time you've looked at 30 or 35 rental units, you'll become a pretty knowledgeable authority on local rental rates. This information is very important so you'll immediately know when you locate a target property whether it's under-rented or not! **Under-rented properties** will allow you to increase the **income** and **potential profits**. Your purchase price should be pretty much based on the income stream the property is producing. Buying an under-rented property with $500 rents when you are satisfied that $700 is the current market rate sets the stage for creating **immediate cash flow**.

Retiring owners are an excellent source for finding these small multiple-unit properties. Another source are units being managed by professional property managers for *out-of-town owners*. In my town, most of these small-managed properties are without an on-site person to help with the upkeep. Without supervision, they tend to go downhill rather quickly. There's often no one around to cut the grass or water shrubs. There's no one available to pick up the accumulating trash or paint the faded buildings – and because these properties are older, they tend to fall into disrepair and become an ugly mess much quicker than newer buildings.

Many out-of-town owners were snookered into paying too much and suddenly find themselves without adequate reserves to pay for repairs and normal upkeep. Eventually, these properties can't compete with the cleaner, nicer-looking units, and managers resort to lowering rents in order to keep them rented. *When you find this situation, be prepared to act quickly!* This is exactly what you're looking for. It's **"The Perfect Storm"** for deal making!

GOOD RECORDS NECESSARY TO WRITE OFFERS

Once you've selected your investment area – it's now time to buy yourself a good county map and start keeping track of properties you find – **target properties**! These properties are generally not for sale. They are properties that have potential! Properties you'd be very interested in acquiring *if they were available*. You are in the **investigating** and **planning mode** right now. You might call this phase window shopping – or creating your wish list!

When you spot a potential property that looks like a good candidate – I want you to make a sketch (free-hand) on an 8 x 11 size yellow pad showing the houses, apartments, mobiles, or whatever! Simply draw little squares that represent the houses or apartments. Perhaps you might show a few trees, driveways or anything pertinent to the property so you end up with a good record (sketch) of your findings. *There's an excellent chance you'll be needing this information later on.* By all means, write down the addresses for each of the rental units so they are easy to identify or talk about later on! It's best to tie in, *or measure*, your property sketch to the nearest street intersection so you can easily match up your drawing with the scaled county parcel map (APN).

As you drive around looking for properties – you must learn to stop and prepare your sketches very discreetly! If dogs start barking, come back later. People don't like strangers prowling around in front of their property. Sometimes preparing your sketch across the street works out better. The idea here is to accomplish this task without other people observing you if you can. With a bit of practice, you'll begin to develop the characteristics of a very sneaky private detective. Rather than park my car in front of a target property, I'll generally park down the street and walk back on the opposite side! Try and look like a tenant, you'll blend right in!

After preparing your freehand, *field drawn sketch*, take it home and re-draw it using a straight edge. This allows you to make it more legible, *proportional*, and easier to read. It will give you a more presentable picture of the property details. Make several copies for your file, and on one copy write (red pen) the estimated rents you believe the units should rent for based on your new market knowledge. By now, you can probably understand why I made you drive around on Sundays lookin' at all those stupid classified rental ads.

The big advantage of having *a detailed property sketch* will become much more apparent during telephone mentoring discussions where both mentor and student will be looking at the same document (sketch) while talking about the property on the phone. This is one situation where a picture (sketch) is worth a thousand words – perhaps a lot more and most certainly, a huge time saver!

KNOWING HOW MUCH TO PAY IS PRICELESS

With a property sketch in hand – and the estimated rents marked in red, it's now time to prepare Jay's INCOME PROPERTY ANALYSIS FORM (see Appendix C). Remember, the rent calculations will be based on your judgment, *or your guess*, as to what you believe the rents should be – *not what they actually are*! You can find out what the actual rents are when you find a property owner who is interested in selling. Right now, however, you are merely preparing a hypothetical purchase plan. Still, you're getting a wonderful education working in the trenches–**agreed**!

Don't forget – most of the properties you'll be preparing sketches for, as well as developing your hypothetical purchase plans, are not yet for sale! Right about now, you're probably beginning to wonder – why in the world should I do all this stupid paper work for a property that's not even for sale? **Several reasons**: first, out-of-town owners with properties being poorly managed by professional managers, and who are quite often receiving pitifully low owner draws (the money left after all expenses are paid), are always prime candidates for **cold-call letters**. Letters suggesting a reasonable price should they ever be interested in selling. Another reason is to establish an active file of properties you would like to own in your buying area – *if and when* they should become available. A third reason is because of all the "real life" experience you'll be getting by setting up these files. *During a 12-year period in my town, 13 of the income properties in my file outta 22 became available for sale.* By having all your homework done – you can act quickly to acquire any one of these properties long before your competition is even outta bed!

Perhaps the best reason of all for this effort and preparation is because it accomplishes the same thing as the U.S. Army does with boot camp or *basic training*. *Ya see*, the Army don't figure a brand new soldier is fit enough, *nor can he shoot straight enough* to meet the enemy head-on without some **advance preparation** or **basic training**. My first eight weeks at California's huge Fort Ord Training Camp was based on this *being prepared theory*. According to the Army, new recruits don't stand much chance of winning many battles or *even surviving* if they don't know what they're doing. My drill sergeant literally screamed this message at us day and night just in case any of us bald-headed, *dorky lookin'* buck privates dared to think otherwise! *Personally*, I feel about the same way as my old Army sergeant did when it comes to basic training for brand new real estate investors. It's very important that "newbies" understand the fundamentals before I send 'em out with real live bullets in the chamber. Investors who know how to estimate expenses, design a mortgage with the right terms, **and draft an offer quickly** are in the driver's seat when opportunity suddenly pops up. Compare how things might work without any training or preparation. I'm sure you get the picture! By now, I'm hopin' you're still not mad 'cause I sent you out chasin' all those stupid rental ads – **lighten up a bit, okay**!

THOROUGH PREPARATION AVOIDS BIG MISTAKES

The combination of constructing an accurate file and discussing the details with a mentor over the phone has proven very successful for many of my students in their quest to *speed up* to become property owners. It also helps them to avoid the most serious mistakes, such as overpaying or getting snookered by an unscrupulous seller or his overbearing agent. It's my mission to help students acquire properties that provide the benefits they need, as opposed to buying properties simply because *they're available* – or for sale. *Properties must fit well with the investors' long-term goals* – and most certainly, with his or her abilities to manage them. A seller's agent couldn't care less about these kinds of issues.

Along with pictures taken by phone, camera, or whatever, which will clearly show all sides of a target property, we can easily discuss matters like the roofs, *pitched or flat*, as well as the overall property condition. I always want to see the building foundations and utility boxes. Does each unit have its own separate utility meter? Show me the picture!

Once we get a nibble on the line – I'm talkin' about a call or some kind of *tip-off* that an owner might be open to receiving an offer – I will generally ask my investor trainee to return to the property and complete his investigation work. *He'll be using my 24-item property inspection sheet* (see Appendix D) to make sure we haven't missed anything important that could make a difference in the price and terms we plan to offer. Sometimes inexperienced investors can easily overlook or forget to ask questions about the sewer system when buying their first income property. This can be a very costly mistake when buying older rental units, because there can be a huge expense difference between having a city sewer service *versus* operating a 60-year-old leach field and a septic tank.

My property inspection sheet will prevent a new investor from making this crucial mistake, as well as offering help to avoid **23 other possible problems** or conditions that could have a big impact on how we might value a property. Writing offers with *contingencies* without knowing the details, as many realtors often suggest, is not a good idea in my opinion. Once you set the price with your offer, then later you discover something that suggests your price may be too high, I can tell you from experience – sellers get extremely emotional about price reductions. Chances are, you'll lose the deal – *plus they'll call you nasty names*!

PROPERTY INSPECTION SHEET

1. Estimate overall condition of property (10 is high)   1 to 10 _____

2. Based on surrounding neighborhood, rate location   1 to 10 _____

3. Full concrete foundations, all living, houses/apts.   Yes/No _____

4. Roofs – Are they flat or pitched, or both   Yes/No _____

5. Type of siding on building, <u>wood</u> or <u>stucco</u> or <u>brick</u>   _____

6. Do houses/apts. have individual electric service meters   Yes/No _____

7. Rate or estimate condition of painting <u>overall</u>   1 to 10 _____

8. Do houses/apts. have individual gas meters   Yes/No _____

9. Find out; determine if units have city/county sewers   Yes/No _____

10. Find out; determine if units served by city water service   Yes/No _____

11. Are houses/apts. served by private septic system   Yes/No _____

12. Are houses/apts. served by private water well   Yes/No _____

13. How many water meters are serving property   (how many) ___

14. Are all units being lived in at this time   Yes/No _____

15. Are any units classified as non-livable   (how many) ___

16. What is roof material - comp shingles(cs), wood(w), metal(m) _____

17. Does property appear to have adequate parking   Yes/No _____

18. Do units – or most units have individual yard space   Yes/No _____

19. Do all units appear to have renters at this time   Yes/No _____

20. Does property sit low or have drainage problems   Yes/No _____

21. Look at property – separation from neighborhood ok   Yes/No _____

22. Rate property overall for rundown and/or trashy   1 to 10 _____

23. Your personal opinion – is neighborhood a safe area   1 to 10 _____

24. Would you personally be ok working on/around prop.   Yes/No _____

DON'T REFUSE HELP WHEN YOU'RE LOOKIN'

I don't wish to gore anyone's ox here, *but I must tell you* – waiting around for a real estate agent to help you find properties will likely be very disappointing. To begin with, if a property is not listed in the multiple listing service – most agents won't know what else they can do to help you. Their efforts won't seem too promising. Having told you this, however, never turn down any help that agents are willing to offer! Who knows, they might just have a contact or a good friend who knows a friend who might just uncover the hidden diamond you're looking for. Long odds perhaps, but it does happen. The fact is that working with an agent who is willing to learn this business can eventually become a valuable asset for you. I've had two excellent agents over the past 45 years and they were both extremely valuable to me after I trained them how they could help me! Naturally, it proved quite lucrative for them as well.

Many new investors who've decided to follow my **colony house strategy** have attended my live training seminars! Most get all "fired up" and they're ready to go! Seems like most beginners or start-out investors are extremely "gung-ho" and have very little patience (which is how it should be) when they first start out! Yet, *speed must never be your goal* – it's **preparation** that will bring you the best results. Part of this preparation for acquiring colony properties is to first determine who owns them! Next, you must learn what motivates the owners who seem willing to sell. *Knowing the answers will help you find the right properties and get the right terms.* It's very important for you to understand what makes these colony owners tick – *and ultimately,* what you must do to create **a profitable deal for yourself.**

There are basically two kinds of colony property owners – by far the largest group are "Mom and Pop" investors who might own anywhere from 5 to 10 or even 20 rental units. Many of these owners have operated their properties for a number of years! They manage the property, collect the rents, fix the toilets, and patch the roofs. They are not like professional 100-unit apartment owners and they operate their properties much differently! Most of these *small-time owners* are quite content with the property they own. They don't usually think much about expanding; they're satisfied to earn a decent income from their rents. These folks are *small-time*, **do-it-yourself investors**.

They also understand what things cost; insurance, taxes, roof repairs, appliances, and they realize they can keep a lot more income by doing the managing and most all repairs. Also, most of these folks are very much aware that mortgages, or any type of bank financing would be classified as *commercial borrowing*; therefore, nearly impossible to obtain. These owners are pretty much resigned to the idea that when it comes time to sell out and retire – **they will need to provide most of the financing and terms to make a sale work**! *As a rule*, their plan for selling is to provide the financing and live off the monthly mortgage payments they receive. Their biggest worry or concern is choosing the right buyer who can keep the property operating! *Having to take back their property once they've retired will always be their greatest fear*!

SEARCHING FOR "HOT SHOTS AND MILKERS"

The second kind of colony property owners is what I call the "hot shots" or *milkers*. They're pretty much cash flow oriented investors and they fully understand that multiple units bring in a lot more money than single-family homes! Their primary objective is more money in their pockets! This bunch is also very reluctant to put money back in the property for improvements or upgrading – *hence the name milker*. Milking the property for every dime they can pull out is the milker's creed!

This strategy is *penny wise* – and pound foolish! Older multiple-unit properties naturally require more maintenance and repairs than newer buildings! And although it's true, these older colony properties will bring in a lot more income every month – the wise investor understands he must give back a portion of his added income for maintenance and upkeep. Failure to do this is the downfall of many "hot shots" and "milkers" and it eventually turns them into "don't wanters" of the highest order! As you shall learn – the disastrous results of hiring poor property managers who seldom check out the property, along with *tightwad owners* who refuse to spend any money for maintenance, **ultimately brings down both the property value and rental income.** When this happens, the property becomes exactly what us colony investors are looking for. *Hang on now* – 'cause I'm about to tell ya how I find these properties.

It's often been said – the good Lord helps those who help themselves! My investing philosophy has always been – **take the bull by the horns and get the job done yourself!** I've never had any reason to change that approach when looking for good colony properties. I drive the streets in my investment area – *a medium size town with a population of 60,000 when I first started out.* The idea was to identify all the **colony-type properties** I would like to make offers on if they suddenly came up for sale! Obviously they're not for sale yet – but I'm getting prepared just in case they might be! Believe it or not, creating your own buying opportunities is a very effective method for acquiring colonies, but you must do something to initiate some action! Allow me to explain what I'm talkin' about!

WEST SIDE COTTAGES ACQUISITION

It was just about noon when I parked in front of eight small houses (cottages) to prepare a rough sketch of the property on the hood of my car! An elderly lady who was watering the front yard plants watched me for several minutes, then gradually meandered on over to question me – exactly what are you doing here, she asked? "We're getting ready to install a new TV cable," I told her, obviously a little white fib (but it usually works)! We then talked about how hot it was that day – "We need more rain," she said. I asked her several other things about the neighborhood and how long she had lived there. She told me almost 30 years and that she was the property owner. I complimented her on how nice the yard looked – and asked if she liked living so close to seven neighbors (her tenants). Great people, she said – some have been here a long time, and I just hope when I retire, the next owner will treat 'em **same as we do**!

"**We**," I repeated. "Are there other owners besides you?" "Oh no," she answered, "Just my husband and I, only he's been laid up for over two years now! He's got an artificial knee and he can't hardly see anymore. The place is just too much for me by myself and my son lives in Portland – has a great airline job, so he's not much interested in owning rentals in Redding! We told our neighbors a couple years ago that if they would like to take over the property, they could just start making payments to us every month. They don't seem too interested, but then again, they like to travel a lot – probably wouldn't work out too well anyway since they're not around very much!" Although we talked for another hour or so, this is how things started out and eventually I was able to acquire the West Side Cottage property – *also I might add*, several other properties much the same way.

HOW TO IMPROVE YOUR LUCK

I have driven through my local neighborhoods and drawn up freehand sketches for almost every colony-type property I would like to own – *assuming of course*, they ever came up for sale! Most probably won't – still, my sketches, as well as my driving trips through areas where I invest, gives me insider knowledge about the properties where my kind of renters wish to live. For example, I know certain neighborhoods where nearly all the renters are young people and mostly single. That means if older tenants were to move there, they likely wouldn't stay more than a couple months. Most older tenants don't mix too easily with young ones! If you'll focus on the kind of neighborhoods where your target customer (tenant) wishes to live, it'll make your management job a whole lot easier.

Not a soul had any idea the West Side Cottages were available (for sale). That's because the owner hadn't listed them for sale and she'd only mentioned the property to her neighborhood friend! You might say I happened along at just the right moment – or as some might claim, I was extremely lucky. There's an old saying that goes – "*the harder I work, the luckier I get!*" I think that best describes how I was able to purchase the West Side Cottages along with several other properties using very similar methods. By going to the source (the property) you'll discover as I have, **lots of opportunities seem to "pop up" outta nowhere**!

Another example: while in the field drawing my sketches, I've started conversations with owners and others, *sometimes even renters,* who have told me about properties they know about that might be for sale. *Believe me,* when you arrive at someone's property around 10 o'clock in the morning on a nice sunny day – you park your car, get out and begin drawing sketches on the hood – there's an awful good chance you're gonna have some company very shortly! If you can learn to engage anyone who shows up in a friendly conversation – slanted toward drawing out the kind of information you're seeking – you can learn a whole lot of things about a property or neighborhood from total strangers. Should you happen to see a *bright 'n shiny* rifle barrel reflecting in the sunlight, I suggest you move quickly to another location!

CREATING YOUR OWN OPPORTUNITIES

Your neighborhood driving and sketch-making ventures will often create an excellent buying opportunity for you while your competition is still home in bed or searching for listings on their computer screen! Had I waited for listings to show up on my computer to acquire my properties, I wouldn't have nearly the number of sheckles in my bank account today, which has allowed me to grow old gracefully and spend my time writing real estate books! Whether that's good or bad – who knows! Let's move on to what I consider my very special method for buying colonies from the *hot shot milkers* – properties that are not listed for sale just yet.

As you observe the multiple-unit properties while driving–you will no doubt see colony-type properties that are being poorly managed! You'll notice some are even going downhill between your trips – dead lawns, hardly any maintenance or upkeep, *rough looking tenants,* too many cars – *sometimes they don't even run!* You'll also begin to see Confederate flags, bed sheets, and Indian blankets covering the front windows. **These properties** are in a downhill spiral and before long they'll be overrun with pit bulls and unlicensed pharmaceutical dealers. I'm not talkin' about slum properties here; I'm talkin' regular *blue-collar* neighborhoods where most investors would normally buy. If you can step in before these properties hit rock bottom, and turn 'em around, you'll discover as I have, your preparation time and efforts will be very well rewarded.

The first thing I'm interested in knowing, assuming it's a property I like – *where does the owner live and who is currently managing the property*? Quite often I've found – when properties are in a rapid downhill decline like I'm talkin' about here, *there's a good chance that out-of-town owners will not even know about it*! Especially if the property manager has been keeping most units rented so the income has remained somewhat stable! Eventually, these properties will run down enough so that vacancies will become a serious problem – sometimes the tenants who live there just stop paying rent! My strategy is to first – *dig out the facts* – as in, **what's gone wrong**! After I learn a few things about the property – it's time for me to write a letter to the out-of-town owner describing what's happening at his property! You must be very careful not to place the blame on the owner or his manager (always blame the tenants). I call my letter writing technique **"cold-calling"** and when my timing is right, it creates an excellent opportunity to begin communicating with an owner about the possibilities of acquiring his property – should he ever decide to sell!

ONE-ON-ONE WITH SELLER AVOIDS COMPETITION

Discovering all you can about a property by learning to be a **property detective** (it might pay you to watch the old Lt. Columbo reruns from the old TV series), will give you enough information to compose a letter to an out-of-town owner. *Your letter stating the facts will establish creditability with an owner* – and will likely get his undivided attention! (See my letter to the Morgan's at the end of this chapter.)

Once again, *these buying opportunities* are being created by **your own actions**. You're not waiting around for somebody else to do something – or for the property to eventually be listed for sale. A key ingredient for creating solid cash flow transactions for yourself happens when you can position yourself **one-on-one** with a seller! Meanwhile, no one else has even the foggiest idea the property might be up for grabs! *Competition is what always drives up the price and limits the kind of terms you can negotiate.* When you are totally **tuned in to** exactly what's going on at the property, you'll find as I have, you are in a very strong position when it comes time to negotiate the **best purchase price and terms**. Obviously, **seller financing** should always be at the top of your negotiating list!

I'm very much aware that out-of-town owners are always concerned about the **net income** they receive every month from their property manager. The net income from the property is often called the **owner's draw**, and it shrinks dramatically when there are vacancies and deadbeat tenants who don't pay their rents. It makes a very compelling argument when I'm able to explain to an out-of-town owner that if he or she were to sell the property to me – *the mortgage payments I'd be sending them every month would likely be as much or **more money** than they are currently receiving from their property manager*!

"More money" are two very powerful words to any owner whose property is performing poorly, and the rental income is in the dumper because of poor management. *You can be sure; it's a very persuasive argument to any owner suffering from negative cash flow.* Friends, you simply can't learn this kind of information sittin' around lookin' at a stupid computer screen – echoing the words from Nancy Sinatra's hit tune, "These Boots Are Made for Walking!" **Here's my advice to you!** Point your boots toward your investing neighborhood and let's get to walkin' and searching for properties! Once you get the hang of this *detective stuff*, you're gonna be extremely pleased with the way you can use this information! **Trust me – this stuff works!**

JAY'S LAUNDRY ROOM INTERVIEW

It's been my experience, when you need to check out a property rather quickly – you won't find out what's happening any faster than by making a personal house call. This is how I began my fact-find-

ing visit at Lemon Street. I call this my "**laundry room technique**."
I usually show up between 7 and 8 a.m. with a clipboard in hand
wearing my "BOB'S CUT-RATE ELECTRIC SERVICE" shirt so I
look somewhat official!

Usually I'll find some "early bird" tenant doing her laundry before
her neighbors are even outta bed! If not, I'll hang out for a while till
someone shows up! When a tenant named Sue finally showed up, I
ask her – *Have you seen Steve yet?*

SUE: **Just who the hell is Steve?**
JAY: **He's my boss, but I guess I got here first!**

That's normally how I make my introduction and present myself!
After introductions, my detective work begins!

JAY: These apartments look like a fairly decent place to live!
SUE: Sure – if you don't mind living around jerks who party
       all night.
JAY: I guess they keep the rents pretty affordable around here!
SUE: Yea, if you think $500 a month is an affordable for these
       dumps! Personally, I think they're gougin' me a bit, *espe-
       cially since management never fixes anything*. They've been
       promising to repair my cooler since last summer, but it's
       still blowin' hot air just like the manager.
JAY: Looks like these apartments are fairly large inside – I
       imagine you've got quite a bit of space to cool down!
SUE: Large she says, *are you kiddin'*! I can barely walk around
       my queen-size bed – *and*, there's hardly any closet space.
       The only decent size room in the place is my kitchen, and
       I don't even cook!
JAY: I'm kinda lookin' around for a place for myself – do you
       know if there's any vacancies here or maybe you can tell
       me where I might find the owner?
SUE: Well, I know there's an empty unit in the back, but I seri-
       ously doubt if it's even cleaned up yet! You'll have to call

Five Star Management Co. – they're over on Hill Street.
The owners live somewhere down near San Diego, I think!

JAY: Would you happen to know if they have some extra parking
around here? I've got a small fishing boat!

SUE: I'd say just go ahead and park up next to your apartment.
As you can see for yourself, everyone here parks their
stupid cars wherever they want! Half of 'em don't even
run. If you ask me, this place is beginning to look like a
damn junk yard!

JAY: Finally I say; thanks for all your help Sue, *I really appreciate
it*. Looks like my boss musta got lost trying to find this
place! If he shows up, would you mind telling him that Bob
went to the next job! Once again; thanks for everything!

My informal interview only took less than 30 minutes – **but I got
more information from Sue than I ever would from the Five Star
Management Co.** Besides, I'm guessin' it's probably a bit more truthful
too! More importantly, it gives me exactly the kind of information I
need so I can *write up an educated proposition* that might just *appeal
to the owners*. Naturally if they contact me, I'll ask them some of the
same information again so I can verify what Sue has told me.

Over the years, I found that most people love to talk – seems
like we all enjoy being heard! My point is, *if you can create a friendly
atmosphere and be a good listener – folks will tell you things you wouldn't
even to tell your mother*! I have always found at least one blabbermouth
tenant who's willing to tell me everything I need to know about what's
going on at the property. *By the way*, Sue even invited me in to see her
apartment. I had to tell her, "No, *but thanks anyway*, my boss, Steve,
would have a fit if I went inside someone's apartment!"

SECRET OFFER TO PURCHASE LEMON STREET

Lemon Street was not for sale. It was not listed with any realty
company, but it was professionally managed (*if you wish to call it that*)
by Five Star Management Co. My informal offer to purchase would

be *totally under the radar*, so to speak, because no agents, *or anyone else*, would have the slightest idea I was even thinking about an offer! **Secrecy** is very important here because I don't want competition if I can avoid it. After all, I'm the one who did all the hard work and research! *I'm the actor who played electrician in the laundry room – RIGHT?* I certainly don't want some copycat competitor learning my acting techniques and overbidding me!

One of the two best ways to make extraordinary profits with income properties is to put yourself in a position so that you and the potential seller are the only two people who know about the deal! **One-on-one with the seller**, I call this! You've totally eliminated any competition. *Okay, I know you're itchin' to know the other way so here it is* – its **adding value** to underperforming properties using my special techniques that will quickly produce more income. You've already been introduced to several of these techniques! However, for right now, let's begin communications with the San Diego owners. My laundry room chat with Sue has given me with all the information I need to write one of my famous **cold-call letters**!

Whoa Jay–*hold on just a minute here.* Pardon the interruption, but you haven't even mentioned anything about what the expenses were at Lemon Street. Aren't you getting a bit hasty even thinkin' about an offer? Friends, if you're not up to speed about what it costs to operate rental units – **please stay with your studies**. And for heaven's sake, don't even attempt to buy anything till you know the answer. Meanwhile, in the interest of moving along – here's my estimated expense number you can use! *Write it down and underline it.* This is my "ballpark" number for estimating the operating costs for any older multiple-unit property (30 years or older). It includes a small vacancy allowance – as well as 05% for uncollectable rents. **For total operating expenses, my estimate is 50% of the scheduled rents.** Lemon Street has seven apartments with scheduled rents of $500 each. Therefore, 7 x $500 = $3500 income. My monthly estimated expenses for operating Lemon Street are **$1750**. Remember, *mortgage payments are not expenses even though they feel like it when you write the check!*

My letter to the San Diego owner was direct – *and purposely quite informal!* I closed with my desire (low key) to acquire the property if and when it should ever become available. I also enclosed **six glossy full color photos** clearly showing the conditions at Lemon Street. Although I make no claim to be an experienced paparazzi, I must admit, *these six pictures were quite revealing!* It's often said a picture is worth a thousand words – however, **the kind of pictures I take** can be worth a lot more than words when it comes to purchasing a property via long distant negotiating. My plan was to mail pictures of Lemon Street to the owners who lived many miles away – *along with my letter or low-key proposition!*

Negotiating pictures are not like regular pictures! The kind of pictures I take for negotiating purposes are staged, sorta like making a Hollywood movie where the timing and each scene is very important – all the actors (the tenants) must be in the right places and *dressed in their native attire.* Needless to say, the pictures I take are not intended to be the least bit flattering! *Their sole purpose is to assist me in obtaining a favorable transaction* should Lemon Street ever become available for sale.

All the actors (tenants) at Lemon Street were pretty much available for picture-taking almost any time because they seldom left the property much before noon. My picture taking began about mid-morning – and took me roughly an hour to snap a roll of film. Unlike making regular movies, my pictures would need to be taken without the actors looking directly into my camera! In fact, my plan was to stay out of sight, completely hidden behind the shrubs and several old storage garages across the street.

FILMING FOR DOLLARS

The two young men living in apartment no. 5 near the back of the property would definitely win my vote for an academy award on this day! Apparently they were raising baby pit bulls inside their unit. Both men were shirtless and both had colorful tattoos almost everywhere. My pictures clearly showed them playing with three small pit bull puppies all being raised inside the apartment. It was summertime and these guys kept the front door wide open. The mom and daddy bulls were chained to a tree in the narrow side yard. Their chains had nearly cut through the small willow tree because the dogs were constantly circling around it. Five pit bulls living in one small apartment – WOW! I've heard about insurance companies cancelling the owner's liability policy with just one of these cute little *"tweaker"* playmates!

Filming like I do takes a little time and patience, especially since I'm trying very hard not to be observed. I shot 24 pictures to make sure I had the property covered, even though my plan was to use only five or six of the ugliest ones for negotiating. *Almost every picture clearly depicted a lack of management.* They revealed just how rundown and unsightly Lemon Street had become. I had pictures showing dead lawns, shrubs turning brown for lack of water, and there were even half a dozen non-running autos jacked up on wooden blocks. A wrecked pickup was sittin' on a stack of old tires. There were so many broken down vehicles at Lemon Street that I decided there would be no need for me to come back in the evening like I normally do. Usually, the after-dark festivities bring out their deadbeat friends – *with even more cars!*

One of my most creative shots was a picture of black mold growing up the stucco wall on one of the rear apartments. A leaking cooler line was still sprayin' water on the wall. I'm guessing the leak had been squirting water for six months or so because the entire lower half of the wall was oozing a dark greenish slime. Apparently, I'm the only one who even noticed! Although it's fairly easy to clean off, color photos always make a wet moldy wall look scarier than it actually is. Obviously, most landlord/apartment owners and their managers are totally aware that even the mere mention of slimy black mold conjures up visions of county health citations, sniffer tests, and lawsuits. Everyone, except the Five Star Management Company, it seems!

FISHIN' WHERE THEY'RE LIKELY TO BITE

You'll notice that my letter is *non-confrontational*. I never blame the owners in any way for the terrible condition of their property! I don't even mention Five Star Management Company by name! I place the blame solely on the tenants so as not to offend any of the parties I might have to work with should I strike up a deal later on! As you can see, my letter offers a rather inexpensive and easy way out for the owners should they even be slightly interested in selling! Take notice that I don't even bring up or mention selling until the fourth paragraph. Before I mention selling, I always offer my **fix-up or rehab services**! Every so often owners will ask me for my cost estimate to fix up their property! As a rule, when I give them my estimate of costs, it generally brings them back to a more serious discussion about the possibilities of selling!

Over the years, my **cold-call letters**, like the one you'll find at the end of this chapter, have been extremely successful by putting me in direct contact with potential sellers. It only takes one profitable transaction like Lemon Street and you'll make my cold-calling technique a permanent tool in your acquisition tool chest!

I only write these cold-call letters when I sense something is drastically wrong at the property! Naturally, I'll do my **house detective investigation** before I ever reach for my pen! At Lemon Street, it was totally obvious from just driving by that something was seriously out of whack! My cold-call **"letter to the owner"** technique is one of my best tools to put me in direct communication with an owner who has a good reason to sell. Obviously, out-of-town investors (owners) are the best prospects, because a large percentage of them are totally clueless about how their properties are being managed. You're gonna love this trollin' strategy when you hook your first big one! **Clap your hands and say Amen!**

JAY'S LETTER TO LEMON STREET OWNERS

Dear Mr. and Mrs. Morgan:

My name is Bob; I'm a property owner-investor in Redding, CA. During the past few years, I've been acquiring small run-down rental properties that need fix-up and rehabilitation work. I have a small crew that does the work – and I've kept most of these properties as rental units. Occasionally, my crew will do fix-up work for other local property owners when they are not busy working on my projects.

The reason I'm writing this letter is because almost every other day or so, I drive by your Lemon Street rentals on my way to my property only three blocks north of yours. During the past year or so, I can't help but notice how junky and rundown your apartments have become. I remember just two years ago – you had the nicest looking property on the block. It's my guess that whoever manages your property, has allowed the wrong kind of tenants to live there. This is exactly what happened to me! I can tell you from experience, the wrong kind of tenants will tear up a property faster than anyone can fix it! I tried four different managers when I had my Sacramento property and things kept getting worse! Never again will I own property where I don't live. It cost me over **$100,000** to learn the hard way.

The big problem is the tenants – but since all property managers are competing with each other, they seem to take almost anyone who shows up with rent money and a deposit. Of course, once the place is rented, that's it! They never seem to have the time to check out how the tenants live! Believe me; the wrong tenants will totally destroy any property. They leave their trash all over – accumulate a bunch of junky cars and of course, almost everyone has pets – *usually the destructive kind*. In Redding, I've never found a property manager I've been happy with! I've tried hard, believe me, but I always ended up taking my property back. I can tell you from experience, owners are the only ones who seem to care about property upkeep!

If you should ever need help with any fix-up or rehab, I've enclosed my business card and telephone number. When you're in town – take a quick drive-by my six houses at 8001 Lemon, just north of yours–also, my 8 units a couple blocks east at 1112 Tenth Avenue. You'll get an idea of how I fix up and maintain my properties. Also, if you should ever think about selling, please allow me to make you an offer. Naturally, there would be no commission to pay, and quite frankly, when seller financing can be used – I've found that owners will often net-out as much or more income from the monthly mortgage payments they receive, than what they're getting now from the property manager!

I've enclosed several recent pictures of your property to show you exactly what I mean about the tenants. They can really mess up a nice property in no time at all when managers allow them to do as they please! As I already mentioned, my expensive lesson was in Sacramento, 160 miles away where I couldn't keep a close eye on my property manager! I'll never make that mistake again. Please call me anytime if I can be of assistance.

Sincerely,
Jay "Bob", Fix-Up Investors
(500)123-4567
Enclosed: 6 Photos

CHAPTER 11

FISHIN' IN FRIENDLY WATERS

*L*et me begin by saying–over the years, through trial and error, wins and losses, following the wrong strategy for too long without making any profits, I've seen the light. I'm now zeroed in on the right kind of investment real estate.

My primary purpose is to acquire properties that will start producing cash flow (**real spendin' money**) in a reasonable period of time. For me, I've long established my time frame should be approximately two years, *give or take a little!* As much as I love buying junky lookin' properties and nursing them back to financial health – I wouldn't give a "rat's hoot" for them if they didn't produce **net-net money** for me after a couple years of hard work. While making money is my primary motivation, I find great pleasure in resurrecting rundown and neglected properties so they will once again provide shelter for countless renters who need affordable rental housing.

Fixing up properties is a highly competitive business with many beginners and amateurs giving it a try! Most start-out investors incorrectly assume they must test their skills with a single-family house to begin with! This belief often leads them to dismal failure and the harsh agony of defeat. The most common reason for this has to do with the *numbers* – **the dollar numbers**. It's very rare indeed when even the most ugly-looking house can be acquired cheap enough to earn positive rental income with an 80% bank mortgage to pay. Of course, very few investors, including myself, expect to pay more than 20% down for rundown properties. During my long career, seldom have I ever paid more than 10-15% as my down payment amount! When you add a hefty mortgage payment to the fix-up costs – understanding that most beginners will likely overspend for fix-up, it's easy to understand why suicide might seem like the most reasonable plan for relief!

You must never take your eye off the ball or lose sight of your objective as an investor whose business is real estate investing – **the goal is, to make money**! This job is way too much work doing it like a hobby! I often hear students who mimic the popular seminar gurus, praising the virtues of a win-win investment philosophy. With very little substance to what many of them teach, the concept of "win-win" sounds almost spiritual, like something straight out of the scriptures. Upon closer examination, however, there seems to be a basic flaw! Have you ever seen two winners in a monopoly game or two winners playing poker? How about two winners at the Kentucky Derby – *or even a baseball game* – I only count one! Likewise, when you invest – your primary concern should be about one winner – THAT'S YOU. My definition of **win-win** *is when my name and my wife's name are both on the deed*!

So far, we've been discussing what works and what doesn't, with a little of my personal philosophy tossed in. It's now time to explore a moneymaking strategy that will work for almost every investor, whether experienced *or a beginner just starting out.* I'm talkin' about a proven strategy I've been using for nearly 50 years – however, it's been around for much longer than that. Let me start by telling you right up front, you're in for some hard work – but if you're willing to learn, work hard, and apply the techniques I will teach you, you'll be able to solve your financial problems while you're still on the planet and have money left over when you leave. Allow me to point out that 90% of all the physical work involved is really what I call grunt work! If you graduated from high school or even a minimum-security reform school, you can no doubt figure out how basic plumbing works – *if not, you can simply hire that part out! What I want you to understand is that most people can do this stuff without too much training.* Willingness to try will be your biggest hurdle!

CHOOSE'N THE RIGHT VEHICLE

As I mentioned earlier, most folks buy properties without nearly enough thought as to how they'll make money with them. Starting right now – **you must correct this mistake** if you ever intend to become wealthy! *An investment property is simply your vehicle in pursuit of making money.* You must never think of your investment property like some prize trophy sitting on the mantle that looks good–*but only earns admiration*! As I sit here with pen in hand, I already have three "how to" books on the shelves of most major bookstore in the country! They all offer easy-to-follow strategies that can make you wealthy. A great majority of folks who purchase my books actually read them – *quite often more than once* – and yet, I still receive a decent number of calls from readers who tell me – I've just purchased my first house using one of your books as my guide!

Friends, nowhere in more than 1000 pages of print, have I ever recommended even once that beginning investors should purchase just one single house. If you happen to be one of my readers – *thank you very much*, but please make this mental correction. **I recommend that you purchase multiple units of some kind – and not just one single house to start with**! Before you've finished reading this book, I think it will become perfectly clear, why *multiple-unit rentals* should be your very first investment property.

DETERMINE THE MARKET FOR YOUR PRODUCT

Before you move forward to acquire any income-producing real estate, you must first determine who your customers will be – and if they can pay you for your product or service (**monthly rents**). Also, what is the outlook for long-term business? Obviously, owning widgets that no one wants to rent or buy is a path to the poorhouse. As I told you earlier, **always think like a business person first**! No successful business person would ever spend money on inventory without first testing the market to determine if his product is financially feasible. Housing may not seem like a product to you since we tend to view it as a basic necessity. Still, investors should consider houses as their product – and like any product, you must always develop a solid marketing plan!

Many years ago, when I first began to understand the importance of marketing as it relates to the investment business, I conducted a local survey of renters in my town. I discovered that nearly 80% of the folks who rent could pay no more than $600 per month. That was tops! Many renters couldn't pay that much! Only 20% of all the renters could afford to pay over $600, and a good percentage of them were only temporary renters because they still continued their search to buy a home. Clearly, it didn't take a rocket scientist to predict where most of my *permanent renters* would be roosting. Given my resources, which were somewhat skinny at the time, it was crystal clear to me that I should invest my money in the kind of properties where the majority of the renters (80%) in my town could afford to live.

BROKE INVESTORS NEED TO KNOW THEIR PLACE

A feasibility study to determine what the majority of renters can afford to pay for rent is also a study about the location and the type of properties where those renters wish to live. Since 80% of all renters must live in units that can be rented for $600 or less, it follows, that if I can supply rental units for no more than $600 – I'll be marketing my properties to almost all the renters in my town. Naturally, this is by far the safest strategy for investors who must count on rent money coming in every month to buy groceries!

The most serious affliction I had starting out was called "lack of money." This affliction is not the least bit uncommon among start-out investors, but it certainly doesn't have to be fatal – it can be if you fail to recognize it, or if you pretend it's not really a problem. To say this another way, *poor investors have absolutely no business investing in wealthy neighborhoods.* Perhaps after you're rich it won't really matter much – *but in the beginning,* when your knowledge is limited and your wallet is newspaper thin, don't do it! *The financial risk is far too great.* House investors who spend all their money on a single rental unit, then nervously pace the floor every month waiting for their rent to come in, are flirting with disaster. Let's assume you lived in my town, where only 20% of all the renters could even rent your house to begin with! Can you begin to see the dorsal fin coming through the waves here? Let's move on, so we can discuss where your tenants are likely to live!

When you purchase properties where 80% of your potential customers (tenants) can afford to rent, it automatically eliminates a whole lot of locations in your investing area. For example, no need to look in gated communities, riverfront properties, or houses bordering the 7th fairway at the Grand Oaks Country Club. When I conducted my rental survey and discovered most tenants in my town could pay no more than $600 per month, average tract or subdivision houses were renting for $800-$1000 per month. Obviously, there was no good reason for me to even look at those properties; besides, I'd never find multiple-unit properties in newer subdivisions with a R-1 zoning classification.

The best locations for my kind of properties are generally the older sections of town – and quite often, a mile or two on the outskirts beyond the city limit sign. Typically, my types of properties are older – built mostly in the 1940s and '50s, some even older. Most of these properties were built long before present day zoning regulations that restrict owners from building multiple-unit structures on their city lot. Back then, if extra units fit on the lot, it was probably okay. During that period of time, families would often purchase a large city lot, build their main family home somewhere near the front, and then as time went along, they would add a couple extra units. Often it was a duplex, or even a four-unit building in the back yard for the sole purpose of providing the family rental income when they retired.

You'll discover that many of these older properties will have a combination of structures like the main family house in the front, two cottages in the rear, and maybe a studio apartment built above the garage. Sometimes you'll even find a couple older mobiles sitting on concrete blocks in the back yard with a separate alley entrance. What's common about these older properties is **they're oddball properties** – *they're a fish in the wrong pond.* The good news about these properties, however, is that they can be purchased cheap enough so that skilled investors can make themselves a handsome profit. These types of properties will generate **cash flow** in the shortest amount of time – also, tenants favor living in them much more than apartments or densely populated properties.

BECOME A STREETWALKER
LOOKIN' FOR ODDBALLS

I have written a great deal already about locations and where you'll have the best results finding these older properties, but first, allow me to repeat myself here and warn you against buying any property in a slum location. **Do not buy rental houses in slum locations.** It could easily shorten your life expectancy! There are many older areas in most cities and towns that are not slums. They are simply the older sections where most people lived before modern freeways and sprawling subdivisions were developed after World War II. As a general rule, these areas are closer to the center of town and often mixed in with commercial and retail development. I have owned many small multiple residential properties where the zoning has long since been re-designated to commercial – however, for as long as these properties are used for residential – *the grandfather rules apply.* From a marketing standpoint, these small multiple-unit locations near mid-town shopping and social activities are high demand properties for the younger renting population who value living closer to their job – many ride bicycles or walk to work! And for seniors, or *people who look a whole lot like me,* it's closer to the emergency room with a large supply of oxygen tanks!

Finding these properties is best accomplished by searching them out on your own. Occasionally you'll be lucky enough to get help from a patient realtor, assuming you can find one who is willing to spend the time. Park your car and walk the older neighborhoods, **identify locations,** and take some notes for future reference. Every now and then, you'll find a property with a "FOR SALE" sign, but I've found it's somewhat rare. The real value of this walk-n-search mission is that you'll discover all kinds of multiple-unit properties you had no idea even existed. Many times during my mid-morning strolls, I've come across people in the yard, **sometimes owners**, who've been thinking about selling. Many owners are about the same age as the properties, and the upkeep has become too much work for them. People love to talk and tell you their stories. If you'll listen, you'll learn a great deal – and if they like you, *no tellin' what you'll hear*! This is exactly the method I used to acquire my West Street Cottages from the owners (Chapter 10). The West Street owners gave me excellent terms and attractive owner financing to boot.

To help you a bit more with location and finding the right kinds of properties, I have broken down all real estate into five distinct locations as follows: See Appendix E.

1. SNOB HILL
2. OLDER RESIDENTIAL
3. SUBDIVISION AND TRACTS
4. SLUMS
5. OLDER COMMERCIAL AREAS

Right off the bat, you can eliminate Snob Hill, subdivisions, and slums. **Older residential** and **older commercial** are the locations where you'll find the grass is greener when searching for small colony-type properties or – *older multiple-unit rental properties*. Quite often, these two locations will overlap or run together. For example, I have owned groups of cottages and houses next door to the neighborhood grocery market and storage units. I have owned small houses between a used car lot and an old furniture warehouse, owned by the local moving company, smack dab in the middle of the downtown retail area. Sometimes you'll find rental units wedged in between long-time downtown businesses. Remember, these properties were built years ago!

DON'T SKIP PAST THE NON-CONVENTIONAL

Do not disqualify older motels, hotels, and motor lodges should you run across a property that lends itself to **creating separate rental apartments**. Most do not, but every now and again you'll stumble across a property like my Hillcrest Cottage property. It was an old 22-unit dysfunctional motor lodge with mostly one-bedroom units separated by carports. This configuration allowed me to arrange for individual power and gas services to create affordable monthly rentals for my local senior market.

If you're interested in knowing a little more about Hillcrest and just how successful that property turned out, just keep reading! Chapter 13 will provide more information about how lucrative these older motels can be. As a general rule, I'm not much interested in these kinds of properties unless they are individual units with space between them, such as carports. Motor lodges were quite popular in smaller towns during the 1930s and '40s. Travelers would stay a few days and do their own housekeeping and cooking before the modern day motels and restaurants existed. These types of structures can easily be separately metered and made *semi-private* with sections of decorative fencing, lawns, and individual patios. They offer affordable housing for seniors who don't require a large living space – **yet they value a small yard with privacy for their poodle!**

You'll find most of these older cottage-type properties closer to the city core because that's where most people lived before freeways and large-scale home developments were built! Also, take a good look near the outskirts of town – *maybe even a bit past the city limit sign!* Years ago, the counties were far less restrictive about the zoning and limits on the number of buildings like most incorporated cities. Taking a closer look at many of the locations I've owned over the years – one might easily observe that the town simply grew up around them. The majority of my multiple-unit properties, both houses and cottages, are two bedrooms with a single bath, but don't fret the size – these are the most popular size of affordable rental units for both young folks who are just starting out, and seniors who are finishing up! They are the highest demand properties for me–**also the most profitable.** When you survey your potential customers, you'll quickly find out the amount of rent most of them can afford to pay. *Your goal should be to provide rental housing at a price affordable to the majority of renters in your area.*

DON'T WEAR BLINDERS WHEN YOU'RE LOOKIN'

I'll assume you can find the older part of town in your own community. When you do, park the car, grab a writing pad, and let's get to lookin' – *walkin' is the best way to start looking!* If you're overweight and under-exercised, my advice might just lengthen your lifespan whether you find any houses or not. Lord knows, with enough walkin', your doctor might even pull you off Lipitor! Downtown, you'll find hundred-year-old trees and mature shrubs growing everywhere. Many target properties are sometimes totally hidden in the trees and shrubs! I'm talkin' about those add-on granny units hidden behind the main house with only a skinny driveway offering access. Large mature trees and overgrown shrubs can hide everything, friends – *you'll have to sneak around and do a little peekin' to find 'em!*

Since it's nearly impossible to look up the skinny driveway to determine what's in the back yard – *here's a couple other ideas!* Take a look at those seven mailboxes on the single post out front! It's hard to imagine that just one resident would be receiving seven boxes full of mail. If at all possible, try and tiptoe up the driveway to see if there are rental units tucked in behind the house. Also, take a good look up in the sky for telephone wires! When you see half a dozen wires or so going from a telephone pole to the peak of the house – *that's way too many wires!* No one has that many phones anymore – *especially with cells.* Be cautious and cover your eyes while looking up – there are a lot of those nasty pigeons flyin' around. Well, you get the picture! Quite often, you'll stumble across several small concrete water meter boxes near the property line or built in the sidewalk just behind it. That's another clue that there's likely more units built somewhere on the property.

Trotting around with a clipboard and writing pad in your hand, while you're looking up in the sky, is bound to draw a few stares from any neighbors who happen to spot you! To begin with, you look like a total dork, so it's only natural the neighbors will be suspicious! **Here's a technique I've used, which seems to work quite well:** tell 'em you're a telephone engineer or a power company estimator if you're asked! You might well look the part anyway – and besides, either one of these jobs will give you a little more credibility – *lord knows, you'll need some!*

Assuming the neighbors decide you're harmless, they'll likely be willing to talk with you, which gives you a wonderful opportunity to listen – *naturally you can ask a few questions of your own!* Act cool! You don't want to blurt out – *I'm here to buy your property.* Still, you're in a good position to ask questions of a general nature, such as do you know how many apartments are behind your house? When you run into someone who loves to talk, you can learn a great deal about the neighborhood from them. Every now and then, someone will say to me – Boy o boy Jay, this doesn't sound like it's a very quick method for finding properties! Here's my answer – **it's a lot quicker than you might think** – besides, you mustn't forget, speed is not the objective here, *finding a quality property with good cash flow potential* is what this neighborhood search business is all about. I have never wandered around very long without someone noticing me and asking – **what are you doing here**? If you'll act like Lt. Columbo, the bumbling detective on TV, you'll do just fine, **I promise**! It might pay you to watch a few re-runs!

CUSTOMER DEMAND KEEPS COTTAGES RENTED

You might be thinking to yourself – why would renters prefer to live in older cottages or houses, as opposed to newer apartment units? There are a number of reasons, but high on the list is **more privacy**, **separation** and **space**. Young single types mostly rent the large apartment complexes. They want swimming pools, tennis courts, clubhouses, and all the latest amenities found in the newer apartments. During the summer months, young gals flash dance around the pool in bikinis – all the young guys will hang over the rails to watch the show. Everyone parades around the complex like they're all one big family. They do laundry together, they park in numbered stalls right next to each other, and they're constantly passing each other in stairwells and common areas.

With apartment living, about the only privacy renters ever enjoy is when they close their front doors at bedtime. **Even then**, rap music and screamin' couples will often rattle the walls well into the late evening hours. However, apartments do provide the most affordable housing for large numbers of renters willing to live close together at a single location. Most older tenants who've already experienced apartment living are looking for more quiet surroundings. Many have already owned their own homes and when it's time to size down – *they're looking for as much privacy as they can afford.*

Apartment living becomes much less attractive for young people when they pair up, get married, and start living together. This is especially true when they have a little baby gomer together. No longer will the girl tolerate her prize male catch sitting around the pool gawking at bikini-clad chicks and *hangin' out!* The tables are suddenly turned – *they've become a family now*, and it's time to seek more privacy and leave all those poolside festivities behind! This is where my older, *but I call more charming* properties offer their greatest appeal! With small back yards and lawns, often totally fenced, they afford my tenants a lot more privacy. With my smaller groups of houses or cottages, renters can now have their own private space. They can even own a small poodle or cat, they can plant a "green thumb" garden out back, and even sun bathe buck naked in their own fenced yard. Mothers feel much more secure when their youngins can crawl around on my lawn (watered weeds) totally surrounded by my six-foot cedar fences.

Both young couples and seniors alike are willing to trade most modern amenities, such as swimming pools, tennis courts, and fancy gadgets, for *more peace of mind, more space*, and *personal privacy*; providing, of course, they can afford my rents. Obviously, I can't compete with brand new rental units offering the latest building technology, but I can certainly beat the pants off them with *privacy and plain ol' fashion charm*. Naturally, I can keep my rents competitive to do this!

Apartments are generally cheaper to rent than separate houses because large numbers of units can be jammed together in a relatively small space with one roof covering several different levels. You're probably wondering to yourself – how can Jay be offering individual houses and cottages at prices that compete with apartment units? How can he offer more space and privacy for the same amount of money? The answer, my friends, is a bit more complicated than I can answer in a single sentence or two. Therefore, allow me to start at the beginning so I can give you a more complete answer. As you might guess, every product or service must start with a discussion about money!

RENTING FOR PROFITS
IS ABOUT PAYING RIGHT PRICE

Business folks fully understand you must **buy wholesale** and **sell at retail** in order to make a profit! Real estate investors sometimes get confused about this simple *truism*. Many judge the value of an income property by comparing it to another property using a "so-called" professional appraisal. Comparisons and appraisals don't mean "diddly squat" when it comes to making money. Real estate tycoons must concern themselves with the **income to value ratios**, terms of the financing, and finally–**will the property earn a profit**? Also, don't waste your time trying to predict the future! For folks who need money to buy groceries, *the future begins immediately when escrow closes*! Investors must pay wholesale prices and earn their money renting or selling at retail pricing! I'm not sure I originated this buying and selling idea, but it sure makes me sound smart! **Don't you agree?**

Buying small groups of houses, cottages, and yes, even an old junky lookin' motel will set you apart from most other investors. *Think about what I just said for a moment*! I would bet my next month's pay that no one has ever suggested you invest this way except me! I don't know of a single seminar guru who even mentions this type of property; much less teach anything about it. The point is, my kinds of properties are not very trendy, they're not sexy or glamorous, and most certainly they're not well known to the masses!

Because of this, however, your competition for acquiring these properties is **greatly reduced**! *Competition is what drives up the prices.* The lack of competition works exactly the opposite way! Unpopular properties like we're discussing here often create extremely "lonely sellers!" They're lonely because very few buyers show up on their door-step to make offers. For fix-up investors, this can be your opportunity to create some magic! I've purchased properties from sellers where I was the only buyer to make an offer. Friends, this is the position you want to be in for negotiating a **super wholesale price** and **favorable financing terms**. Never forget the importance of this paragraph. It's called the *contrarian strategy* – it means going in the opposite direction from everyone else. The reward is – **you'll end up a whole lot richer than everyone else if you can pull it off**!

EVEN DUMMIE BANKERS DON'T LOAN ON JUNKERS

Small colonies of older houses, duplexes, cottages and/or motor lodges, fall into "never-never land" when it comes to institutional financing. When you explain to your banker about six or eight rundown cottages down behind the soup factory and ask for a mortgage – he'll likely throw up. Of course, more than four units of any multiple-type properties requires a commercial loan – they're almost impossible to find anywhere. My kinds of properties are "ground zero" when it comes to seller financing, because in most cases – **that's all there is**! If a seller wants to sell, he'll most likely have to carry back the financing himself. This is exactly the place experienced buyers wish to find themselves in – negotiating the selling terms, **one-on-one with a seller**.

Negotiating *purchase terms* with the seller is a world apart from asking your friendly banker or mortgage broker for a loan. Most bankers or brokers will advise you that even if you're credit worthy, they have only three or four products or mortgages available! To do business with us, they explain, you must choose one of our loan products that will hopefully work for you. With seller terms, you will have dozens of choices – *in fact*, there is really no limit to your choices because the terms are whatever you and the seller can negotiate and agree to. **Friends, this is how you end up with cash flow when you purchase a property.** You design the financing (the mortgage terms) with the seller so that the mortgage payments and expenses can be paid from the available income generated by the property. **Memorize that last sentence** – it's the key to cash flow. **Raise your hands – say Hallelujah!**

FACE TO FACE WITH THE SELLER

Okay Jay, even if I agree with you, my sensitive real estate agent almost cries when I say I'd like to meet with the seller. She says it's not very professional and it's simply not done anywhere to her knowledge! **First**, you must get her full attention – tell her there are no rules that say you can't! You might even mumble under your breath like – *maybe I've chosen the wrong agent*! Once she stops whining and sniveling, explain it to her something like this: Sally, I think there's a real good chance this seller will carry some financing even though the listing agreement says he needs all cash.

No one pays all cash for six dumpy little cottages with deadbeat tenants hangin' out the windows. The agent who listed this property and told the seller he could get all cash is guilty of doing his client a huge disservice. I believe if I could just talk to the seller one-on-one, I could persuade him that I'm a very credit-worthy buyer. Plus, I have lots of experience fixing and managing these kind of properties – and I can even offer additional collateral to guarantee the seller gets all his payments. I'd like for you to call the listing agent and explain what I've just told you. **Here's how I'd like you to say it:**

MR. LISTING AGENT: My buyer wants to meet with the seller! He would like you and I to both attend – I think you should make the appointment since you listed the property and you're much better acquainted with the seller. My buyer promises he won't kill the deal. He's very experienced, and owns several of these kind of properties himself. You already have our purchase offer and price, which you have said is totally acceptable to the seller – the problem is, finding a new mortgage is simply out of the question. There's no lender I know of who makes loans on these kind of properties. My client wants me to let you know, if our visit works out, he's all set to close within ten days without additional contingencies – and as you already know, **his down payment more than covers our commission.**

Obviously, this whole idea or strategy takes a bit of practice, and most real estate agents will automatically fight you "tooth 'n nail" because that's what they're taught to do. They believe the worst thing they can do is to allow the principals (buyer and seller) to get together in the same room! It's their greatest fear that the principals will blow the deal if allowed to meet and talk to each other! **It's a deal killer, they claim.** Still, in the end I've found that most agents will reluctantly give in! The temptation is simply much too great for them to pass up the opportunity to **close escrow in 10 days**, knowing the **full commission** is within their grasp!

YOUR FIRST COLONY PURCHASE
PUTS YOU IN THE GAME

Like anything you accomplish in life – *you'll always start with number one!* So go ahead, buy your first colony and see how it goes! This first purchase can be your "getting acquainted" period, much like going on your first date – take it slow and easy. You'll be getting your first real taste of what multiple properties feel like to own. You might call this the "petting stage!"

Meet the tenants, paint a couple buildings, and cut the grass! This will be your first "guinea pig" property so you can measure yourself. **I honestly believe you can do this** – *others have, so why not you!* Do your very best to follow my advice in this book. **Make the property a nicer place to live.** When you do, you'll get the respect and admiration from most of your tenants. This, in turn, will make your property management a whole lot easier. Give me a call after your first full year! If you're doin' fine, I'll suggest moving on to your second colony – if you're not, let's figure out what's gone wrong!

If you've been a single-family house investor before, *you're gonna be very impressed with additional cash flow*! If you haven't, then you won't know the difference anyway – **no harm, no foul**! You can thank your lucky stars that you bought my book and saved yourself a lot of time working for peanuts. At any rate, you're off to a good start and you're on the right path to **a sound financial future**! That, I can **promise you!**

SEARCHING OUT COLONIES

When you consider investing in a particular location, always ask yourself these important questions. Make absolutely certain you're okay with **Items 1 and 2**.

1. Would I personally feel comfortable working in this part of town?
2. Do I believe this location is safe at night, relative to the general neighborhood?
3. Does the area look like it's reasonably stable and not going downhill?
4. Are city or private services – such as buses, police protection, schools, fire department, hospitals, and decent shopping available within a reasonable distance?
5. Does this location look like a good rental area where I can attract the kind of customers (tenants) I'm looking for?

Assuming you answer **YES** to all five questions – it sounds like your property selection is working out just fine! Now all you have to do is find a few more like this first one and you'll end up filthy rich!

CHAPTER 12

SHOOTIN' FOR
THE PRIZE CATCH

I often use the term "*ski bum*," it sorta conjures up an image of how some folks in my town view my existence today! They never see me on the freeways going to work. In fact, most people who only know me by sight don't even figure I have a real job! Every so often, some brave soul will walk up and ask me – **what exactly do you do?** Most 9-5 working stiffs are totally baffled when they see someone they recognize, who don't seem to have any particular purpose or place to be! Being a real estate entrepreneur is completely different than working down at the sawmill!

To start with of course, I'm my own boss! There's no one else to please except me. There is no alarm clock in my life – no freeway commutes, no specified time for me to take trips – because I can juggle my schedule on a daily basis to fit whatever I'm doing. *For heaven sakes*, don't get the idea I don't work – or that I sleep all day! I work plenty – but I only work at things I choose to do–and **only when I want to**. Obviously, you can't operate 200 rental units without having responsibilities; however, being responsible doesn't mean I'm doing all the work myself. My biggest responsibility is making sure my "helper bees" do what they're supposed to be doing – **so I can do what I choose!** Can you see that my having total control over all my affairs allows me to enjoy the freedoms most people can only dream about?

FIVE WEEKS VACATION
– ONLY TWO WEEKS WORTH OF MONEY

Years ago (I've almost forgotten now), when I had a legitimate 9-5 job, my boss controlled my schedule. Like most jobs, mine was pretty much structured. I had to be there at 8:00 a.m. every morning, rain or shine, five days a week. I eventually earned five weeks' vacation time, but as a rule, taking it required choosing the date many months in advance. The biggest problem I always had with my five weeks' vacation – five weeks was too long for the amount of money I had. *Looking back*, I remember telling my friends, I've got five weeks' vacation time – but only two weeks' worth of money to enjoy it! This problem is not the least bit uncommon for employees working for big corporations!

Working for myself is a whole lot different than working for the other guys! *For starters*, even though I earn a good deal more money now, I get to keep almost everything I make. At my corporate job, I lost about 40% to the tax man – and even more to various charities sponsored by my company! The phone company believes that management employees should donate a portion of their earnings to worthy causes! Naturally, they decided what cause was worthy! Also, managers were required to dress the part. White shirts, suits, and ties were the standard dress for me! Image is very important to big corporations – still, I don't recall any special clothing allowance to help me promote the company image.

WORKING SMARTER REQUIRES CONTROL

To achieve wealth, you must *control your time*, and of course, *the amount of compensation* you're willing to accept for your services. Working as a W-2 employee for most corporations, these controls are pretty much in the hands of others. **If building personal wealth is your goal**, *as it was for me*, you must take these controls back for yourself. In Chapter One of my best-selling book, *Investing in Fixer-Uppers* (available at most bookstores), I explain to readers how

I was able to earn $300 per hour fixin' up Hillcrest. You simply can't get rich by working more hours on a regular job. The answer lies in earning more money for each hour you work. In practical terms, the best way to accomplish this is **working smarter** – *not longer or harder.*

Control by itself can only help you when you select the right vehicle that can deliver the additional money you seek. For example, when I fix up houses, which adds more value to them, there's actually no limit on how much money I can earn. **Earning $300 per hour at Hillcrest was a perfect example.** No matter what I did, it would be absolutely impossible to earn that much money working for the phone company. Even robbing the company pay phones won't pay that well!

MY HIGH PAYING VEHICLE IS HOUSES

The Haywood houses (*Investing in Fixer-Uppers*, Chapter Two) is another excellent example of "the right vehicle" for making more money without any restrictions. Readers may recall how I earned $150,000 for just one summer's worth of fix-up work. During my ownership, the houses paid me roughly $10,000 every month from start to finish. You should also keep in mind; Haywood was only one of the properties I owned at the time! Still, it was nowhere near a full-time job! Once again, allow me to emphasize a point here! **Big money properties like Hillcrest and my Haywood houses were great opportunities for me because I had absolute control over my time** – plus I developed the skills necessary to fix up the non-complicated stuff.

When you work for the corporation as a *W-2 wage earner*, you cannot work at building your personal net worth the way I can as **a full-time real estate investor**! You simply don't have enough time! Wage earners are not just slaves to their bosses; they're also slaves to the tax man as well. Working full-time for yourself, like building your personal net worth, allows you to escape both masters and chart your own course towards much bigger earnings! Allow me pause here for just a moment to say – *you should gradually build up your real estate holdings before you start thinking about becoming a full-time investor*! I strongly suggest you don't walk away from your day job hoping that real estate investing will set you free and end all your financial worries. Without a well-conceived transition plan, you can easily find yourself on the welfare wagon instead the financial freedom train!

INVESTORS CAN DEVELOP MANY SKILLS

I'm a strong believer that every do-it-yourself real estate investor should learn a variety of different ways to earn profits with real estate. I don't believe you can reach your full potential as a real estate entrepreneur until you learn a variety of different **income-producing strategies**. These should include buying single-family houses, creative financing, foreclosure properties, rundown apartments, option techniques, wrap-around installment sales, buying discounted mortgages, *and of course*, **you must learn landlording**. Just in case I missed anything, add it to the list, because as time goes along, you'll need all the knowledge you can get! This might seem like an impossible task at first glance. However, because these strategies and skills are all closely related, you'll find that learning this stuff is much easier than you might think! **Knowledge is what makes you a total investor** – it's also knowledge that keeps you ahead of your competition and earning the biggest paydays!

Before I unintentionally mislead anyone, allow me to say this loud and clear! **I feel very strongly that successful investors must develop their own specialty.** I define *specialty* as a strategy or technique that you can do better than anyone else in your area. We might call it your "ace in the hole" **moneymaking plan**! It's a *special skill or technique* you can always count on to earn money when everything else stops working. For example, I specialize in fixing ugly rundown properties generally occupied by ugly tenants. I've learned how to quickly turn *ugly duckling houses* into beautiful swans – *and at the same time*, I can generally resolve most problems with any tenants who live there. This specialty always works for me – I can almost smell the money on the day I begin!

When I first began buying investment properties, there was absolutely no question in my mind about where I might find a few extra dollars to tide me over in case my properties didn't generate enough cash flow. The answer was – **nowhere**! Even though I was successful at keeping my cash down payments reasonable, they still took all the money I had. I knew very well that there was nothing left over in my bank account to make up for any cash flow shortages. The only funds I would have available to pay my *mortgages and operating expenses* would be the rents I received from my tenants every month. Buying properties this close to the belt can be both challenging and rewarding at the same time! Obviously, I didn't have much wiggle room estimating my fix-up costs – in short, I had to make certain that my mortgage payments and expenses did not exceed what I was collecting in rents. When you're investing this tight, you had best make sure your cash flow plan is not "pie in the sky"! *And most important, do this before you sign any deal*!

PREDICTABLE INCOME IS ALWAYS #1

What I'm strongly suggesting here – especially for new investors itchin' to get their feet wet – is that it's a much smarter strategy, and a whole lot safer to acquire a property with a somewhat uncertain future, *but with predictable cash flow,* than to pay top dollar for a property with *more potential*, but not enough cash flow to pay the bills. Don't misunderstand what I'm saying here! Future potential is great, but the future is still the future! It's still "pie in the sky!" In my opinion, the first three reasons for owning income property in the first place are – INCOME, INCOME, and INCOME. All the other reasons must start with number four!

BUYING THE MOST UNITS
YOUR DOWN PAYMENT CAN AFFORD

Nearly every investor I've met has paid too much money for an income property. It happens more frequently when they first start out! There is almost no defense against paying too much, *at least once or twice anyway*! I've done it more times than I like to admit. However, in most cases for me – *buying the multiple-unit rundown properties* has allowed me to **add value and improve the income** much faster than if I had *overpaid* for nicer looking properties.

Fixing up properties and adding value quickly gave me the opportunity to increase rents and recover from paying too much! The best lesson in the world for speeding your education along is to learn what true values are, including rents, and what the real expenses are. You'll learn very quickly once you begin buying and operating your own properties. Remember, I'm not recommending single-family houses to start with! My recommendation is to acquire just as many units as your down payment will allow you to purchase. Try for five or six, I know you can!

When I first started buying, I quickly discovered that multiple-unit fixer properties can often be bought for about the same down payment it would cost for a single non-fixer, non-owner occupied house! As you might guess, the cash flow potential is many times greater. Also, there's an extra-special bonus involved – most multiple-unit fixer-type rundown properties can be purchased with **seller financing** to boot!

CHEAPEST RENTALS PROVIDE BETTER CASH FLOWS

Although I have diversified my portfolio over the years, my primary investment vehicle has always been affordable rental units. *I buy properties that my customers (tenants) can afford to pay for.* These properties provide me with "eating money" or what most folks call **cash flow**. Affordable rental houses are still my biggest source of income today. Lower-end rental units provide a much higher profit return for investors, but there are some trade-offs for more cash flow upfront. My multiple-unit properties don't appreciate quite so fast – nor would there be as many buyers should I decide to sell them quickly. However, I do not consider these trade-offs to be a disadvantage! The reason – I'm a firm believer in first things first! **To me, cash flow has always been first!**

Allow me say this another way – investors like myself who start out with hardly any money in their pockets need a crystal-clear vision about who they are (**poor investors**) and what their buying capacity is (**not much**). Once you can focus – and clearly visualize where you stand – *a struggling investor trying to acquire real estate with very little money*, it should come as no big surprise–**cash flow must always be your number one priority** if you intend to be an investor very long.

Much of my own success has come from keeping my investments as simple as possible – **and paying particular attention to the basic fundamentals**. That means, I thoroughly analyze all the expenses (money going out) – and I make certain there's enough money coming in from the rents. You don't need to be a rocket scientist or know what the *internal rate of return (IRR)* is on your duplex to make a profit with real estate. You're far better off knowing whether the toilets flush or not! Later on, when the money starts rolling in – you and your accountant can have a pow-wow and figure out what the IRR is. In the meantime, you might ask him to help out with the plumbing while he's not fiddling with the books!

USING PERSONAL SKILLS
TO PRODUCE FASTER EQUITY

The most important reason for buying unattractive rundown properties is because you can quickly add to their value with *sweat equity*. Investing in these kinds of properties means you should be able to buy them lots cheaper – and sell for a decent profit in the shortest possible time. You should also be able to increase the rents and generate more monthly income much faster with these types of properties. This is a whole lot different than buying *pride of ownership* properties at top market prices where your only chance for profit is appreciation. Quite often, that can be a very long wait! The big advantage with fixer-upper properties is you can immediately start making obvious improvements, **the kind that will improve the looks and force the value up**. By forcing up the value yourself, you won't be stuck waiting for appreciation in order to make your profits. **Controlling profits** is a much more predictable strategy than trying to figure out when prices might go up on their own! **Agreed!**

With many rundown properties, it's not the least bit uncommon to do a quickie cleanup and paint job along with bringing in new tenants willing to pay higher rents almost immediately. As you increase the income, you're also making the property more valuable. Several of these deals can "pump up" your equity very quickly and allow you to build wealth much faster than you could otherwise. I call this strategy **"fast-track investing."**

Most investors will never develop these *equity-building skills* because they incorrectly believe they're not handy enough to deal with rundown properties. Many new, and even more experienced investors are reluctant to tackle jobs they've never tried before. They're afraid they might screw something up they can't fix, or make a bad situation worse! For this reason, I strongly encourage new do-it-yourself investors to acquire at least one rundown property as their own personal "guinea pig." *With rundown type properties*, I've found that most investors are not nearly so afraid to experiment. In fact, I feel so confident that the majority of my readers can handle most "run of the mill" fix-up jobs that I'm willing to refund the price of this book if you try and end up a total flop!

BUILDING CONFIDENCE IN YOURSELF

I will promise you this much: if you can muster up the courage and at least make a good effort, you'll learn to do things you thought you could never do! And perhaps more important – **you'll have proven to yourself that you really can do this stuff**. The best test to find out what you are really capable of doing is to jump in and give it your very best shot!

Finally, there's one other extremely valuable benefit you'll get from working on your own property. *This one is quite possibly the most important benefit of all.* **It's called confidence in yourself**. Once you actually experience **more cash flow or bigger profits**, you'll suddenly step back, take a deep breath, and realize you're doing some pretty powerful stuff! Wow, I'm really making big things happen! **Having confidence in yourself is worth more than money** – yet, strange as it might seem, more money builds confidence faster than anything I know of.

TAKING ADVICE FROM SKILLED PRACTITIONERS

In his timeless classic, *The Richest Man in Babylon*, author George S. Clason writes: **"Gold is reserved for those who know its laws and abide by them."** *The fourth law of gold states*:

> "To the man who has gold, yet is not skilled in its handling, many uses for it appear most profitable. Too often these are fraught with danger of loss, and if properly analyzed by wise men, show small possibility of profit. Wise, indeed, is he who investeth his treasures under the advice of men skilled in the ways of gold."

Often when I counsel students, I'll ask them why they've decided to invest in real estate. *Then while they're thinking, I'll ask*: How do you propose to do it? Tell me about your investment **plan or strategy**! *Have you started using it already* – if so, how is it working for you? Is your plan producing cash flow yet? Tell me more about it – *and, let's take a real close look at your numbers*!

Most people have great difficulty trying to explain their plan or investment strategy to someone else. If you can't explain what you're doing, you need to hold up until you can. The biggest problem I encounter is impatient investors who don't do near enough planning before they close a deal! *That's a big mistake*, which generally accounts for overpaying. As a rule, overpaying means there will be little or no cash flow – worse yet, you might end up having to feed the property with out-of-pocket money every month because it won't earn its keep from rental income.

Let me emphasize that investing in real estate, *the way I suggest* does not require perfection. There is ample room to make a few mistakes. Most are fairly easy to fix – and as time passes you'll become a lot more skilled! What's most important in the beginning is that you learn from each mistake – *and then do better on your next transaction*. Mistakes are natural, and will provide some of the most valuable lessons on the road to success. When you read the autobiographies of successful people as I often do, you'll find that hardly anyone becomes successful without making their share of mistakes as they develop their skills!

Never forget what I told you earlier about your wealth-building education. It will pay you big dividends to seek out and learn from successful investors who are already established. *They should have a verifiable track record* from doing the same kind of investing you'd like to do. Stay away from gurus who simply talk it – *but they fail to walk it*. After all, a teacher who doesn't use his own advice is not very credible – **wouldn't you agree?**

YOU WANT PROPERTIES THAT PAY YOU

Many beginners have told me – they don't see much **long-range potential** in the kind of properties I've been discussing here! *First, allow me to say this*: there is no need to worry about long-range investing potential unless you first get a handle on your short-term investment needs. The most important one, of course, is **positive monthly income**. Over the years I've transitioned from single-family houses to small multiple-unit properties with up to 22 rental units. I've owned a 100-room hotel with commercial storefronts. I still own many single-family houses and duplexes. I've converted old World War II motels to monthly apartments along the way! Finally, I've made some very profitable sales and carried back the financing using wrap-around mortgages. **Still, the most important part of my investment strategy** has always been to *only buy properties that will pay me to own them*.

Finding *the right properties* with high potential for profits and cash flow is the first step for developing a successful investment plan. It's also important that you don't take advice from traditional thinkers, or as I call them, the amateur investor crowd! Serious money is made by those who study their marketplace and develop the ability to spot bargains that others never see. I don't suggest you ever purchase run-down properties below your comfort level, but I can promise you, investors who have the courage to step outside the box and push the limits **generally earn the biggest rewards.**

During my many years investing and working to help others get started, a somewhat interesting fact pops out! It seems to me that investors who have the least amount of money for a down payment, and a brain that's not occupied with pre-conceived notions about what constitutes a real bargain, tend to have a lot more success with my kind of properties. **They also seem to end up with cash flow much faster.**

In short, it's the poorest folks who follow instructions well that tend to reach their investment goals much faster because they have fewer opportunities to stray from the target! Being about half smart, and having a few extra dollars to play with, often gives the new investor a false sense of security – and too much time to think! It also gives him or her time to make up lame excuses for not accomplishing anything! **Action is what it takes to become a millionaire investor.**

SWITCHING JOBS REQUIRES MUCH DISCIPLINE

Frequently I'm asked – how long will it take me to start earning enough money from real estate so I can quit my regular job? Unfortunately there is no single answer! The reason, of course, is because investors are people and people are all different. Most folks are in a big hurry to hit a home run – especially right after they've been "pitched" by some traveling "hot shot" real estate guru who promises riches in 90 days. Think very hard about what the pitchman said for a couple days or so – or at least till the guru's paisley colored mini-bus leaves town. Look around and see how many people you can find who made it big without knowledge, skills, and hard work. I think you'll agree – *90 days is cutttin' it a bit close!*

The truth is – building real estate wealth must always begin with a solid foundation! Once that's accomplished, you can start adding additional bricks as you learn more – *at a pace you can handle*. Naturally, the more bricks you can add, the more wealth you'll acquire! **You must never forget that step one of any plan is to achieve positive cash flow.** Getting rich will take care of itself so long as you keep cash flow coming in!

In chapters 10 and 11 of my best-selling how-to book, *Start Small, Profit Big in Real Estate*, I discussed two properties (good examples) that generate cash flow in the shortest period of time. *Both properties* are the kind I recommend for creating long-term wealth. Both properties provide spendable cash flow and you can quickly add more bricks to increase their values. You may wish to study both of these excellent examples during your planning and educational phase.

When you think about my "ski bum" analogy, *and apply it to a real estate investing*, there's probably a good chance you know someone around you who fits this description. *Here's a tip* – they always seem to have enough money to do whatever they wish to do! They never seem to be involved with any kind of normal type of work, and they never have to be anywhere during so-called business hours. Every so often, you might even hear them mention something like buying or refinancing investment properties. It's likely the only way you'd ever know about these *real estate "ski bums"* would be if someone told you they were full-time real estate investors. If you happen to be around one very much, you've probably already observed – whatever they do for a living seems to pay well enough so they don't need a regular job. Believe it or not, this is what many folks have thought about me over the years. To the majority of local residents who occasionally recognize my face at the mall, or see me during my daily post office runs, I'm still a big mystery because most have yet to figure out what I do.

BUILDING PERSONAL NET WORTH
TRUMPS REGULAR JOB

Folks who attend my lectures and investor training seminars know how much I emphasize the value of *multiple real estate benefits*. It's the combination of these benefits that make real estate investing so rewarding. **There are many different ways to extract profits from the kinds of properties I recommend.** Some of these benefits allow investors to take home huge profits without sharing with the tax man. Earning money in a way that allows you to keep 100% for yourself is a mighty powerful wealth builder. Uncle Sam does not require you to pay taxes when you spend your time working to increase your personal net worth.

For example, let's suppose I use my buying skills to acquire an income-producing property with an estimated value of $500,000. As you already know, I happen to be an accomplished Lt. Columbo style negotiator, so using my skills I convince the owner to sell me his property for **$400,000.** *Why in the world would he do something stupid like that, you ask?* Because he was dumb enough to allow his property to become rundown and ugly – now he's having great difficulty keeping it rented! Over the years I've purchased properties from sellers who were absolutely frightened to death of their tenants. You'll find there are many reasons for selling out cheap, but it's up to you to discover the truth! If you buy everything a seller tells you – stop right now and practice your interrogation techniques in front of a full-length mirror before you try it on the seller. Otherwise, someone will sell you the famous Brooklyn Bridge!

Obviously, this purchase will make me $100,000 richer because I have the knowledge to fix the sellers' problems. The question is: **Who will pay the taxes on my $100,000 profit?** The answer, my friend, is nobody! *I'm building my personal net worth, and it's not a taxable event, even though I'm now $100,000 richer!* Building your personal equity, while at the same time, steering clear of the tax man, is one of the best kept secrets why the rich get richer! I simply call it **working smarter!**

On the other hand, let's suppose you happen to be a real estate agent working for commissions – or a W-2 wage slave earning the same amount. I can guarantee you'll pay Uncle Sam taxes on your $100,000. Chances are, you'll get to keep about $60,000. This powerful technique is merely one of the many wealth-building benefits available to real estate *"ski bums"* who have discovered the gold in real estate. **The way you earn money is just as important as earning it!** Learn more about this in Chapter 13.

WORKING THE BENEFICIARIES

One of the most rewarding of all my **profit-making techniques** is buying back my own mortgage debt for big discounts! For several years, I didn't buy, sell, or trade one single property! *To the folks around me*, it might appear as if I were slowly going broke! The truth is, I was busy as ever negotiating for another kind of benefit! Like most landlords, I have tenants' rent checks coming in every month – but to the casual observer who doesn't see me actually doing any real estate transactions, it might appear as if I were going broke, or at least, headed in the wrong direction! But in reality, nothing could be further from the truth!

One of my most profitable techniques is to buy rundown properties from sellers who agree to finance the sale, or at least part of it! Over time, I've accumulated quite a number of seller carryback mortgages. *These are mortgages or notes I make payments on every month.* Frequently, when I purchase properties, I will also assume or take over existing seller carryback mortgages from previous sales. It's not the least bit uncommon for me to purchase a property and assume or take over three or four existing seller carryback mortgages on the same transaction. This sets the stage for one of the most **exciting and profitable opportunities** in my business.

BANKS SELDOM FINANCE DUMPY PROPERTIES

Most sellers who own rundown dumpy-looking properties must provide *seller carryback financing* in order to sell their properties. That's because most banks want no part of financing these junky lookin' rental properties, so sellers must finance the sale themselves. Sellers who finance their own deals and carry back mortgages or notes are called **beneficiaries**. They're the folks who receive my mortgage payments every month when I purchase their properties! *We are in direct contact (by mail) every month because I send them their mortgage payments!* About now, you're probably startin' to wonder – where's the benefit to sending out mortgage payments? **Pay very close attention here, to what I'm about to tell you!**

Many beneficiaries (the folks I pay monthly) would rather have a lot more dollars in their wallets – and a whole lot faster than my monthly mortgage payments dribbling in. This is even more so when the beneficiary is 80 years old, and the mortgage payments still have 17 years left to go. Quite often an elderly beneficiary will pass away long before a mortgage is paid off, and my debt will then be inherited by family members who don't value monthly payments dribbling in for 17 more years! There's no big secret to what they want – **cash, and they want it now**! Many of these *inherited beneficiaries* will agree to take a lot less cash right now rather than waiting around for the mailman every month. *How much less*, of course, will depend on their personal financial situation at the time. Naturally, I'll begin using my Lt. Columbo detective skills trying to figure out exactly the proper time to dangle a bucket full of green foldin' money in front of their nose. **Timing is everything** when you're trying to buy back your mortgage debt for a substantial amount less than what's owed. In other words, **I'm looking for a steep discount!**

YOU MUST LEARN
BENEFICIARIES' FINANCIAL STATE

For example, let's say you offer to buy back your $100,000 mortgage debt from a beneficiary you haven't taken any time to investigate. Had you done a bit of homework, you could have easily discovered that the beneficiary just won the "big spin" lottery four days ago – *if you should ask for a big discount now*, chances are, he'll tell you to go stuff it! *On the other hand*, if your cash offer arrives smack-dab in the middle of a nasty divorce – or he's just been laid off at the pretzel factory – **now $40,000 to $50,000 cash** might easily buy back your mortgage with a $100,000 balance!

During my slow year, when I didn't buy or sell any properties – many folks around my town thought I'd totally given up on real estate investing! Most observers wonder, when they don't see you wheeling and dealing or making deals, how in the world can this guy survive – he can't be making any money! However, here's what the observers are not seeing!

During my slow year, three separate mortgage holders (beneficiaries) accepted my cash discount offers! This reduced my mortgage debt by a total of **$109,000**. Besides creating $109,000 worth of mortgage discounts, my payments dropped by $811 per month. That meant my cash flow earnings increased by almost $10,000 annually. Obviously, my net worth was improved by $109,000 from the debt reduction. Close observers thought I slept through the entire year. They had no idea I had generated over **$100,000** in profits because they couldn't see anything happening!

SELLING PROPERTIES FOR EXTRA FULL PRICE

Most buyers who purchase my *"nice-n-clean"* fixed up properties are tickled to death when they discover I'm willing to accept only 10% cash down payments – **and also provide attractive seller carryback financing**. Assuming my potential buyer is credit worthy, I'm happy to offer very attractive financing – with payback terms up to 20 years or so – often with *interest only* payments. Easy payback terms are always far more important to investors than the selling price – *within reason of course*!

I always tell my potential buyers right upfront – I'm willing to give you nice and easy payback terms, but I won't discount my selling price. **I get my full price and you get great terms**! My definition of *full price* is what some folks might call **"extra-full"** – sometimes up to 20% higher because of the easy pay terms I'm offering! Since good terms are always top priority for most buyers, rarely has my **extra-full price** been much of an issue. Buyers want monthly mortgage payments they can afford to pay without reaching in their pocket every month to make up for cash flow shortages.

Naturally, when I sell for top price and easy payback terms using seller financing, my buyers have no idea that my future plan might be to trade my new carryback mortgage or promissory note for the down payment on my next rundown property. Sellers of ugly rundown multiple-unit properties, *the kind I'm looking for*, will often take my seller carryback mortgages in trade as part of their selling price.

Quite often, I've found sellers would much rather have "hassle-free" income from my mortgage payments rather than trying to collect rents from their deadbeat tenants. As you can probably see, selling my property for the highest selling price, in exchange for giving liberal payback terms, gives me a **bigger mortgage** for my trade. Also, remember the liberal payments I gave to my buyer? Well, they're gone now – they've been transferred to someone else in exchange for my next income property.

For example, let's say I own a $500,000 property, which I'm able to sell for $595,000 (20% extra) because I gave my buyer excellent easy-pay financing terms. **That means I'll have a $95,000 bigger mortgage to trade for my next purchase.** Obviously, I'll gain an extra $95,000 worth of equity on my next deal as well! *This means less new financing will be required* – therefore, I'll end up with more cash flow on my next property!

Right about now you're probably thinking – okay, I understand when Jay sells his property and gives the buyer special easy-pay terms, he can then jack up his selling price by $95,000 – *but is that really legal*? The answer, my friends is YES, YES, YES! Buyers are happy to pay more for **good terms** and **seller carryback financing**! Think about the last car you bought! Weren't you the most concerned about terms? If you could own that brand new shiny red Mercedes for the same monthly payment as the puke green Chevy coupe, **which one will you choose**? The Mercedes cost twice as much, but the payments are exactly the same! I'll bet I can guess which car you'll drive away! Terms work exactly the same with **real estate investing**. As far as a legal analysis, well I'm no cop, but I can tell you that everyone I've ever sold properties to were very happy with the deal. I call this "**creative money-making**." *You must create this deal yourself* – this is not some "blow dried" packaged deal you'll find on the shelf at Sears!

ACQUIRING PROPERTIES WITH SMALL LOANS

As you begin to stack your financial bricks higher – or building your personal real estate wealth – *chances are*, you'll begin to accumulate a few extra dollars which are not earning their keep. Real estate entrepreneurs, as well as us "ski bums," don't put our extra money in bank passbook accounts, low paying CD's and we certainly stay away from buying risky stocks! One solution I've found for investing those extra bucks is to offer small **hard money loans** to other investors who purchase the same kind of properties I do. *Rundown type properties that I wouldn't mind owning myself!* As a rule, I've found that folks who need to borrow money against their rundown properties are struggling *financially*.

My loans are generally in the $15-$30,000 range – and I will only loan money when the total debt (including my new loan) does not exceed 60% of the property value (in my judgment). I simply do a personal drive-by appraisal – *and the value is what I say it is!* For example, let's say my drive-by appraisal determines the value to be $100,000. Let's say there are two existing mortgages secured by the property; a first of $30,000, and a second of $10,500. My loan offer, *in this case*, would not exceed **$19,500** – which when added together with the other two mortgages equals 60% of the property value.

I realize my mortgage will be a third loan – and most lenders would consider it too risky; **however**, you mustn't forget the business I'm in! Let's say that 30 days wiz by and the very first payment fails to show up in my mailbox! Should I start looking for the borrower, *you ask*? **No sir**, *I've never been very good at finding someone I don't want to find!* I'll simply begin foreclosure and take the property instead! Where else can I purchase a property these days for only 60% of its value? Can you begin to see how powerful my $19,500 loan can be? In reality, *foreclosure* feels almost like I'm purchasing a **$100,000** property with a $19,500 down payment – **but at a whopping 40% discount**! I don't believe you'll need to ask me if I consider my third mortgage too risky or not – but if you do, you need to re-read these last two pages a little bit slower and let it sink in!

My lending terms are generally for five years and most likely I'll ask for monthly payments of interest only – *at a respectable rate of course!* If usury laws are involved, you can avoid any problems by originating these loans through your licensed real estate broker to be on the safe side. This is yet another way for us "ski bum" investors stay afloat. Can you begin to see why casual observers in my town have never figured out what I do – or how I can possibly survive? **Don't ya love it when you've got 'em all baffled?**

CHAPTER 13

THE SMARTEST FISHERMAN

Rich folks get that way, in part, because of how they earn their income. You've no doubt heard the old adage: "It's not how much you make that counts – **it's how much you get to keep for yourself**." Taxes inhibit the ability for most working folks to become rich, because as their earnings go up – so do their taxes. Our progressive tax system – *the tax ratchet, I call it*, only goes in one direction – and that's up! Unless you can somehow control or eliminate increasing your taxes as you earn more income, it's almost impossible to rise above middle class earnings – which of course, ain't rich.

W-2 wage earners pay the lion's share of income taxes. In fact, if the government should ever decide to pass out gold medals to the real tax heroes – all the regular working folks who swap their time and energies for W-2 earnings would surely get one. However, I haven't quite figured out exactly where they should pin it just yet! One of the important lessons that the super-rich learn from the very start is that their income or earnings must be invisible to the taxing authorities! Okay, now don't throw up your arms and get all nervous thinkin' I'm talkin' about something illegal – I promise you, I'm not! What I'm discussing here is all perfectly legal – *and in fact*, it's your right – still, it's you who must decide how to arrange your financial affairs to pay the least amount!

INVISIBLE INCOME

About now, you might be thinking to yourself – Jay's been watching too many reruns of that ol' time radio-television show called *The Shadow*! You may recall that The Shadow was a completely invisible man. Obviously, if you're not a senior citizen like me, you probably missed all those exciting episodes of yester-year. Mr. Shadow was a very cool guy – he could suddenly appear out of nowhere, hit you in the mouth, and you wouldn't see a thing. That's exactly how you need to earn your income – so the IRS and state taxing authorities never see it. Stay with me here – you might discover this is easier than you think!

In my business of buying properties, and adding value to houses, I'm constantly looking for properties that I can acquire for substantial discounts. What's that, you ask? To me, substantial discounts range anywhere from 20-50% below the true market value of a property. Let's say for example, I find a house that I believe has a true market value of $250,000. Using my Columbo-style negotiating skills – I'm able to convince the owner to sell his property for $150,000. That's a substantial discount (40%).

Let's assume for a moment that it took me 50 hours of my time or labor to put this deal together! How much am I getting paid? If you divide my 50 hours into the $100,000 discount, the answer is way too much! ($100,000 divided by 50 hours = $2,000 per hour) Naturally, there will be clean-up and fixin' expenses to bring the property up to its market potential ($250,000), but as you can clearly see, my earnings will still be substantial! More importantly, whatever the amount is – it's totally invisible to everyone, including the tax man! Suddenly, I've become like "Mr. Shadow," so far as my profits are concerned. Keep in mind here – we're talking about personal income taxes – those nasty deductions they take from your paycheck if you happen to be a W-2 wage earner.

It's obvious – if you purchase an asset for $100,000 less than its true market value, you've somehow got to be a little richer, even with your fix-up expenses, to make the property market ready. The point is, my $100,000 discount feels like I'm earning $100,000, but yet, **its tax free to me**. There's no line on the 1040 federal tax form to report one nickel of my $100,000 profit! In fact, the government is not even asking me to report any earnings from this activity! As far as they're concerned, the extra $100,000 I earned using my negotiating skills is a total "free-bee." This is what I call **working for my personal net worth**! *I'm building – or increasing my equity*, which in turn will earn more rental income for me. Rental income, the kind I earn, is called passive income. For the most part it's sheltered by my depreciation expenses, leaving little or nothing to pay for personal 1040 taxes.

EARNING PAYROLL WAGES IS MUCH DIFFERENT

If you're an upper class wage earner making $100,000 W-2 wages – your payroll earnings will receive a far different treatment! Obviously, **you're not the least bit invisible**. Everyone knows exactly how much you earn and they plan to share it with you. Depending on your marital status, number of dependents, etc.–your tax deductions will vary somewhat. Still, you'll end up with substantially less money than the amount you actually earned. Federal income taxes, state taxes, and your share of FICA (Social Security taxes) will gobble up at least 35-50% of your paycheck in my state – leaving you far less than the amount you earned.

Payroll wages are very easy to track, since employers are required by law to keep perfect accounting of every nickel you earn. Your annual W-2 form shows exactly where all your earnings go! Naturally, a copy must be sent to the IRS and state taxing authorities along with your regular tax forms. If you should toss it in the garbage by accident – there's no need to worry, because your boss has already mailed the tax folks the very same information that's on your check stubs. After all, that's how he's able to claim an expense deduction for the wages he pays. If you are a W-2 wage earner – you're essentially trapped! You can't hide one thin dime of your earnings from anyone – especially the tax folks who stand ready with open hands, eager to grab their share!

Keeping as much of the money you earn is just as important to your financial well-being and overall wealth building as earning it to begin with! Many moons ago, while I labored at the telephone company, my average tax deductions would automatically trim about $15,000 every year from my paychecks – before I ever received them! I say *automatic*, because my employer withheld the money without ever discussing the matter with me. That's the beauty of payroll deductions! If somehow

I'd been able to keep my annual tax deductions back then and invest the money for my personal benefit, I'd have ended up rich a lot sooner! My state and federal tax deductions invested at a piddly 05% would have made me a millionaire during a normal 30-year telephone career. Since I quit after 23 years of service, I would have had to settle for a measly $700,000. Still, that's a sizable wad of dough compared to the worthless pile of check stubs I received.

IT'S NOT WHAT YOU EARN – IT'S HOW YOU EARN

Everyone gets to choose how they will earn their income! Obviously, knowing a little something about the way taxes work can greatly influence the decision! Three different people can be earning exactly the same amount of income – *and yet*, be paying far different amounts of personal income tax on their earnings. Without a full-blown discussion on revenue Tax Code 469, let me simply say that all income is divided into three different categories. As you might have guessed, each of these three categories gets taxed differently. Let's take BILLY BOB for example! Figure 13-1: he's a single taxpayer who earns $40,000 annually selling T-shirts and popcorn at local county fairs. He has a special trailer he tows around to operate his mobile T-shirt business. When tax times rolls around, he takes the standard deduction of $6100. He takes another deduction of $3900 for being a single dependent. This reduces his taxable income to $30,000. He now pays 15% federal taxes – plus another 15% for Social Security tax (30% of $30,000 = $9000 taxes). This means Billy Bob gets to keep just **$31,000** of his $40,000 gross earnings.

SLICK WILLY (Figure 13-2) has $40,000 income same as Billy Bob! The difference is – Willie earns his income from promissory notes and mortgages! He's also a single tax payer, so he gets the same standard deduction of $6100. He also deducts $3900 as a single dependent. Willie's taxable income, same as Billy Bob's, is $30,000. His federal tax bracket is 15%–but because his income is what IRS calls **portfolio income**, he's not required to pay Social Security taxes. Therefore, 15% x $30,000 = $4500 taxes, which means Willie gets to keep **$35,500** of his earnings – or $4500 more than Billy Bob.

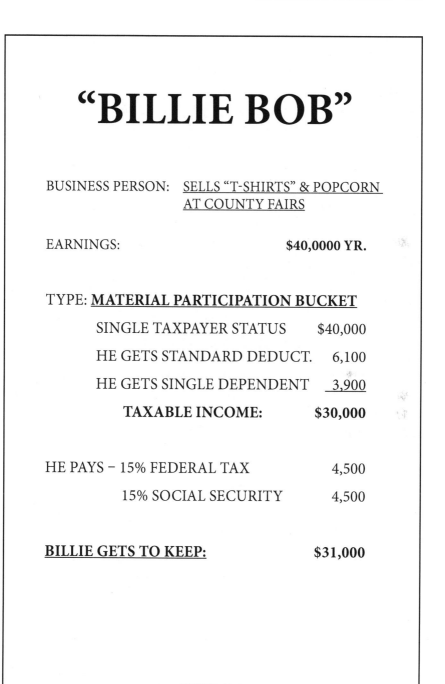

"BILLIE BOB"

BUSINESS PERSON: <u>SELLS "T-SHIRTS" & POPCORN</u>
<u>AT COUNTY FAIRS</u>

EARNINGS: **$40,0000 YR.**

TYPE: **MATERIAL PARTICIPATION BUCKET**

SINGLE TAXPAYER STATUS $40,000

HE GETS STANDARD DEDUCT.   6,100

HE GETS SINGLE DEPENDENT   <u>3,900</u>

TAXABLE INCOME: **$30,000**

HE PAYS – 15% FEDERAL TAX   4,500

15% SOCIAL SECURITY   4,500

<u>BILLIE GETS TO KEEP:</u>   **$31,000**

FIGURE 13-1

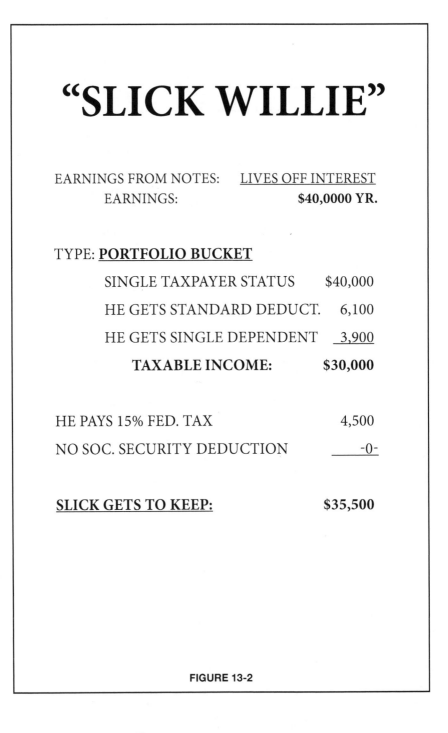

"SLICK WILLIE"

EARNINGS FROM NOTES: LIVES OFF INTEREST
EARNINGS: **$40,0000 YR.**

TYPE: **PORTFOLIO BUCKET**

SINGLE TAXPAYER STATUS $40,000

HE GETS STANDARD DEDUCT. 6,100

HE GETS SINGLE DEPENDENT 3,900

TAXABLE INCOME: **$30,000**

HE PAYS 15% FED. TAX 4,500

NO SOC. SECURITY DEDUCTION -0-

SLICK GETS TO KEEP: **$35,500**

FIGURE 13-2

LANDLORD LOUIE (Figure 13-3) also earns $40,000 annually just like Billy Bob and Willie! His income, however, comes from rents, which the IRS calls **passive income**. Like the others, Louie is a single tax payer and therefore takes the standard $6100 deduction. He also gets $3900 as a single dependent. That reduces his taxable income to $30,000; however, Louie owns $800,000 worth of income-producing real estate, which nets him 05% annually. Louie, just like Billy Bob and Willie, is in the 15% tax bracket – but first, he's allowed to deduct $680,000 worth of depreciable assets, which gives him $30,600 annually in depreciation write-offs – or tax shelter ($30,000 taxable income less $30,600 depreciation = **0 taxes**). Therefore, **Landlord Louie gets to keep every single nickel he earns**!

As you can see, three separate taxpayers earning exactly the same amount of income, all in the same tax bracket, have substantial differences in what each one gets to keep. Landlord Louie's income is earned from the assets he owns, and because of his depreciation expenses, his $40,000 income is pretty much invisible to taxing authorizes. Acquiring hard assets like rental houses and small apartments, which produce income sheltered by depreciation, is a much more efficient method of building wealth, because you don't have to share your income with the tax man. In my examples, Landlord Louie gets to keep $9000 more of his earnings than Billy Bob and $4500 more than Slick Willie! Should Louie decide to reinvest his $9000 tax savings to buy more real estate each year, he could reasonably expect those funds to earn him a million dollars or so in the next 10 to 15 years.

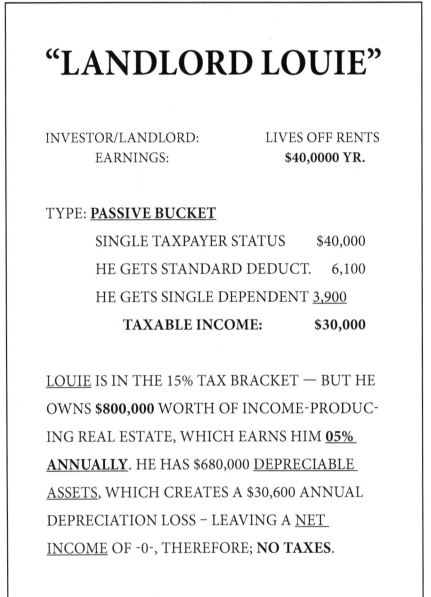

"LANDLORD LOUIE"

INVESTOR/LANDLORD: LIVES OFF RENTS
        EARNINGS: **$40,0000 YR.**

TYPE: **PASSIVE BUCKET**

>   SINGLE TAXPAYER STATUS $40,000
>
>   HE GETS STANDARD DEDUCT.   6,100
>
>   HE GETS SINGLE DEPENDENT <u>3,900</u>
>
>   **TAXABLE INCOME:**   **$30,000**

<u>LOUIE</u> IS IN THE 15% TAX BRACKET — BUT HE OWNS **$800,000** WORTH OF INCOME-PRODUC-ING REAL ESTATE, WHICH EARNS HIM **05%** **ANNUALLY**. HE HAS $680,000 <u>DEPRECIABLE</u> <u>ASSETS</u>, WHICH CREATES A $30,600 ANNUAL DEPRECIATION LOSS – LEAVING A <u>NET</u> <u>INCOME</u> OF -0-, THEREFORE; **NO TAXES**.

<u>LOUIE GETS TO KEEP:</u>   **$40,000**

FIGURE 13-3

THE AWESOME POWER
OF KEEPING WHAT YOU EARN

When I quit my telephone job, I can still remember how frightened I was about giving up my dependable income to become a full-time real estate investor. Although my gross rents far exceeded my telephone paychecks, I still had a bucket full of expenses and mortgages to pay. For the first several months or so, I constantly worried whether there would be enough rents left over for me – somehow there always were, and eventually my worries faded away.

After a couple years or so of being on my own, I began to realize there's a huge difference between gross income and the **amount I got to keep**! I also became aware that many of my personal expenses could legally be paid from my real estate business. Accountants call these expenses – *above the line deductions*. It simply means that items like my computer, automobile, telephones, and transportation expenses could now be paid from my rental income. Working at the phone company, these kind of expenses were always paid from my personal *after tax earnings*, – what accountants call, below the line deductions.

Working full-time in my own real estate business allowed me to transfer many personal expenses to *business expenses*. Also, many of my old personal expenses simply disappeared! Things like buying brand new suits for work quickly became a memory of the past! Today I often refer to myself as a walking, breathing, expense account. What became very obvious to me as a full-time investor–many of my old out-of-pocket expenses now qualified as legitimate business expenses. I also began to save money from dumping old habits like buying lunch every day, five days a week with my telephone buddies – *money not spent is the same as earning more.*

SPENDING WISELY

When my long-time student and friend Ralph M. told me his son's student loan would exceed **$60,000**, I nearly fell off my chair. That's enough money for two or three down payments back when I was acquiring lots of properties. *For the life of me*, I can't understand the thinking or rationale for spending $60,000 on school loans when my friend's son still doesn't know what he wants to be! I have no problem with borrowing money, but I certainly want to know what I'll be getting back in return before I agree to sign up for a long-term debt!

Students are always asking: how much money can we expect to earn *fixing up or adding value* to properties the way you suggest? Obviously, there's no single answer I can give you – however, let me explain it this way! If you follow my teachings for searching out, locating, and acquiring rundown properties, with a high potential for adding value – the sky is the only limit I can think of! I will promise you this much: regular everyday Mom and Pop investors who will dedicate themselves to learning the ropes–then doing this stuff, can make themselves **a million dollars** in a reasonable time! Here's what happened to me once I realized I could clean and fix up two or three units at a time – I figured I could do even more. Soon afterwards, I purchased an old dilapidated motor lodge in my town that no one else seemed to want.

HIGHEST PROFITS ARE MADE SOLVING PROBLEMS

When students attend my seminars in Redding, I always drive them past my **Hillcrest property**. Besides all the money it earned me, I still feel a real sense of pride and accomplishment. Without question, Hillcrest was truly a "first class" pigsty when I bought it. Students never fail to ask me the same question when they visit Hillcrest today. Doesn't it take a lot of skills to convert junky rundown buildings to these attractive-looking cottages like you have here today? Of course, it takes some skills, but the nice part about it – *you can learn many of these skills as you go along*! It's kinda like the "poor man's on-the-job" training program. You certainly don't need to have all the answers at your fingertips on the day you start! This is one of the major advantages of investing the way I teach. *You can be learning new skills and be making money at the same time* – and it certainly doesn't have to cost you $60,000 before you even start.

I can't think of any job that rewards your creative skills more than fixing up crappy-lookin' properties for profits – *and besides*, even a eighth grade dropout can pretty much learn as he goes! When you stop to consider what it costs for a decent education at a respectable college, and compare the amount of income you might expect to earn, fixing up rundown properties just might be pound for pound the best paying job you'll find anywhere. Obviously, the fix-up business is not for everyone, and it certainly favors those with an entrepreneurial spirit. *Self-discipline* and *stick-to-itness* are the major ingredients of course – but if you have them, then you've got pretty much what it takes! If I told you – you could earn **$1,000,000** with just your **personal skills**, would you believe me? The truth is, many of you who are reading this book already have more than enough talent! Your problem may be that you simply lack enough confidence in yourself!

GOLD IS OFTEN BURIED IN THE DIRT AND GRIME

My **million-dollar story** begins when I first found out that Hillcrest Cottages, an old rundown motor lodge (motel) in my town was for sale. I was told that the sellers, two investment partners, were highly motivated. On a scale of 1 to 10, these guys were about 12, I soon discovered! What got them there was a series of "nightmarish" events, none the least of which was the unholy state of their two-man partnership. They acted like they despised each other! One had a good job and was a responsible citizen; the other was an unemployed deadbeat who lacked much responsibility. Worse yet, he was the on-site manager whose job it was to collect the rents from tenants who seemed to have more commonsense than he did. Obviously, both partners were on a collision course headed for self-destruction. Both the property and the partnership situation seemed hopeless on my first visit to the property.

This story is mostly about **creativity** – making what you have fit the situation at hand. *Allow me to explain*! About a year before I first laid eyes on Hillcrest, I had purchased an older three-bedroom house located on a large commercially zoned lot. The property had frontage on a major thoroughfare. I had paid $80,000 to buy the property, which included my $20,000 cash down payment. If $20,000 cash sounds like a lot of money to put down for one house, don't forget I actually had a legitimate job back in those days with the telephone company. The twenty grand came from my bell system savings plan.

When I arrived at Hillcrest – I was financially "tapped out" as you might guess! I had no cash left for even a small down payment. After haggling a bit over the selling price, we finally agreed that Hillcrest was worth about **$234,000**. There were three existing mortgages against the property, totaling $142,000. All had delinquent payments, plus late penalties owing. The equity was $92,000 – calculated as follows: $234,000 value less $142,000 mortgages = **$92,000 equity**. The sellers were looking for a cash down payment to "bail out" their delinquent mortgages (two were already being foreclosed)! They also had several mechanics' liens against the property for "stiffing" the neighborhood hardware store. Since I had no cash to give, I was not exactly the seller's ideal choice as a "buyer." Fortunately for me at the time, I was their only choice!

Both partners had simply fiddled around too long and the mortgage holders were quickly closing in–and if that wasn't bad enough, the city abatement committee had the property all measured up for a "full scale" demolition party! The city claimed the buildings were dilapidated and had become a public nuisance! The owners had ignored repeated threats from the city to make the needed repairs. Finally, the day of reckoning was at hand, and the sellers knew it! It wasn't long before I knew it too!

YOU CAN HELP YOURSELF BY HELPING THE SELLER

One of the most important ingredients for acquiring a bargain property is **high motivation** on the part of the seller. At Hillcrest, you could actually feel the motivation. I could tell that almost any concession I asked for, *within reason of course*, would be acceptable to the partners. Sensing the urgency – I sorta milled around the property with the sellers trailing me, asking every question I could think of like Lieutenant Columbo used to do on the ol' TV show. In fact, I've patterned my own negotiating style after Lt. Columbo! In case you're not familiar with Columbo, he's that "dumb like a fox" TV detective who wore the old wrinkled-up raincoat on the once popular series – (channel surfers can often find the re-runs). Columbo's style is exactly the opposite of "winning through intimidation!" In fact, he solves most of his cases because the bad guys can't possibly imagine how anyone who looks and talks so sweet like Columbo could possibly be any kind of a threat to them; therefore, they trust him and they blab everything!

I have found that most property owners who are seriously motivated to sell their properties will tell me their innermost secrets–**if I'll just ask nicely in a non-threatening way**. That's what Columbo does, and it works. At Hillcrest, the owners and I put our heads together to work out a plan that would give them relief – fully understanding it would have to work for me too! *Always remember*, nobody will sign your deal or cooperate with you unless they see themselves benefiting. **You must help them first in order to help yourself!**

The key to what I'm telling you here is simple! **You must listen very attentively to all the sellers' problems**. Forget momentarily what it is that you want, and just concentrate on providing the seller immediate relief from his problems. If you make his problems your first priority, I'll guarantee you'll be taken care of in the long run. Hillcrest was not nearly so much about buying a bargain property as it was solving a "giant-size" problem for the partners! And as you shall learn, solving giant size problems sets the stage for "**giant-size paydays!**"

MAKING AN OFFER THAT BENEFITS EVERYONE

After I had thoroughly stomped over every inch of Hillcrest's three rolling acres and asked every question I could think of, I decided that Hillcrest had a tremendous "upside potential" for profit-making! Obviously, I could see it was a real mess and would be a "king-size" job. Still, it was my gut feeling that if I could somehow buy the property, without spending any "upfront" money, the most I could lose would be my personal labor and, of course, whatever money I spent for materials.

I calculated the risk of losing my personal labor against my estimate of the high-profit potential for fixing up the 22-unit apartment and concluded–**why not "go for the gusto."**

Basically, what I said to the partners was this: if we can all put our heads together and come up with a plan that will get you guys totally off the hook, *meaning*, sell me the property and get all your debts paid off – **would you be willing to sell?** They agreed they would; just show us where to sign! I reminded them that we don't quite have our total plan worked out just yet. We gotta couple more details!

Getting these guys off the hook meant catching up their payments on delinquent mortgages. It also meant paying off their local trade accounts to satisfy several mechanics' liens. The total cash needed to pay these bills added up to almost $15,000. That's exactly **$15,000** more than I had in my bank account at the time! No one ever said this job was easy; still, you'll have to admit, there's a wonderful opportunity to be creative here! What I needed was a little *voodoo economics* for this acquisition. Turns out, my offer would be quite creative, so I summoned the partners so I could explain.

Here's the deal guys: I will purchase your "scum-bag" motor lodge for **$234,000**. That's **100%** of your asking price since we've already agreed on the value. In order to buy Hillcrest, I will trade you, straight across, (under rules of tax code 1031) for my lovely three-bedroom house located on Opportunity Lane (not real name), which is in the city's booming commercial area. I have scientifically determined the market value today is **$150,000**. It has a current mortgage balance of $58,000, which means my current equity is exactly **$92,000**. "Gentlemen," I said, "If I'm not mistaken, that's a perfect match for your Hillcrest equity. **What a surprising coincidence!** What we have here gentlemen is a 'straight across the board' equity trade. *No cash down payment is required!*"

NO DOWN PAYMENT DON'T ELIMINATE NEED FOR CASH

The partners went along with the voodoo value I established for my three-bedroom house. They quickly agreed to the straight across the board trade for Hillcrest! But we still had the problem of finding the cash to pay off their delinquent bills. Naturally, they didn't have two dimes to rub together between them! Here's where I got a little bit more creative with the financing; **that is**, me and the Beneficial Finance Company.

I then asked the partners this question: would you guys be agreeable to borrowing **$25,000** from me so you can pay off all your delinquent bills – mortgages, foreclosure costs, liens, etc.? They were more than delighted! I said okay guys, *here's what we can do* – I will borrow the money from Beneficial Finance Co. and loan it to you for that purpose. I'll deposit it into a separate escrow account. You must agree to pay approximately $15,000 for all your delinquent bills and the balance of $10,000 will be yours to keep. The loan will be for a period of five years, with annual interest payments to me of 10%, payable each year until the principal is paid back. The loan will be secured with a deed of trust **against the three-bedroom house I'm trading to you guys**.

Once the deal was written up, I visited my friends at the local Beneficial office. I explained that once this trade happens, I'll have **$92,000 equity** at Hillcrest. I would like to borrow $50,000 to fix up the property! They did a quick appraisal, which meant they verified that I still had my 20 plus year job at the phone company, and said, okay Jay, **we'll do it**!

Quite often when folks ask me about this transaction, they say "WOW" Jay–beneficial really charges outrageous interest rates. How can you afford to pay that much? **My answer** – *you must earn big enough profits to make the payments*! **It's simple arithmetic.** If your interest payments are at 18%, but you can earn 40 to 60% with the money, you'll have no difficulty! On the other hand, if you use high cost financing on properties that lack the high profit potential like Hillcrest, you'll crash and burn. As a general rule, the **biggest profits** will be earned on properties where the **biggest problems** can be solved! **Don't ever forget this!**

Selling has never been my favorite thing to do! However, this sale was made years ago when my two primary goals were staying in business and paying my grocery bills. As you shall see, the Hillcrest sale helped me a great deal with both.

The doctor who purchased Hillcrest Cottages, along with five other small rental units I owned, immediately fell in love with my newly fixed up Hillcrest property. The doctor was like many other high-income earners–he was making tons of money, but he didn't wish to part with any for a down payment! This was completely acceptable for me at the time, because I needed a stable monthly income. We basically agreed to a no down transaction with higher monthly payments. Back then, the doctor as able to save a bundle on taxes, which lessened his quarterly burden! The Doc also asked me to manage and oversee the property! I agreed for 7.5% of the monthly gross rents. My management fee would earn me an additional $600 every month, which I considered an excellent fringe benefit for putting our deal together.

MAKING MONEY OFTEN DEPENDS ON HOW YOU COUNT

Often people tell me – you really don't make any profit unless you sell for all cash! When you sell over time, *they explain*, your profits are eroded by inflation. It's the period of time versus the value of money thing, *they claim*! Certainly, I'll be the first to agree – a dollar in the hand today is worth two in the bush tomorrow! But what about five or six dollars in the bush! When I sold the property, I carried back a note for **$594,000**. The deal was a no down transaction for the doctor, with payments to me of **$6,000** per month at 12% interest rate. My note was a wrap-around secured by an all-inclusive deed of trust, which kept me responsible for paying the existing underlying mortgages on the property.

Just how lucrative was this particular deal, you ask? Plenty, I'd say, but you needn't take my word – instead, allow me rattle off a few dollar numbers so you can judge for yourself! If you happen to be a calculator bug, I'm probably not giving you quite enough information for all your buttons. Just put it away for the moment and allow me to paint you the big picture! The property sold for **$594,000**. Payments were **$6,000** per month, including 12.0% interest. The nine underlying mortgages on the properties totaled **$333,055**. Naturally, I was responsible for paying all the underlying mortgage payments from my $6,000 monthly check!

REWARD VS. RISK – YOU BE THE JUDGE

In the beginning, my net annual earnings were only $23,460, but as the underlying mortgages began to pay off, my net earnings increased dramatically. The note was written to pay off in slightly under 27 years. Altogether, I would take in total payments of **$1,878,000** and would pay out a total of **$677,978** to retire the underlying payments and interest. When the smoke cleared, (**$1,200,022**) *was mine to keep*! I've always felt I was pretty well paid for my two years of fix-up and a little dab of voodoo financing! Regarding the long wait for my money – I'll let you be the judge for yourself!

The following page (Figure 13-4) shows a diagram of my **$594,000** Hillcrest wrap-around note. You can see the *annual note receivable payments* along the left side of the chart. That's the amount I took in. The annual mortgage payments paid out are listed across the top. The lower left hand corner shows the total payments received: **$1,878.00**. The lower right hand corner of the chart shows the net amount I got to keep: $1,200.022. Not bad earnings from a sale that was only **$260,945** more than what was owed on the property when I sold it! Had I sold the property for cash, my profit would have been **$260,945**–$594,000 minus nine mortgages at $333,055 equals $260,945. By waiting for my money, I earned a whopping $937,077 more. **It doesn't pay to hurry – say Amen!**

WRAP AROUND MORTGAGE
HILLCREST TRANSACTION – $594,000
Schedule Of Payments Receivable & Underlying Mortgages Payable

YEARS	ANNUAL PAYMENTS INCOME	ANNUAL PAYMENTS • OUT-GOING UNDERLYING MORTGAGES (9)									NET INCOME TO JAY
		GBRL-TR.	DEMPY	ERNIE	BENE#1	BENE #2	RUSS	MAHOY	RICE	BENE#3	
1	48,000	4,800	2,400	4,000	3,752	3,752	2,400	3,504	2,000	5,752	15,640
2	72,000	7,200	3,600	6,000	5,628	5,628	3,600	5,256	3,000	8,628	23,460
3	72,000	7,200	3,600	6,000	5,628	5,628	3,600	5,256	3,000	8,628	23,960
4	72,000	7,200	3,600	6,000	5,628	5,628	3,600	5,256	3,000	8,628	23,460
5	72,000	7,200	3,600	6,000	5,628	5,628	3,600	5,256	3,000	8,628	23,460
6	72,000	7,200	3,600	6,000	5,628	5,628	1,200	5,256	1,000	8,628	27,860
7	72,000	7,200	3,600	6,000	5,628	5,628		5,256		8,628	30,060
8	72,000	7,200	3,600	6,000	5,628	5,628		5,256		8,628	30,060
9	72,000	7,200	3,600	6,000	5,628	5,628		5,256		8,628	30,060
10	72,000	7,200	3,600	6,000	5,628	5,628		5,256		8,628	30,060
11	72,000	7,200	3,600	6,000	5,628	5,628		5,256		8,628	30,060
12	72,000	2,000	3,600	6,000	5,628	5,628		5,256		8,628	35,260
13	72,000		3,600	6,000	5,628	5,628		5,256		8,628	37,260
14	72,000		3,600	3,500	5,628	5,628		5,256		8,628	39,760
15	72,000		3,000		5,628	5,628		5,256		8,628	43,860
16	72,000				1,876	1,876		5,256		2,879	60,116
17	72,000							5,256			66,744
18	72,000							5,256			66,744
19	72,000							5,256			66,744
20	72,000							5,256			66,744
21	72,000							5,256			66,744
22	72,000							5,256			66,744
23	72,000							5,256			66,744
24	72,000							5,256			66,744
25	72,000							5,256			66,744
26	72,000							5,256			66,744
27								1,314			28,686
	$1,878,000	78,800	52,200	79,500	84,420	84,420	18,000	136,218	15,000	129,420	1200,022

CHAPTER 14

CAREFUL WHEN YOU'RE SHORTA WORMS

Regardless of whether your plan is to acquire single-family houses, duplexes, or multiple-unit properties, which is my favorite – **cash flow should always be your immediate goal**! Naturally, I'm assuming you're an investor with limited funds who can ill afford to pay out extra money every month to keep your property operating. Certainly that describes me in my earlier investing years! That's why I've always favored **fixer-uppers** or properties I could begin adding value to as soon as I closed escrow.

With almost every fix-up or adding value transaction, the key is to acquire the property at a substantially lower price than the equivalent *fixed-up* property would sell for. The investor is hoping to benefit himself from what we call "sweat equity." This generally means that the investor will be doing most all of the labor himself – using his fix-up budget for only materials and supplies. *The goal is to do only what's necessary to make the property more valuable.* By providing the labor himself, the investor can save expenses and hopefully rent or sell for a profit. Personal labor is where the biggest savings will come from starting out.

DIRECTING YOUR DOLLARS AT THE TARGET

Below you'll see a 20-item summary of what I consider the most important improvement of add-on value items. Obviously, some things are more important than others, some are basic necessities, and some are Jay's "FOO-FOO" items to improve the looks. Remember, first impressions are worth big bucks!

1. Paint exterior. Includes siding or stucco repairs, whatever shows poorly.

2. Fix yards or landscaping. **Front street view is most important.** Back yards: cut grass, water, that's it! Re-seed lawn areas, plant cheap shrubs and trees for improved looks. Re-build and repair existing fences when possible to save them. Best evergreen shrubs for front yards are pyracanthas; they grow fast, they're cheap, and they have thorns, which keep kids from pulling them up. Also, colorful red berries add to looks.

3. Paint interior of houses as tenants move out, not while the existing tenants still live there. Semi-gloss latex, off-white is best.

4. Replace carpets and linoleum **only** as required. Save, repair, and clean existing floor coverings if they can be salvaged. However, it must look good after cleaning. Do this work between tenants moving out and new ones coming in.

5. All water valves, faucets, toilet assembly (guts); shut-off stops must work properly. Best to replace if they are old and ugly. Same for shower and tubs. Replace ugly dinged up sinks – also, ugly toilets with slow discharge.

6. Replace all ugly light fixtures with new but cheap (economy) fixtures. All switches must work easily; otherwise junk them.

7. Make obvious repairs: holes in walls, busted doors, door hardware, broken windows. Exterior doors must have good working locksets, preferably with deadbolts. Re-key as needed to have a single key that works in all exterior doors. This will save you on copies, plus the hassle of too many keys.

8. Replace old ugly countertops with new ready-to-use Formica tops. Kitchens mostly – some bathrooms will need them too!

9. Window coverings are big payback item – plus, it saves you the heartache of watching tenants split window moldings by driving

16 penny nails to hang bed sheets and Indian blankets over your windows. Most houses can have full window treatment; plastic mini blinds or drapes in living rooms, bedrooms, dining rooms, or family rooms – cheap colorful curtains in kitchen and bathrooms. Always add a rod and shower curtain. Window coverings add a touch of class, plus they tend to hide minor flaws always found in the older houses or apartments. If your money is running out, **do street side windows only.** Let tenants do back of the house windows where it doesn't show from the street.

10. It goes without saying; however, I'll say it anyway! Heating units and coolers or air conditioners must work properly! In my town it gets over 100 degrees in the summer. I use evaporative coolers (swamp coolers) in my lower priced economy houses – forced air heating and cooling systems in higher scale houses. I furnish kitchen ranges, either good re-conditioned or economy model new ones. I do not furnish refrigerators unless it's an upstairs apartment where it's difficult to move appliances in and out. Most (95%) of the time I let tenants furnish refrigerators in my lower-income rental properties.

11. Naturally, rotten wood or windows that can't be fixed must be replaced. Most older windows can be repaired and re-puttied without much cost. Mostly grunt type labor – paint will fix most anything on a house that looks ugly.

12. Frills are okay as long as they are cheap (inexpensive). One of the best is ceiling fans. One or two ceiling fans add a lot of class to older houses and its money well spent because it attracts the attention of renters. They like fans!

13. Big-ticket repairs like bad roofs, especially if they look ugly from the street view, can be replaced in several stages. For example, on pitched-roof houses, it's seldom that both sides leak! Generally the south side or weather side leaks first and the other side doesn't! Patch or do only half a roof on phase one of your fix-up projects. Roofs on the street side that are old, weathered, and ugly may not leak yet. However, the ugly roof distracts a great deal from the property. Replacing the street side because it's ugly

may be justified. Do the back side later in Phase II. Remember, however; you can't get higher rents for new roofs. Roofs are simply to keep water out. That's it!

14. Extra sizzle items that cost very few fix-up dollars are exterior shutters. Install them on front street side windows. They manufacture plastic shutters for various size windows in white, brown, and black colors. Check any handyman do-it-yourself store. I buy mine at Sears!

15. I always recommend white picket fences. Build them three feet high around front yard areas! White picket fences show off the property – **both to renters and potential buyers alike**! They create a soft homey atmosphere, especially with nice green lawns, or as us landlords call them, "mowed weeds." Fences in back yards are also hot seller items. They keep kids and dogs inside the property. Mothers like fences and mothers make the decision to rent or buy. Need I say more? If money is tight, do front white picket fences first; back yard board fences can wait till Phase II!

16. While you're working on the property, train yourself to water front yard areas while you are there. Always carry a hose and sprinkler with you at all times. That way, when you arrive at the job you can set up your sprinkler and water dry areas. The idea is to make all front yards green! Toss out some lawn seed where you have bare ground. Lawn seed and weeds grow together to become a durable lawn when they're cut and watered enough.

17. For multi-unit properties, most of your inside fix-up work should be done as the units become vacant. This will happen when you raise rents! You should begin to increase your rents after the outside painting is done and the yards start looking nice. Your original tenants will begin moving away, one by one, until you have new ones. This process is what I call tenant cycling! Multi-unit fix-up jobs normally take about a year to 18 months when you do it this way!

18. Exterior painting can make a drastic difference in the looks of any property. I recommend medium quality exterior latex. Use a light color for the main body of the house, with darker trim

color. With off-white or tan, almost any trim color goes well. The trim can be doors, window surrounding and the fascia or eave board. A two-color combination is very attractive. Painting the exterior is the first thing you should do because it immediately changes the character of the property from a dirty dingy mess to clean attractive property! This change needs to be done quickly so everyone – tenants, passersby, and potential customers, get used to seeing the "new look"!

19. Most rehabbers and most all contractors will save the painting until last! They do all repairs inside first – then paint the exterior as their last parting effort. To everyone who observes the property, it continues to look ugly no matter how much work you do inside. People don't see inside – they judge the property on how it looks outside. This sequence is very important, **so get it right**! Don't forget, we're in the profit-making business!

20. Old dilapidated garages, carports, and storage sheds can be made to look attractive by installing new light-weight metal pull-up garage doors and exterior paneling (wood or Masonite). Do this on the front only or whichever side shows! Old-style heavy wooden doors with those hard to adjust springs and bent hardware should be junked. The idea is to fix up the building enough to have a nice exterior appearance. **That's the goal here!** Tenants like garages, not for their car – mind you! *They love to store junk.* The good news is that most renters are willing to pay $35-40 per month additional rent to have a garage. As a landlord, I like that for two reasons. First, *it's the money*, of course. Secondly, *if they don't have a garage, the junk will end up all over the yard instead.* With garages you can always persuade tenants to keep their stuff inside or face a rent increase! **Ya got it!**

OVER FIXING IS DEADLIEST SIN

The difference between "successful fixers" and those who have difficulty figuring things out, financially speaking, is learning **where** and **how** to end a fixer project! Fixing rundown properties can cost you all the money you have today – plus, every dime you earn in the future. However, it doesn't have to be that way. Don't forget, it's not much fun fixing up junky houses and fiddling with deadbeat tenants if you don't get paid well. **Over-fixing is the most common problem you must guard against.** By far, the most difficult group of investors for me to teach is building contractors. Contractors are taught from day one of their contractor education that buildings must be plumb and dry rot must be annihilated from the face of the planet! Technically they are correct; however, nobody said we're living in a perfect world?

ALLOW ME TO REPEAT MYSELF ABOUT LOOKS

Fixer properties should always be fixed outside before inside. The reason: potential customers (tenants and buyers) judge a property on the basis of what they see when they drive by. Doing fix-up where the property is located on a main thoroughfare or a heavily traveled road – what everyone sees is even more important. You must always remember, the world judges almost everything on how it looks! That definitely includes ugly houses and apartments!

THE PROPER SEQUENCE FOR HOUSE FIXIN'

Forget any nonsense about introducing yourself the first day you arrive at your newly acquired fixer property. The tenants couldn't care less about who you are or where you came from. *In fact*, some would be tickled pink if you dropped dead! You need to understand that junky properties and uncaring tenants go together. They know you'll likely make some changes, *but most of all they can smell a rent increase coming before you ever arrive.* Even if that's not your plan, people instinctively resist change, even though your goal is to improve their living conditions! Your best introduction to the property is to leap out of your pickup and begin cleaning up the mess! *That's the only introduction you'll ever need!*

What I'm about to tell you next is one of my most valuable house fixer tips! You should remember this well because if you'll do what

I'm suggesting here, you'll save yourself tons of grief – plus you'll make better allies of all your tenants instead of having to work around uncooperative deadbeats! **Don't even begin to think about rent increases until you've done something that benefits each of your new tenants.** What do I mean, you're probably wondering? Fix the leaky faucets, repair the window locks, and replace those two burners on Jeff's stove top the former owner promised him months ago. You might even toss in a partial paint job or a new bedroom carpet (cheap carpet, of course). The point is – make 'em smile – and win them over. **You'll win a whole lot more tenant battles with love than with your new set of rules.** I've seen the most obnoxious tenant you can ever imagine melt like warm butter after I repaired his non-working fan and installed new guts in his toilet so it quit running water all night!

FIX-UP SPENDING NEEDN'T BE ALL AT ONCE

Doing fix-up the way I recommend is always ongoing – *it never ends.* Naturally, there's a significant economic benefit for doing fix-up my way! *You don't need a ton of money saved up to begin with*! If you begin by working on **safety problems inside – and improving the looks outside**, you'll find as I have, the less urgent stuff, *plus other improvements you are planning*, can be scheduled over a longer period of time. This method will allow you to partially fund your improvements with cash flow coming in from **rents** and **vacancy fill-ups**. Many fix-up investors, especially contractors, mistakenly believe you must fix up everything in one big expensive splurge! **That's not true!** When you do it my way, *one phase at a time*, you can reduce the heavy strain on your *Visa card.*

There are some folks who believe that fixing rundown houses is a job that only experienced carpenters or contractors can do. Nothing could be further from the truth. Almost anyone can do this job! In the final analysis, it matters very little who performs the physical "fix-up" work, so long as **the right things get done** and **at the right cost**!

Investors who do their own fix-up work can enjoy a money saving advantage if they'll fix the **right things** at the **right time**. Both are equally important! As you shall learn with experience, **knowledge** is what earns the big money. Swinging a hammer or swishing a paintbrush will merely earn you average wages and save you money when you can't afford to pay someone else.

WHO NEEDS A LICENSE ANYWAY

Frequently I'm asked two questions about fix-up: first, does fixing up houses require any special licenses or professional skills? Second, do you feel it's best for new (start-out) investors to do their own fix-up work on the properties?

As a general rule, **no licenses are required** by owners who fix up properties for themselves. However, if you do it for someone else – for example, as an employee or independent contractor, that's different! It's very likely you will need a license to be perfectly legal. However, my books are not exactly the best source of information on doing everything perfectly legal. After all, you've never seen a rich cop, have you?

Having fix-up skills can certainly be a big advantage because it's one less thing you'll need to learn about; and of course, you can save yourself the cost of hiring outside labor! But having said that, let me tell you something you should immediately underline, and never forget! It's very important to your success!

BIG PAYDAYS DO NOT COME FROM FIX-UP SKILLS. THEY COME FROM REAL ESTATE SKILLS AND SPECIALIZED FINANCIAL KNOWLEDGE.

When I first began fixing rundown houses, I had no idea how important this really was. It took me several years of hard work before I began to understand. To illustrate my point, just think about all the thousands of licensed building contractors who can do almost anything to a building – they have plenty of skills. Now try and think about what most of them don't have plenty of; if you answered **money**, you're right! Believe me when I tell you, fixing skills alone are not enough if you intend to make **the big money** in this business. Still, I don't want you to quickly decide that fixing rundown houses is not for you simply because you can't make a toilet stop running. Just let the damn thing run for a while, while you study my chapters on **financing** and **arranging your financial affairs**! When you understand the dollar numbers and how to negotiate high profit deals, it won't be long before you can hire the highest paid plumber in your town. **I'll betcha ya never dreamed you'd be takin' financial lessons from a high school dropout, now did ya?**

FREE BONUS:

4 Free Copies
Fixer Jay's TRADE SECRETS Newsletter
How-To Secrets for Investors & Landlords

INCLUDES: Jay's "Christmas Letter"
How to Create Profitable Sales Directly with
Sellers & Avoid Outside Competition

---

1. **Seller Financing By Design**
   *Creative Terms Set Stage for Cash
   Flow Now - Then Future Profits*

2. **Buying Debt – A High Profit Strategy**
   *Fix-Up Investors Can Improve Cash
   Flow 30-50%*

3. **Investing Works in Boom or Bust**
   *Success Is About Investor Skills - Not
   Timing or Location*

4. **How to Earn $100,000 Annually**
   *Financial Security Comes from Choosing
   Right Property (Vehicle)*

Go to: www.fixerjay.com/bonus

CHAPTER 15

CHOOSIN' YOUR FISHIN' GUIDE

Real estate agents are the eyes and ears of the real estate business! I'd be hard pressed indeed to think of any successful investors I know who got that way without benefiting from their services! At least 50% of all my business over many years has been directly involved with real estate agents who were paid to make the transactions happen. I've had several situations where an agent referral about a non-listed property, or a special tip about an owner who needed to sell, was all it took to create a big payday for me. Don't get me wrong here; this is not some hyped-up promotion for real estate agents. I'm just saying we need them for the investment business we're in!

More than once I've heard so-called real estate gurus tell their audiences that an excellent strategy or technique for getting rich is to completely avoid paying commissions! Certainly I'm not one to recommend throwing your money away, but I must tell you here and now – paying commissions should be helping you make more money; otherwise you need to re-think your investment plan. Even in the worst-case situation for me, assuming I paid a full 06% commission, I would still have 94% of the value left for me! I'd also get all the benefits from acquiring a high-profit property. To me, that doesn't seem like such a bad trade-off! **Agreed!**

SAVING COMMISSIONS IS PENNYWISE, BUT POUND FOOLISH

Right about now someone always asks me —- Why would you give a tinker's damn about paying commissions when you are buying properties? After all, they point out – it's really the seller who pays commissions! Technically, that's true, but you mustn't forget who's putting up all the money to close the deal. The seller can't pay one lousy nickel's worth of commission until the buyer agrees to pony up the money! Real estate agents account for approximately 95% of all the real estate sales; therefore, anyone who thinks going around or bypassing agents is good business, needs to rethink the issue. In my own case, I would have nowhere near the amount of properties I own if it weren't for my two real estate helpers – Merv and Fred. These two agent-brokers have been involved in about 60% of all my activity, both buying and selling. **Believe me, in this business you'll need help if you expect to make some serious money anytime soon**!

Personally, I stand ready, willing, and able to pay real estate commissions (even full commissions) if agents bring me good deals. Real estate wealth has nothing to do with "stiffing agents." In fact, just the opposite is true! If you get the reputation for being a "tightwad," you could possibly lose out on valuable tips and attractive deals simply because the agents don't want anything to do with you. When you think about licensed real estate agents, consider reversing the chairs for a moment! How much effort would you spend with a client who thinks you don't deserve to be paid? **See how easy the answer comes!**

Enough kisses and bouquets for the agents, now let's "rip 'em" apart! First of all, no agent alive will make you rich! The fact is; no other person can do that for you unless of course, you're lucky enough to inherit your fortune from them. Here's the bottom line: if you seek wealth and riches, **it's up to you**! You alone are the driving force to make it happen. It's you who must make the right decisions to get you there. However, real estate agents can be powerful helpers if you'll teach them what you want done! More specifically, you must give them clear instructions about what constitutes a good deal for you. They must be properly instructed on what you will buy when they find it – *and of course*, how fast can you close the deal so they can get paid!

MEETING YOUR AGENT FACT TO FACE

The best way to begin your search for Mr. or Mrs. Right is to visit local real estate offices in the area where you plan to invest. Ask the receptionist if she knows which agent sells the most apartment buildings or rental income properties. Get yourself introduced and tell the agent exactly what you're trying to accomplish. The interview will be your opportunity to learn what the agent thinks he can do for you! **Always remember: he must know exactly what you want done in order to respond in a meaningful way**.

Much like a budding romance, the first thing that has to work is chemistry! It will do you no good in the long run to force yourself into working with an agent who disgusts you, no matter how good you think he or she might be. Obnoxious agents are best left to work with *obnoxious house buyers*, since there's no shortage or either one. I mention this because it's very important to develop a relationship that can last for a long time. Lasting together is much easier when you like each other. I've had only two agents in the past 45 years. Merv passed away and along came Fred.

If you're a beginner just starting out your search for an agent, or you're relatively new to investing, you'll need a more experienced agent to help you. I'd suggest you seek out an agent whose specialty is income property or investment sales. In the smaller offices, agents will take on everything that comes through the door. Many times you'll find the most experienced agents working by themselves in these smaller offices. Larger firms always have a ton of new agents cycling through the learning process to get experience.

If you concentrate your efforts, it shouldn't take you too long to find an agent who appears to be more interested than the others. He or she will begin calling you more and likely bring you a few deals to look at! If a special interest begins to develop – it's just possible you may have found yourself the right agent. If not, keep repeating this same process till you do. Finding a good agent is not a whole lot different than finding a good wife or husband. It's simply a matter of "weeding 'em out" till you find one who starts kissing back!

Naturally, the worst part will be breaking the ice – introducing yourself to complete strangers who you hope might be able to help you. I don't know of any way to short-cut this procedure, so it's best to simply charge ahead and get it done! When you eventually find an agent who appreciates your goals and is willing to spend time helping you achieve them, you'll begin to realize you've added a powerful new tool to your wealth-building kit!

Real estate agents are the eyes and ears of the real estate business! About 95% of all sales and trades involve licensed sales agents and their brokers. It would be very foolish indeed to harbor any serious notions about excluding them from your investment plans. The best thing you can do for yourself is to diligently begin searching to find a good one.

AGENTS MUST EARN A LIVING LIKE YOU

Before I get started on the reasons why selecting the right agent is so important, first let me discuss the issue of commissions. **Commissions are what agents earn when they help you buy and sell real estate!** You must first understand that there is no such thing as a standard one-size-fits-all commission! They come in all different flavors.

For example, in my town, most agents charge about 6% for selling houses. However, that's not basically the market I'm part of. House buyers generally represent a one-time "Wam-Bam" transaction for most agents. On the flip side, I'm a buyer and sometimes a seller anytime a worthwhile deal pops up! Unlike the guy who buys a house and that's it – I'm good for many transactions. **Naturally, I represent a far greater source of income for my agent.**

Understandably, agents can work for smaller percentage commissions when **multiple transactions** are anticipated! To give you an idea of what I'm saying here, I'll share my own experience. The average commission I've paid for all my transactions during the past 45 years is slightly less than 3% of the purchase price. That's roughly half of the *so-called* going rate in my town. I find it's best to negotiate the commission fee in advance of every deal I do. Just remember, it must be fair for the amount of work your agent does.

Agents won't hang around long if you're simply a *looky-loo*. That's a person who wants to see everything, but never buys anything because nothing ever seems to be what he wants. No agent worth his salt can afford to fiddle around with a "fuzzy-eyed" investor like that! Fred works for me for one simple reason – **it's profitable!** He knows I can close fast if he does his job. Fred's job is to know exactly what I will buy so he doesn't waste time calling me about every property that pops up for a sale! A trained agent will immediately qualify the property to determine if it has the potential I'm looking for! Fred knows already I don't generally want properties where new bank financing is required. He also knows I'm looking for sellers who will carry financing or at least part of it! I've told Fred I'm especially looking for properties with 5 to 12 units on a larger lot! When Fred hears about these properties, *he knows exactly what to do and who to call.*

TRAINING YOUR AGENT HELPS YOU

Fred's job is to learn everything he can about the property. I want to know if the seller is having any sort of financial difficulty. Does he live out of town? Is the property being managed for him? Are unruly tenants causing the owner problems? Fred tries to determine if there are serious reasons for the seller to be motivated to sell – i.e. retirement, going broke, bad health, poor management, dying, etc. *These are the things Fred will be looking for!* Its detective work, like Lieutenant Columbo does on TV. Fred obtains a property profile from the title company and asks for copies of all deeds of trusts (mortgages) on the property. He verifies rents, vacancies, and liens – *and finally*, he uses my INVESTMENT PROPERTY ANALYSIS FORM (See Appendix C) to finalize the information. All this stuff takes time and it costs Fred money. The only way he gets paid is when I buy the property.

Fred doesn't make very many dry runs. He knows what I want and determines quickly if a property has the **right stuff**. How did Fred get so smart, you ask? Where did he learn all this detective stuff anyway? When Fred and I first started working together, we spent a lot of time discussing what I wanted! **Investors must be very clear with agents**

about which properties they'll likely buy or least write an offer on when it comes along; otherwise, agents will quickly become discouraged and tell you to "buzz off!" It gets even worse when they're mad!

Once again, I strongly recommend that all new investors simply walk in the door at several different realty offices. Sit down with any agent who introduces himself and tell him or her exactly what kind of properties you would like to acquire. Some agents will jump through hoops to help you. Others will shine you on. As with any meeting, personalities will always play a role. Some people will like you – others won't. Just remember, both of you will be learning from each other!

WORKING WITH MULTIPLE LISTINGS

Only licensed real estate agents have access to the multiple-listing service. That's the reason I never tell anyone how I get mine! I'm mostly interested in the older listings or what most agents call – *seasoned listings*! It's perfectly okay with me if they're six months old or even a year or two for that matter! **Here's why!**

First, you need to understand that most *income properties* in the multiple-listing service would have already sold before they ever got there if they were truly bargains! If they're really good deals – they'll be sold by listing agents before they ever reach the multiple listing service. What you will generally find in the multiple listings are overpriced apartments and "dog properties" that the owner can't sell without lots of help!

The multiple service agreement provides for selling agents to split the commission with the listing office when a sale takes place. Obviously, for a property owner the multiple-listing service provides the maximum exposure for his property, because every licensed agent is a potential seller. The real value to me is keeping an eye on properties that stay in the multiple listing for long periods of time, at least six months, sometimes several years. Sellers who can't sell in that length of time often become *extremely motivated*! Offers they would have never considered when they originally listed their property somehow become much more acceptable after a long dry spell without any offers!

I've had pretty good luck buying properties that nobody seems to want from the older (seasoned) multiple listings. On several occasions, I found old listings that had already expired and I was able to purchase directly from highly motivated sellers. Picture yourself in the seller's position; if you can't sell your property in six months with all the exposure of the multiple-listing service, obviously, more drastic measures are called for. **Usually it's lowering the price and offering better terms.** I've done approximately 10-15% of my business as a result of tracking down these older multiple listings. I consider it well worth my time and efforts.

BENEFITS A GOOD AGENT PROVIDES

Once you find an agent who seems like he or she talks your language – and of course, demonstrates they are truly interested, say like jumping in quickly and finding you several properties that seem to fit what you're looking for – you'll be off to a running start.

One thing to remember here – both you and your agent are new to each other! *Don't make the agent do all the work.* You should help every way you can, especially while you're in the "getting acquainted" mode. For example, if the agent is showing you properties in "top notch" condition and you've already told him you want rundown junkers, reiterate your instructions and make sure he understands! By helping your agent, who in turn is trying to help you – **you'll end up helping yourself the most**!

The benefits you'll receive by taking enough time to develop this relationship will be worth big bucks to you over the long haul! Following are five of the most valuable benefits to me!

1. Your agent will have **immediate "pipeline" knowledge** about when a bargain property is first listed for sale – either as a member of the multiple listing service or by networking through his associates and contacts. You'll get this information quickly so you can write up an offer fast, assuming the property is what

you're looking for. **Being first to know about the property is very important!**

2. A good agent will do **"weeding out" for you automatically** once he or she becomes accustomed to what you really want. My agent, Fred, always brings me everything I need to know for making an educated evaluation about the property. The information Fred provides is normally a property profile, *copies of existing promissory notes,* and either a filled out INCOME PROPERTY ANALYSIS FORM (see Appendix C), or at least the necessary information to fill the form out. This is valuable "time saving" work for an investor – **yet it's needed before any intelligent buying decision can be made.** Obviously, it moves Fred into a quicker commission if I'm able to purchase the property.

3. My agent provides **a middle-man "buffer" between the buyer and seller**. This is a valuable service to me or any real estate investor who owns several properties already. "Mom and Pop" real estate owners (the folks I buy most properties from) will often feel intimidated negotiating with me one-on-one. They seem to feel that because I own a number of income properties and because I appear to be successful, they'll automatically end up on the short end of the stick! It's a perception that's hard to work around, regardless of whether it's true or not. Fred can generally diffuse this problem by stepping in as a neutral third party. Sellers often feel that a licensed professional will be much more sensitive to their needs, as opposed to negotiating with a "ring-savvy" buyer.

4. **A good agent will never let his commission block a sale!** The good ones are always creative! Often they'll take a fraction of what they have coming in order to close the sale. Good agents will allow you to pay the balance later on, *perhaps making monthly payments*. My first agent, Merv, would allow me to pay him 50% of his commission at closing, and on the balance, he agreed to take promissory notes, anywhere from $50 to $250 per month, *depending on my projected cash flow*. At one point I was paying monthly commissions of $1750 per month to Merv. In addition to helping me, Merv was very happy to have the steady monthly

income, plus the 8% interest he normally earned on his notes.

5. **A good agent can put you in contact with money lenders**, both the private "hard money" guys and institutional lenders with special loan programs that might just fit what you're doing. Many lenders shop real estate offices looking for qualified borrowers who might become future customers. This can be a valuable benefit for investors who are always in need of money for upgrading and acquiring more properties. Naturally, you and your project will need to qualify in order to take advantage here. **Still, money is always the ammunition that keeps us investors in the hunt.**

As you might guess, benefits must always flow both ways between an investor and his agent! Never forget the person who helps you become rich – **it's a two-way street.** Here's what you need to do to help your agent if you're serious about developing a profitable relationship!

A. **Don't chippy around!** Use your agent for all your transactions unless you have some special agreement or exception you've both agreed upon. **Loyalty will move mountains.**

B. **Don't try to squeeze the commissions.** If you are like me, that is, you wish to negotiate commissions, **do it before the agent goes to work** – not after the deal is written up and already in escrow.

C. **Don't' send agents on "wild goose" chases.** The veterans will dump you if you try – *but don't even do it to the inexperienced dummies.* They'll soon catch on and will have nothing more to do with you. I've heard several *"so-called"* real estate seminar gurus instruct their listeners to have their agent draft up and present or mail out "low-ball" *shotgun offers* to purchase every property in the multiple-listing book. Ask any respectable agent what he thinks of this advice! **Take it from me**; don't waste your agent's time with such nonsense.

D. **Don't make a ton of offers without ever closing anything.** No agent can survive without "paydays" *same as you.* Take better aim and hit the target – **close some deals –okay!**

E. When other real estate agents call you direct – **always refer them to your agent**. Naturally, some sellers will insist on dealing direct. They don't want any agents involved, period! That's fine, but tell your own agent about the exception. Sometimes I pay Fred a small fee, $500-$1500, to help me do the background legwork. **If you take good care of your agent, you will always benefit the most in the long run, believe me!**

WHAT ABOUT AGENTS WHO
SHOP FOR THEMSELVES

I sometimes hear seminar instructors advise new investors to seek out real estate agents who buy and sell properties for their personal investment accounts. They explain that an agent with this kind of experience will be able to serve you better since he knows the ropes! To me, this advice is akin to leaving your fiancée at an all-night bachelor party, with your friends hoping they'll take good care of her!

I can see no advantage to having my own agent competing with me to acquire bargain properties. I once accused Fred of doing exactly that. We were both looking over the numbers on a small (HUD) subsidized apartment building for sale, when suddenly and unexpectedly I had to leave town for a week. When I returned, Fred had already purchased the building. He claimed, since I hadn't told him I was interested just yet, he just assumed I wasn't. What Fred couldn't explain very well, however, was why he didn't wait until I returned home before he opened the escrow. Suddenly, he began treating me extra-special nice! He even bought me lunches for a year or so trying to make me forget. Eventually I did!

AGENTS CAN NEGOTIATE MORE IMPARTIALLY

Negotiating to purchase real estate can be a downright intimidating experience for new investors, especially the weak hearted! *Worse yet*, the results can end up a total disaster, leaving both parties wondering exactly what went wrong! What mostly goes wrong is that emotions become involved. Poor communication skills are often the biggest problem! Sometimes personalities clash, making it nearly impossible for either side to stay objective. For these reasons, **a good third party real estate agent**, who is knowledgeable about the deal, can be worth his weight in gold or at least a reasonable commission!

More than three centuries ago, Sir Francis Bacon wrote an essay, *Of Negotiating*, in which he advised: "It is generally better to deal by mediation of a third than by man's self. Use bold men for expostulation, fair-spoken men for persuasion, crafty men for inquiry and observation, forward and absurd men for business that doth not well bear out itself – in all negotiations of difficulty, a man may not look to sow and reap at once."

Fred often deals with sellers who have over-financed their real estate by paying too much in the first place or by adding additional borrowing during their ownership. Regardless of the reason, it hardly matters, because these sellers are not in a financial position to make us a very good deal! The only way they could make a deal would be to pay down the existing debt or to pay me money to take over their property! Obviously, these are not very attractive options for most sellers. The simple truth is, when too much money is already owed on a property, it can rarely be a good deal for me or anyone else! Fred has learned not to waste much time fiddling with deals that don't show us a clear path for making decent profits.

Properties that have been owned by sellers for a substantial period of time, *say 10 to 20 years for example*, will offer far greater opportunities for negotiating a reasonable selling price. The reason for this is because the existing mortgage debt has most likely been paid down over the years. It's much easier to negotiate a reasonable purchase price when the seller has substantial equity in the property.

TRAINING YOUR AGENT TO BE SNOOPY

The very first thing we do when either Fred or I hear about a property that's suddenly available, assuming I'm interested of course, is to begin what I call "detective work!" Fred will usually perform this task. Remember, it took him four years with my coaching before he became snoopy (skilled) enough to suit my taste. Brokers and sales agents typically don't do the exhaustive research or "snooping around" like I insist having done.

The biggest difference between Fred and most other agents is that they accept the word of sellers as being mostly true! I convinced Fred to accept their word as being mostly exaggerated and generally untrue! **It's never considered true until it's proven to me.** I'm not trying to be overly critical here, but you must never forget this important rule of an investor's life.

> **Once the escrow closes and everybody gets paid, it's you alone, all by yourself, who must live with the deal you signed! If for some reason you've failed to uncover the true property expenses and it turns out they're considerably higher than you were led to believe, guess what? It's you alone who have now become the STUCKEE!**

That's the reason I taught Fred how to become a very snoopy house detective and its paid big dividends for me since he's learned how.

TOOLS REQUIRED FOR PERFORMING DETECTIVE WORK

The first thing we (Fred or myself) do is visit the local title company, where we do most of our business. We request a parcel map, the tax roll, and copies of all the deeds or mortgages recorded on the property. Many title companies provide this service free for their repeat customers and **to real estate agents**. Some folks refer to this information as a PROPERTY PROFILE. It's the best way to start your file on any property you have an interest in owning, because these few documents will provide you with most of the following information:

A. A parcel map gives you lot size and often shows easements and right-of-ways.

B. The tax roll shows who owns the property and where the current tax bill is being mailed each year. It will also show you how much the taxes are now and how much value the county assessor has appraised the land, improvements (buildings) and personal property for (dollar amounts).

C. Additionally, with the parcel map and tax roll you can also find out who owns the properties around the parcel you're investigating.

D. Copies of trust deeds or mortgages will show the amount of debt against the property at the time of the last sale or transfer of title. It also shows who owes the debt (trustor) and who receives it (beneficiary). *For trust deed states,* the due-on-sale clauses normally show up on trust deeds also. Obviously, deeds or mortgages are part of the chain of title with recording dates and notarized signatures.

E. The documentary transfer tax, which is a state tax on the sale of real property and is based on selling price or equity transferred, is generally stamped on the grant deed. The current California tax is $1.10 per $1000 of property transferred. When you have a copy of the grant deed, you can easily determine what the current owner paid for the property. For example, if the documentary tax is $55.00, computed on the full value, then the purchase price would be $50,000 ($55,000 divided by $1.10 = $50,000). Sometimes knowing what the owner paid can help you develop your offer to purchase. Sellers dislike offers for less than what they paid, no matter how motivated they are. Always keep this in mind when negotiating your deals.

KNOWLEDGE ABOUT PROPERTY
AND SELLER IMPORTANT

Even motivated sellers are not generally "stupid idiots" like many "fly by night" seminar gurus might lead you to believe. Mostly they're just folks who've gotten themselves in a financial bind. Also, high on the list motivated sellers are folks who for whatever reason are lousy landlords. Their tenants are driving them "bonkers." I've purchased several properties from sellers who were actually afraid to drive me out to their property for a showing. **Their own renters frightened them**! Having this kind of information is extremely helpful to me when I'm negotiating to purchase a property.

I hope I've convinced you – that if you intend to be a successful real estate investor, it makes little sense whatsoever to "shut out" the professionals, the local real estate offices. Most people with real estate to sell will ultimately list their property with licensed agents. That's who mainly gets the selling job accomplished; therefore, **you must have a contact**. Do this by developing a relationship with a good sales person in an office that subscribes to the multiple-listing service. That gives you access to virtually every property that becomes available in every real estate office in your area.

As I told you earlier, it will pay you to be loyal to the agent or sales person you pick! **Always remember this** – your goals are to make profits and build personal wealth. Your real estate agent will have similar goals with respect to his commissions. Just think of how much money you'll make for yourself if you're able to make your agent rich by acquiring profitable deals from him. Never lose sight of the fact: **good relationships are a two-way street**. Once again I'll repeat myself, **always take good care of those who help you make it.**

JUST HOW VALUABLE IS A GOOD AGENT?

Approximately 60% of all my transactions involve real estate agents. If you count *telephone tips* and indirect help, agents may be involved 70-75% of the time. Can you imagine how much it would have stymied my personal wealth had I avoided using agents? **It translates to several million dollars!** *There is simply no way to become a wealthy investor in a reasonable period of time without help.* A trained real estate agent working with you doesn't cost you money – **he or she makes you money! Train them well, and they'll make you rich!** Enough said already, it's now up to you! Find yourself a fishing guide and let's get on with the fishin'!

CHAPTER 16

FISHIN' WITH A PARTNER

*M*y personal investment strategy has constantly changed over the years as I've discovered what works, what doesn't, and how to "tighten up" my deals to maximize cash flow. I've always felt that investing alone is better than splitting the pie and sharing my profits! However, I've had several excellent partnership ventures over the years and I must tell you, when they work, you can achieve your financial goals many times faster than doing deals alone! But remember, I said **when they work**, and that's the tricky part – don't ever forget it.

There is only one good reason I know of to take on an investment partner. It's when you don't have enough financial horsepower to do the total deal by yourself. In other words, you need some help! Most often, it's financial assistance you need. However, there might be other legitimate reasons. We'll discuss a couple as we go along. Equity sharing and time-share contracts are two examples of partnership investing. Both arrangements are specifically designed for investors who can't purchase the whole "enchilada" themselves, or at least they don't think they can!

SELECTING A PARTNER FOR THE RIGHT REASONS

If you are fortunate enough to choose the right kind of partner and make it work – partnership investing can speed up your financial plans and help you reach goals much quicker than investing alone. However, the downside of selecting someone who doesn't work out can be a serious setback for even the best of plans. You must not take the selection process lightly.

Partnerships are like marriages – there are some good ones that last a lifetime and many that don't last till they're paid for! Like marriages, partnerships stand a much better chance of working and lasting if the partners are selected for the right reasons. When I talk about partnership investing, I'm not necessarily meaning you should form a legal partnership. I'm talking co-ownership or two investors owning real estate together for the purpose of making money. One of the biggest reasons that small-time investors end up filthy rich is because they learn how to use the powerful law of leverage. It is written that the Greek mathematician who discovered leverage once claimed he could lift the entire world all by himself, with a long enough lever and a place to stand. Real estate investors can do exactly the same thing with the assistance of other people's money or physical skills.

Many small investment partnerships are created almost entirely on the basis of friendships between people who work together, attend the same clubs and churches, or perhaps enjoy the same social activities. Regardless of what mutual involvement brings folks together initially, partnerships founded solely on the basis of friendships are most likely doomed to fail from the very start. No matter how compatible people might seem to be as friends and social acquaintances, they will almost always change when their money or labor becomes involved. The selection process is without doubt the most important consideration for developing a lasting and profitable partnership. Individual needs, contibutions, and skills must be considered and balanced effectively, but the selection process deserves by far the most thought. It's much too important for quick decisions or snap judgments. Get rich schemes with little thought are generally predictable failures from the very beginning.

PARTNERS NEEDN'T BE BEST FRIENDS

Contrary to a popular myth shared by many, investment partners need not be good friends to be successful partners. It might help a little getting started, but it's simply not a requirement. Obviously, enjoying the same social activities has nothing to do with a profitable real estate partnership. My number one consideration for establishing a strong and lasting partnership has to do with my own *self-interest*. Do I really care if my investment partner gets rich? **I certainly do** – *but only on the condition that I get rich too*! If it sounds like Greed Provides the Need, then so be it! Let me caution you here, don't let your mind wander or overact! Just think about what I'm telling you. Later on, I believe you'll understand why partnerships will turn out better with this kind of thinking.

My "no compromise" business rule for finding an investor with money when I need financial help is the same rule I use for landlording. *It's called my 60/40 rule*. It means I'm willing to give more than I take! Here's the way I apply it to partnership investing.

I've always felt that broke investors should be willing to give up at least 60% of the co-ownership benefits in order to attract the money. This means if I'm the broke partner, I'll be content with taking 40% of the deal for myself. Always ask yourself this question about the partnership. Who could most likely make it on their own – *the partner with the money or the one without*? Don't over-analyze my question here! I think it's quite clear, considering all things equal – the party with the money will always have a much greater opportunity than the one who's broke – if you're not sure, just go ahead and agree anyway!

PARTNERSHIPS CAN SOLVE
YOUR MONEY PROBLEMS

Developing partnerships to pool individual resources, knowledge, and experience can provide an excellent vehicle for acquiring wealth at a much faster pace than would otherwise be possible. I've discovered that in most successful partnerships, the partners themselves will often have very little in common with each other except their desire to make money together. Sometimes an accountant will team up with a carpenter or handyman. A doctor might select a contractor or a schoolteacher with some extra hours. A person with mechanical skills might work very well with a real estate broker. Sometimes the best way to find investment partners with the particular qualifications you need is by advertising in the HELP WANTED ADS of your local newspaper.

Many folks would like to create a profitable partnership, but don't have any idea where to start! The first thing you must determine is – *what you can provide to the partnership*! Will it be **investment capital**, **your time**, or some specialized skills you possess? Write it down on paper, and then advertise for a partner. There are many people looking for what you have to offer, but they don't know you exist so they can't respond. You must "speak up" and let them know!

The biggest problem I've observed about these small investment partnerships is that they are almost always engineered or thought up by the partner who doesn't have any money! This person has all sorts of wonderful ideas, but in order to make them work, he must find someone with a few dollars in their purse. The typical arrangement I see is where one partner is asked to **put up hard cash** and the other is supposed to contribute an equivalent share of **personal service**.

I don't know how you think, but let me share my own thoughts – **I'm very skeptical about anyone who proposes a joint venture using my money, while risking only personal services themselves**. My first question to anyone who proposes using my money goes like this: *if you're so smart and if your ideas are so good, then why is it I've got the money and you don't*? There are several good answers to this question, which I will consider reasonable and acceptable, but unless the question gets answered to my full satisfaction, I will not consider going forward and neither should you!

THE COURTING PERIOD REQUIRES HONESTY

The biggest mistake that no-money partners make while trying to entice a money person is to **over-sell** and very often, **overstate** the benefits the money partner is supposed to receive. If I were to show you all the proposals offered to me, and if we added up all the profits I've been promised, backed up with several boxes of computer spread sheets I was given, I would need to rent the Bank of America headquarters building to store all my money. Fortunately, or *unfortunately*, whichever way you view it, I did not invest my money, so I'll never really know for sure! I can tell you this much however: a very high percentage of those proposals went bust!

Since I have experience on both sides of the partnership investing team, i.e. the broke party and the one with money, I feel qualified to pass on a few tips that can help you structure a partnership which might just survive the high fatality rate. Because there are so many more want-to-be investors without any money, I'll concentrate on helping no-money partners first.

In the beginning, the money partner is always the most important member of your investment team. It's called "The Golden Rule" of investing. **He who's got the gold always rules**. Look at the situation like this and ask yourself: who do you think might be more successful acquiring real estate – a rich investor who's a lousy painter and don't know a toilet from a vacuum cleaner – or a self-taught handyman without any money who paints well and knows that toilets are supposed to run downhill? My question was not meant to be a quiz, but rather a pointed reminder that *money always makes things happen faster* – the opposite doesn't.

Years ago, my fascination with retailing and entrepreneuring took me into the world of "Women's Fashion." I incorrectly thought my sweet lady friends and the people I knew quite well would be the first ones through my door to support me. How wrong I was! The only time I saw my friends in the store was on "Super Sale" days or when they wanted me to order something for them wholesale. People who made my store successful and kept the registers ringing were total strangers! They wanted what I had to offer and were willing to pay me for it. **It was a very valuable lesson.**

It works exactly the same way with real estate partnerships! Your best bet is to find a partner who can give the partnership something you can't provide – either the money or the skills and "know-how" to operate the property. Also, you want a partner with a strong desire to make money for himself, because in doing so, he or she will automatically make money for you! **Perfect strangers** are more apt to be better business partners than friends, I've found!

PARTNERS WORK BEST WITH SEPARATE SKILLS

Partnerships originated solely on the basis of friendships are seldom very well thought out and most always lack the key ingredients absolutely essential for any kind of success! You might be thinking right about now – what's with Jay and all this *ingredient baloney*? Does he think we're learning to be "fry cooks"? Okay friends, let me be as serious as a heart attack here – **be very careful**! If you're half asleep right now and somehow miss my message here and get yourself hooked up in a bum relationship with a shyster partner or a *street-wise deadbeat*, "fry cooking" will seem quite heavenly by comparison.

Keep in mind here, we're talking about **small-time investment partnerships or co-investors**! The kind typically associated with *do-it-yourself investors*, generally involving two or sometimes three investors pooling their resources together. We're not discussing formal partnerships requiring separate federal tax reporting (1065 forms) and the equivalent state tax forms – although much of my basic wisdom can be applied to all partnerships and joint ventures!

I often make the analogy that small partnerships or co-investors work something like an electrical circuit – *that is*, electrical current only flows when there's a positive and negative side! No current will flow when both sides are equal or have the same potential as they call it. Small partnerships won't flow very well when duties are alike or the partners all do the same things! **What makes them work or flow well is having different responsibilities for each of the partners**. Let me explain!

LIKES MAY ATTRACT BUT SELDOM MAKE MONEY

Have you ever been around an amateur partnership or had the occasion to observe two investor buddies who both contribute $10,000 cash and agree to share all the painting and yard work on weekends? Usually things go well for a month or so, *then one weekend*, **partner A** doesn't show up to paint. He informs **partner B** that he always takes the kids to Disneyland for two weeks in the summer. At first, partner

B is only slightly disgruntled painting by himself; however, by the second week, he's downright mad. He expects partner A to do some makeup painting when his vacation is over, but instead, he only does one day of makeup and then misses the next weekend with the flu!

Both partners have $10,000 in the pot and they're both supposed to paint on weekends! They're both equal, they both perform the same tasks, and both share the same responsibilities. Remember the electrical current – *we don't want likes with the same responsibilities* – what we need is **unlikes** to make current flow. Thus, Jay's first rule for partnership investing is as follows:

> **Each partner must bring something different (contribution) to the partnership that the other partner needs but doesn't have! Partnerships seldom survive when all the partners are responsible for the same duties.**

Like all my teachings, my rules and techniques for investing with other people have been developed from my personal experiences over many years of trial and error. That means I've actually done this stuff and I'm not passing along ideas that might work just fine on a clear day in a perfect world! Friends, there ain't no such thing as far as I know, but even if there was, **partnership investing would still require the extra precautions**.

Attempting to convince others to trust you with their hard-earned dollars requires extra special skills. I think you can understand why co-investing and partnership arrangements are almost always horrible failures for **the naïve** and **inexperienced**. The following story will help you remember how easy it is to be deceived!

In the southwest plains, a young Indian boy climbed to the top of a very high mountain. There he found a rattlesnake shivering in the cold. The snake said to the boy, "Please put me under your shirt and take me down the mountain where I will be warm and comfortable. I promise you no harm." The young boy protested: "But you are a rattlesnake!

You will bite me and I will die." The snake promptly reassured the boy that he would not be harmed, so the boy then did as he was asked. When they finally reached the valley below, the boy reached into his shirt to bring out the snake and as he did so, the snake bit him! The young boy cried out: "But you promised not to harm me!" The snake calmly replied. "You knew I was a rattlesnake when you put me under your shirt. **You, not I, chose to ignore the danger!**"

Please don't conclude that all partnerships are bad and that co-investors and money partners are all *rattlesnakes*. It just ain't so! That sort of thinking would be something like the comments I often hear from property owners concerning their wayward tenants. Deadbeats, they claim, always have the upper hand in evictions because they know all the legal technicalities about stalling and staying in the house without paying rent. Certainly that's always a possibility, *of course*, but a far bigger problem that I observe, working with lots of stressed out owners – **it's their own lack of knowledge** that's causing most of their problems. Ignorance is causing the problem; likewise, ignorance can cause all sorts of problems with small-time partnerships for the very same reason.

I have written a great deal about my personal investment philosophy and the techniques I use – but I must tell you, nothing requires more planning or preparation than when you become a partner and take on responsibility for spending other people's money. Your plan must be well thought out, and when you make promises, **they must be kept**. If you "short change" your money partner, you've committed the most serious of partnership sins! You must do everything humanly possible to make sure your money investor gets what he or she is promised. Obviously, this is why **preparation** and **planning** are absolutely essential before you sign on to the deal.

A SIMPLE TWO-PARTY INVESTMENT PLAN

Partner A has money to invest. **Partner B** has the time and skills to operate a real estate investment. Let's suppose for a moment I'm Partner B. I'm looking for Partner A or "Mr. Money Bags" to put up

$25,000 for a down payment on the "Super Deal Apartments." I find "Mr. Money Bags"! He is willing to invest his money, but first he will need some assurance that I can operate the property and eventually turn a profit. He will need a satisfactory answer to four basic questions that any investor with money (Partner A) wants to know about the investment and his partner who will operate the property.

1. What's in the deal for me?
2. What is my risk if I invest $25,000?
3. What assurances do I have that Partner B can manage property?
4. What will Partner B lose (risk) if he or she can't manage the property?

Once negotiated, **everything the partners agree to must be formalized**. That means you need a written document, which I call "THE AGREEMENT." Do not operate your partnership business on verbal promises. You'll end up on the short end of the stick if you do. The agreement need not be the size of a Sears catalog for a small two-party association. However, you must "spell out" the terms of your acquisition. For example, how will you purchase the property? How much money will it cost? Who pays for what and when? You'll need a statement about the purpose of the partnership (what you're expecting to accomplish by investing together).

Next, you need to draft the rules for a CO-OWNERSHIP AGREE-MENT (see Appendix F). These are the important terms (rules) the partners must live by. When partners agree to invest their time, skills, and money to develop a good workable plan – you should write down the rules you'll conduct business by. **It's very important to have everything in writing; a good contract** is what protects the partners. My own co-ownership agreement is only three pages long with 14 terms or rules and it's held up very well for me over many years. By the way, one of my long-term partnerships (co-ownership partners) happens to be an attorney. Naturally he fiddled around with my wording, but basically kept it three pages long with my *14 original terms*. He added a few lawyerly words, but that's about all!

HE STOPPED LOVIN' ME TODAY

Although my co-ownership agreement is a *no-nonsense*, tightly drafted set of rules, some terms are much more important or carry heavier weight than others! Perhaps the granddaddy of all my 14 terms is the **termination clause** – or you may choose to call it: "The Buy-Sell Provision." You wanta know how in the world can I get outta this mess if my partnership love affair turns sour?

When you trap a rat in the room without cutting an escape hole in the baseboard – you leave the rat no alternative but to attack and possibly bite you! This happens all the time when small-time investors get mad at each other and wish to call it quits! Without a hole to escape, the partners have little choice but to fight each other in a lawsuit using up what little money or equity they may have accumulated. *Believe me*, calling each other nasty names in court is a "no win" situation for everybody! My agreement provides a nice big hole to escape for either party.

Termination or Buy-out Provision

This agreement shall terminate upon the sale to either party as follows:
(This is not the exact legal wording but you'll get the idea.)

Here's my own explanation: The party who wants out shall prepare an offer to purchase the property for *x number of dollars* and submit the offer to the other party. Upon receipt, the other partner will either accept the offer and notify his partner of acceptance – or prepare a counter-offer (higher bid) indicating his willingness to purchase the property. The first partner can accept the counter-offer or repeat the process by presenting a higher offer. Each offer and counter-offer shall be granted 10 days for acceptance. Finally, without a higher bid or counter-offer, and after 10 days have elapsed, the highest offer shall be deemed the winning offer. The buyer (winning offer) shall immediately open escrow and proceed to purchase the property within 30-90 days from the time of submitting the winning bid (final purchase offer).

As you can see, my **termination agreement** allows either party a fair and equitable way to end the partnership without going to court. A variation of this same procedure (opportunity for buy-out) is also included in my **Death of the Parties** provision, allowing this simple buy-out arrangement for terminating the partnership in case of a death.

My **Telephone Mentoring Service** provides me many challenging opportunities to help small partnerships with their struggles to *un-ring the bell*. Without any rules drawn up, and often without any documentation whatsoever, it's easy for both sides to make up their own rules as they go along. Thousands of dollars are wasted because no one has taken the time to initially set up the operating rules before jumping in bed with a total stranger (partner).

IT'S POSSIBLE TO SOAR WITH THE EAGLES – BUT!

Nothing in the world can add as much horsepower to your real estate investment program than a partner who's willing to pony up the money. Certainly, I'll be the first to agree that partnerships are tricky business, and I'm told that eight out of every 10 will fail. Still, I've experienced several good ones and although I completely acknowledge the high failure rate – **it don't have to be you or me.** I will tell you from experience, plain ol' common sense can help you about as well as anything, starting with who you select to do business with. That should be a very heavy decision for the reasons we've already discussed. Even eharmoney.com analyzes each new customer with a 29-point compatibility checklist to determine likes, dislikes, and common characteristics. I would hardly think checkin' out your investment partner should be anything less!

The following information (topics) needs to be seriously thought about and addressed! Each topic should be discussed and answered to your total satisfaction before the wedding date. After acceptance by the partners, each of these items should be formalized and drafted into your **co-ownership agreement**. My agreement (Appendix F) should help you.

A. NAMES OF PARTNERS – place of business – dates.
B. FORM OF BUSINESS. Example: General partnership, LLC or co-investors.
C. CAPITAL CONTRIBUTION – who puts up the money – when and how?
D. SHARING INCOME, expenses, profits. How will they be divided?
E. WHO IS IN CHARGE of daily management of property?
F. WHO CAN SELL, encumber, transfer or purchase a new property.
G. What to do about **disagreements**.
H. WHO WILL KEEP BOOKS, records and do taxes?
I. DEATH OF A PARTNER – what will you do?
J. INDEMINIFICATION of each partner against debts of other.
K. VIOLATION OF TERMS of agreement. What will you do?
L. RESTRICTIONS OF THE PARTNERS. Don't allow borrowing, for example; pledge property.
M. TERMINATION – when, how for what reason. Is extension okay?
N. WITHDRAWAL by any partner. How to split assets and what percentage–when.

TAKING TITLE TO PARTNERSHIP PROPERTY

Formal partnerships have many disadvantages for small "Mom and Pop" investors! They can also be quite expensive to set up. To start with, a formal partnership is a separate entity when it comes to tax reporting. Federal taxes are prepared on a Form 1065 with a Schedule K-1 form for each partner. Aside from being an added expense and pain in the neck, 1065s are yet another source for government tax audits. Also, partnership statements and fictitious business name documents (DBA) must be filed in each county where partnership property is owned. Perhaps the most serious reason to stay away from a formal partnership is because you cannot exchange partnership interests using tax code Section 1031. For this reason alone you should give serious thought to keeping your association informal.

Finally, most institutional lenders, banks, and mortgage brokers will not make direct loans to small partnerships. **Individuals** have a much easier time borrowing money. Having partnership information on file will likely require you to purchase a business license for rental properties, and if your partnership is a separate entity like a LLC, you won't be allowed to do your own evictions. Instead, you'll be required to hire a licensed attorney. The problem is, the type of associations or partnerships I'm writing about here are generally shoestring operations. Seldom do they have enough money for extra accounting expenses, tax returns, licenses, and eviction attorneys. Most investors feel lucky if they can scrounge up the down payment to buy a property.

The best way to take title, in my opinion, is **tenants-in-common**. Don't confuse this with being a renter who might seem very common or joint tenancy, which is generally used by a husband and wife when they acquire jointly owned properties. Tenants-in-common investors can benefit from 1031 exchanges. Each partner does his or her own tax reporting on an individual tax form 1040 for federal taxes. There are no extra tax forms requiring information about the partners. As tenants-in-common, each partner can own any percentage of the property they agree to. It can be 50-50, 20-80 or 90-10! Whatever it is should be specified on the deed that gets recorded. When a tenant-in-common dies, his share or percentage of ownership in the property is passed to his heirs. That's different from joint tenancy, where surviving joint tenant inherits the share of the one who passes on.

SOME FINAL ADVICE TO CONSIDER

Some counselors claim that marriages work much better when the participants have many things in common. For example, they like doing the very same things. However, for investment partners who join together for the purpose of **profit-making**, you'll find the rules are quite a bit different! Personal traits, common activities, and likes or dislikes don't really count for *diddly squat*. Ask yourself this question: do you give a "rat's hoot" about what you and I have in common if our joint investment together provides you a very lucrative income every month? **Yea, that's my answer too!**

In my opinion, co-investors need only a couple common ingredients to be successful. They both must possess a very strong, *almost selfish* desire to earn profits investing together as a team. Also, both must fully understand that their *different or unlike contributions*, when added together, are what produces a successful investment! Rich, poor, different religions, or whatever club someone belongs to matters very little to me if they are willing to put up the money on a property I can't purchase by myself.

Quite often, investors will say to me – Jay, I'm sorry to disagree with you, but I didn't become an investor to share my profits with someone else. *Fair enough* – but hold that thought for just a moment! Remember what I told you earlier about my personal investment philosophy! **I don't share deals with anyone else unless I don't have the money to do the deal myself.** Quite often, borrowing more money is not a good option because it's too expensive and uses up all the cash flow to pay the additional debt. *This creates far too much risk in my opinion.*

CASH FLOW – MONEY IN YOUR JEANS
MOST IMPORTANT

Survival requires **cash flow to pay the bills** and keep going! Cash flow is always the most pressing concern for investors who start out with little more than a wing and a prayer. Small down payments result in high balance mortgages, which suck all the cash flow from leveraged investments. In my early years, basic survival meant a great deal more to me than **becoming rich someday in the future**! I was always pressed by the need to create more income just to keep the lights on! You'll find yourself passing up lots of super deals if you have no money in your pockets.

Sometimes it might be better to find a money angel from heaven and share the profits. I will tell you from experience, the investment doors swing open much wider and offer far more opportunities when money is no longer your major problem. My final advice, be very cautious before taking on any partner. Also, **be completely sure that you are in a position to keep your end of the bargain**. Finally, make sure either of you know how to find that big rat hole in the baseboard to withdraw (buy-out provision) should things go haywire! **See how easy this is?**

All things said, there are still plenty of good partnership candidates out there. It's your job to weed 'em out! Besides, **fishin' with a partner** can be lots more fun and keep you warm and cozy when **lack of cash is your problem**!

CHAPTER 17

SHUCKIN' OFF
BOTTOM FEEDERS

Not too long ago I was the featured guest on a radio talk show! The announcer, *my host*, had promised me earlier no "hard ball" questions if he thought I might not know the answer, just the regular "cream puff" stuff he promised! We need to keep the program moving along, he said! Our first topic went slick as a whistle! For 15 minutes or so, we talked about how to set up **seller financing** – all the pro's and con's, and benefits for both the buyer and seller. We even discussed various precautions each should take and how to check the buyer's credit and the different clauses both parties should use in their deeds and promissory notes. Everything seemed to go quite well, I thought. Looking back, I should have used up all my time because the next round of questions were about the **different ways for beginners to start out and become successful investors** – WOW! Where should I begin?

Suddenly the air went dead! Radio hosts hate silence – "Good grief Jay," you've been teaching seminars and "how to" workshops for over 30 years! Please say something! The silence seemed like forever, even though it lasted less than 10 seconds max! Still, I felt I needed a few seconds to think about my answer before blurting something out. I told the host afterwards I probably wouldn't do very well on those late night infomercials! Those guys can always give you fast answers – *they've got everything memorized.* Success, they claim, can be almost instant if you'll give up your Visa card right now and purchase our "super-duper" magic course. Seems like you don't see near as many "late night gurus" these days. Most are trying to figure out how to qualify for another extension on their unemployment benefits.

YOU MUST THOROUGHLY
CHECK OUT YOUR TEACHER

Unfortunately – *or otherwise*, depending on how you view it, there are many salesmen masquerading as teachers – but there are also some excellent teachers and they all sell their educational products. To the beginner, they look very much alike. I have listened to many self-proclaimed real estate gurus who could sell snow to Eskimos! When they speak in Arizona, they can do the same thing with sand! For the most part, these folks are nothing more than roving salesmen living off their product sales. Many have never signed a deed or come face to face with a real live tenant. As salesmen, *these folks are very good*! But as trainers or real estate experts – well, I think you already know the answer!

No matter how good they sound, or how convincing they are, every promoter or real estate guru can easily be checked out! One self-appointed real estate expert, Wade Cook, was known as an "all-star" back in the '80s and '90s! I personally could sit for hours listening to him! He was extremely convincing, and an excellent speaker! He was also very likeable, funny, and had great wit! The problem was Wade was also a *notorious bandit*! While he was selling millions in real estate seminars and books, he would later need his money to pay for attorneys defending embezzlement charges. At the end he wrote one last book titled *Investing For Christians*! Wade had a big heart and never forgot his religious friends. For several years, it was quite easy to check Wade out! Both he and his wife were in the federal penitentiary serving time for fraud and security violations. I have no doubt that Wade will talk his way out of prison if the guards ever get close enough to hear his well-rehearsed pitch!

A true real estate investor who teaches others should have no problem whatsoever proving that he or she is what they claim to be! Any real estate investor should be able to show a prospective student at least one or two of his properties. A quick visit to his personal office should contain files with **escrow closings**, copies of deeds, and most certainly, his *landlording and management* records. You can't be very much of an income property investor without having these basic documents around – **agreed**! Most real estate gurus *who are not really investors tend* to shy away from talking personally to students on the telephone, unless of course, they're making another sales pitch. Try asking any imposter what he thinks you should do when your tenant goes *bonkers*. I've found some of the answers to be quite humorous! Still, I don't consider this a wasted telephone call because in the real "honest to goodness" landlording business – there's just not enough stuff that's really humorous! A little extra laughter is always good for the soul! **Don't you agree?**

FINDING A TEACHER YOU CAN COPY

After many years in the seminar training business – my advice to any guy or gal who is serious about learning to invest – **you should thoroughly check out your teacher**! You can call real estate investor clubs, or find out where you might hear them speak. Don't pick the first person you hear – **listen to several so you can compare.** You will also want to find a teacher who talks like he's doing the same kind of investing you'd like to do yourself. I call this research **the teacher selection process.** Keep checking till you feel good vibes about a particular teacher you believe knows what he's talking about! Also, make sure Wade Cook's still locked up! Once you settle on someone you feel can teach you – start checking 'em out a little more thoroughly!

Any teacher worth his salt has successful students. Ask permission to talk with several. For club members, I suggest you ask around at the meetings. One of the major benefits attending local real estate clubs is that newer members can learn a great deal from the older members who've been around a while! They'll likely know **who's real and who's not** in the real estate teaching circles. There's also another *check-out source* on the web, operated by John T. Reed. Mr. Reed is a real estate author, investor, superb writer, and very well respected.

He's also pretty much of a straight shooter, in my opinion! However, I must warn you, he's a tough interviewer, hard to get along with, and reserves his most favorable opinion for himself. Still, *that being said*, Mr. Reed is honest and not a bit shy about sharing his personal opinions! Many well-known economists and real estate journalists seek out his advice! John is also the *unofficial* "self-appointed" high priest of real estate guru evaluations. He shares his opinions of just about every real estate educator you've likely heard of. Be warned, however, he's not much for flattery, praise, or **blowing kisses**! My advice, take a look and judge for yourself: www.johntreed.com/Reedgururating.

AFTER A THOROUGH INVESTIGATION – SELECT A TEACHER

Once you decide on a teacher you'd like to learn from – your next step is to decide exactly **how you plan to learn**. Regarding teachers who conduct seminars and sell home study courses, you must decide how fast you wish to learn and how much education you can afford. Contrary to what some folks may think – learning the real estate investing business from a skilled trainer is not free. I am absolutely amazed during my frequent conversations with wanta-bee investors when they inform me they've already invested heavily, *sometimes $15,000 to $40,000* with popular seminar groups. Most of these groups are nothing more than roving bands of *dream merchants*. Unfortunately, the wanta-bee investors I talk with haven't been taught quite enough about how to get started investing or they wouldn't be calling me. Sadly, many of these excessive seminar fees are the penalty for not thoroughly seeking out a qualified trainer. Most of the good ones I know are far less expensive!

A SUCKER IS BORN EVERY SECOND

Harold Smith, the long-time owner of Harold's Club in Reno understood selling dreams very well. Referring to his gambling customers, he often said: "*There's one born every second!*" He was right of course – *still*, there's absolutely no good reason for any wanta-bee investor to become the next *real estate sucker*! Do your homework and check out the players! My advice, like always, is to use basic **common sense**, and apply **sound judgment** before choosing your mentor!

You should always investigate your teaching choices thoroughly before deciding whose right for you. Finding a teacher who will assist you in acquiring your first investment property is a tremendous advantage for new investors. Not only from the ownership standpoint, but from the **self-confidence** you'll gain when you acquire your first property. I suggest finding a teacher who will assist you all the way through your first purchase. This will greatly advance your learning experience and speed up your success **by tenfold or more**!

FINDING THE BEST EDUCATION VALUE TODAY

Learning the **building blocks of investing** is much like learning how to become an auto mechanic or a skilled plumber. You'll end up light years ahead if you seek out a qualified teacher who does what he teaches – someone who teaches from experience and can show you how he does it for himself. Trying to invest without a reasonable understanding of the basics is like attempting to sail across the ocean with a broken rudder. Many beginners often use the "try it myself method" or they'll take advice from their local pastor or golf buddy! In most cases I hear about, the costs of early buying mistakes will far exceed the expense of attending a few good **investor training seminars or one-on-one teaching**!

I have found that when a new investor makes early buying mistakes (such as paying too much), it's much easier for him or her to become discouraged and often give up! Folks who buy properties that fail to generate income or profits will seldom stay the course. I will tell you from my personal experience, it's extremely difficult to stay in a positive mood when you work your tail off fixin' your property, and you still need to cough up money every month to make up for a cash flow shortage. It destroys your confidence when properties fail to produce at least some income to reward you for all your efforts!

Alligator properties *or negative cash flow* happens because you don't know what you're doing! **The problem is lack of education!** The good news is you can avoid the worst problems if you'll be realistic about the need for obtaining a proper education to start with!

The difference between success and failure often lies with *one's personal thinking* about how they can achieve their goal! **For starters, it's completely naïve to think that anyone can suddenly jump into real estate investing and start doing things correctly without any help or education.** The idea that someone can read a *motivational* real estate book and miraculously be transformed into a *successful investor* is "tooth fairy" thinking! Obviously, being totally honest with yourself will give you a much stronger platform to launch a successful investment plan. I don't mean for this to sound too heavy – or that successful investing is beyond the capabilities of anyone – **because it's not.** But education is what makes successful investors. Trying to explain what I'm telling you here was the reason for my 10 second lapse on the radio show. When I finally started talking, here's the advice I passed along to my listeners.

JAY'S RECOMMENDED LEARNING SEQUENCE

Don't even think about buying an investment property until you've studied a comprehensive real estate course or attended a training workshop or seminar offered by the trainer you've decided is qualified to be your instructor. A study course should explain how to develop the **right price for your offer** so you don't overpay. For example, in my study courses for *income-producing properties*, I provide an INCOME PROPERTY ANALYSIS FORM (see Appendix C) which when filled out properly, eliminates much of the guesswork about **paying the right price.** Using my form and the accompanying instructions will automatically keep you from acquiring properties with negative cash flow! A simple lesson, yes, but it's extremely important for inexperienced investors so they start out on the right foot! Buying properties poorly (paying too much) is not only costly in terms of wasted money, but it can also take several extra years to sell or trade-out of a negative property while losing money along the way. Both your **time** and **money** are much too valuable to waste in the early years when your cash is in short supply!

STARTING SMALL WITH INEXPENSIVE HOUSES

Starting with small rundown houses will work for most people whether they're handy or not! Being a bit handy can certainly help – but if you're not, it's still much cheaper to make your early mistakes on small fixer-type houses rather than more expensive properties. Cheaper houses are also less expensive to repair and they're much easier to rent if you keep them like I strongly suggest. Why small houses, you ask? They're much more affordable to a greater number of renters – or buyers! Common sense will tell you there are more poor renters than rich ones. Also, poor renters are not nearly so critical about your crappy-lookin' sheetrock repairs!

The inexpensive houses I recommend are generally older houses built many years ago. Many are desperately in need of rehabilitation – plus a whole lot of clean-up. About 80% of the fix-up effort required is what I call *grunt work* or non-skilled labor. New investors normally have a lot more grunt power than financial power. Obviously, doing all you can to save money should be a big part of your early learning experience.

Fixing up or *adding value* to older properties takes a few special skills – but on a positive note, these older rundown houses provide a wide range of practical do-it-yourself training lessons for new investors. It has always been my opinion that operating inexpensive fix-up properties is the fastest way to learn the real estate investment business. Perhaps even more important – fixing rundown houses provides the quickest path to profits and cash flow. **Obviously, cash flow is always the top priority for new investors.**

Adding value to properties tends to level the playing field when it comes to investor competition! Almost every new investor starts out about equal regardless of where they come from. High school dropouts, jailbirds, and life-long geeks all fare about as well as the so-called professionals, including PhD's, building contractors, and lawyers! The reason for this is because the serious money will come from **financial skills** rather than hammering on boards or fixing a leaky toilet. Obviously, it's very helpful if you possess decent hands-on skills – and you know the difference between a grant deed *and General Grant*! But regardless, these are not the things that will make you rich!

INVESTING WITH MINIMAL RISK

Lots of small-time investors go out of business and lose everything they have when the market stops appreciating – or when bank financing dries up. To me, dependence on appreciation or bank financing is speculating – *it's not investing*! I want more control when I own the property. My first rule of investing has always been **to control the profits and cash flow**. That's almost impossible when you're dependent on the economy (appreciation) or available bank funds (mortgages). My investing strategy is to earn money year 'round regardless of mortgage funds or appreciation. When they're available, I'll consider them as icing on the cake – but never the cake itself. Minimizing risk is an important part of becoming rich. It makes very little sense to make a bundle of money and then lose it to circumstances beyond your control.

Education is your map to the gold mine. There are basically two ways to learn about making money with rundown properties, and both will cost you a few bucks. The first is to start out on your own using the trial and error method. I call this the *no money down training technique*. No money that is, until you make a costly mistake. Obviously, when that happens, any savings you may have had is money down the toilet! Then of course, there's the question of time – as in, how long before I'll be rich? This requires some serious thought – **how many years do you plan to practice real estate investing**? You need to come up with some answer for yourself.

The second method is to hire someone who knows the business and can teach you the ropes! Seminars or special group training will be the least expensive. Don't expect to learn this business in just two or three days of classroom instruction at a single event. **Remember what**

I said about practice – on-the-job training! Mixing formal education (seminars) while actually working on your investment property at the same time is best! For learning this business, that's about as good as it gets. Naturally, you'll need to pay a few hard-earned dollars upfront for your training, but you should learn enough to avoid the most expensive pitfalls for your money. Soon you will realize that **your time equals money** – paying a few dollars upfront will be much cheaper in the long run. Young folks can keep starting over for a while, but when you're older, you must move more quickly and avoid the biggest mistakes.

SEARCHING FOR GOLD MINE HOUSES

Much like the gold miners of *yester-year*, today's investment property seekers can always use a few good tips about where to look, what to look for, and of course, the main reasons why. Your search for houses, *much like looking for gold*, is more easily accomplished when you have some idea about where you should dig!

Older rundown houses are found in the older sections of most cities, so don't waste your time driving through modern day subdivisions. In rural areas they might be scattered almost anywhere, but generally you'll find they were built surrounding the main commercial areas, close to stores and other retail activity. You won't find the houses I'm talking about in the newer tract developments. Non-conforming properties like a group of single-family houses or cottages on one large city lot are often found in commercial zoning locations. Zoning didn't matter much when they were built! These properties can make top-notch investments, so long as the houses are kept in decent repair and occupied. Their current usage will be "grandfathered in" regardless of current zoning laws.

FINDING GOLD MINE HOUSES

Once upon a time – many years ago, before present-day zoning laws, home buying families would often build or purchase their home on a giant sized lot with the idea of building a few rental houses in the back. Sometimes they even built apartments above the garage. Their plan was to supplement their future retirement income. 401K's and today's lucrative pension plans were not in the picture back then, so families had to plan for their own retirement incomes. Most of these properties are at least 60 to 75 years old today – and many look tired, they sag a bit and they're generally rundown! These houses can be hidden gold mines for smart investors willing to breathe new life back into them.

Forget looking at multiple listings on your computer screen and don't be waitin' around for your real estate agent to call. The few agents who actually understand this business know that even if they found one – today's rigid disclosure laws would be a can of worms and the financing would likely end up a time-wasting nightmare! Naturally, most sellers want all cash because their agents have convinced them it's the way business should be done today! Pay no attention to this nonsense, it's totally depressing. Finding these properties is much easier if you take on the task yourself. What you'll need is a good pair of walkin' shoes and a car that runs good enough to get you around.

In average sized cities – start looking in the downtown area. Try to find five or six junky lookin' houses on a single lot between the old theater and the RV sales lot. Look a few blocks away from the downtown mall, in the old commercial or industrial areas, and perhaps you'll find a group of rundown cottages hidden in the tall brush behind the soup factory. The idea here is to look for these kinds of properties on your own – stompin' through the weeds yourself. Notice, *I've never once mentioned slums or the hood*! Stay away from well-documented slum areas. You'll no doubt find cheaper prices – but you ain't gonna like meeting your new tenants. Worse yet, you'll never get the value to increase regardless of how many times you fix broken fences or repaint the buildings. **Stay away from the slums! Are we clear on this?**

DOING THE LEG WORK ON YOUR OWN

Folks often ask me when they're lookin' at rows of older houses downtown – how would I ever know if there's more houses or apartments in the back yards? From the street, all I can see is one old house! Everything else is covered by trees and overgrown shrubs – I can't even see what's up the driveway! Here's the deal gang, I want you to look for groups of mailboxes or addresses like A, B, or C after the main number. Sometimes you'll find several water meter boxes in the sidewalk, along the property line. I always look for multiple telephone service wires, and more than one electrical service – even lots of TV cables. When you spot big bunches of wires, obviously they've got to be going someplace! When you suspect there are multiple living units on the property but you can't quite tell for sure – draw yourself a little sketch of the property. Take a measurement (stepped off) to the nearest street intersection. Go to your county tax and map department to find the APN parcel number (tax ID number); then take a look at the assessed property value (tax bill). With multiple units on one lot, the tax assessment will be much higher than surrounding houses in the neighborhood, indicating more houses (improvements) on the property or tax parcel.

In bigger cities, select an area where you think you might be productive. There's no need to drive all over the entire city. In rural areas, groups of houses, duplexes, or various multiple-unit combinations might be found just about anywhere. Remember what I told you, you won't find older properties in the newer tracts or subdivisions.

SALT WATER AND HIGH PRICES GO TOGETHER

High-price seacoast towns are tough for new investors who are just starting out! The basic problem is – *too much money chasing too few properties!* Competing investors will drive up the prices and many will pay all cash for fix-up properties. If you live in a seaside location, my suggestion is drive out of town a ways till you can no longer smell salt-water air! 50 or 60 miles can make a huge difference in terms of **prices** and **buyer competition**! No matter which location you choose, you must learn the local tenant customs in addition to the **market rents** and **property values**. *Learning the local customs meaning –* where do the majority of tenants in your particular price range choose to live. Learning this information to begin with will keep you from buying investment properties in drug-infested neighborhoods that some sellers and agents forget to tell you about! **You must know the amount of rent you can charge in your buying area**. This will help you determine the amount you can pay for the property *and still earn a profit for yourself*. **Very Important!**

GOLDEN ECONOMIC BENEFITS

I love real estate investing with all my heart, but there's nothing more distressful to me than a rental house that won't earn a profit after I buy it, fix it all up, and rent it out! This happens to investors all the time who don't learn how much they can pay and still make a profit! **Remember, if my tenants can't pay my bills, I don't want the property!**

Buying a few of these negative income houses will almost guarantee you'll eventually end up at your local AA meeting. Although they might not always smell so good, small rundown gold mine houses (in groups or bunches) have major financial advantages over most single-family tract houses. The biggest advantage is that **the unit price is cheaper** when you buy them in bunches. The *cost per unit* is an extremely important measurement when you're trying to buy properties that will generate a positive cash flow.

REVIVING OBSOLESCENT PROPERTIES

We live in an age where most everything operates with the flip of a switch, or goes up and down when you press a button! Even the television shuffles through 75 channels, leaving hardly any reason to get off the couch except to grab another beer. We have automatic icemakers and special pots that have dinner cooked before anyone even gets home. Today's hi-tech houses must be designed and built with every imaginable convenience or they simply won't attract buyers. 65 years ago, no one had ever heard of a garage door that opened all by itself! The only way it would open is if someone reached down and manually pulled it up or they backed through it with the family car.

Times have changed, and houses without all the push button gadgets are no longer attractive to home buyers – however, **home buyers aren't the only folks who pay out hard-earned money for housing.** *At least 43% of the folks in my state live in rental housing at all economic levels.* A great majority, however, are young families and seniors who must get by on very restrictive budgets. These folks are my primary customers and the *hi-tech push button technology* doesn't rank anywhere near the top in terms of what they want for their housing dollars! *They want clean and safe housing they can afford.* For many young couples and seniors alike – two bedrooms with one bath, a single car garage, and a small back yard makes an ideal rental property that will fit their lifestyle – **and more importantly, their budget**! The problem is, they're not building these kinds of houses anymore – and the only thing comparable is apartment house living with a lot less privacy and a list of restrictions that many tenants don't like.

ADDING VALUE OPPORTUNITIES

Older rundown properties are available everywhere. There is no shortage of fix-up opportunities. The fact is that *more houses are becoming rundown fixers than are being fixed up!* The U.S. Department of Housing and Urban Development (HUD) estimates that 600,000 units of residential housing are falling below minimum habitability standards annually. That figure is quite shocking given all the money HUD spends annually on rehabilitation projects. The good news for investors is – fixing up and **adding value to older properties is a job with a very long-term future**. Small time, Mom and Pop investors are desperately needed. Unlike blacksmiths, steamfitters, and vacuum cleaner salesmen, the fix-up business is on the upswing. It's a specialty that needs all the help it can get. If you'll learn the ropes, and develop a plan to acquire these gold mine properties – they'll make you a very wealthy investor for your efforts. **Re-read Chapter 8**, "TROLLIN' FOR A COLONY," so you get started on the right foot!

A MOTIVATED STUDENT –
A BEAUTIFUL SIGHT TO WATCH

The year was 1988 when Dan showed up at my **Investor Training Seminar**. He explained how he had *grossly overspent* trying to bring back the charm to a grand old San Francisco Bay area Victorian! His computer job supported him quite nicely back then, but Dan had a much **bigger and bolder vision**! Determined to stop spending more money than he could ever get back, he came to my **Investor Training Seminar** to learn a few cost saving tricks. Lots of water has flowed under the bridge since the day I met Dan, but my KJAY SEMINAR records reveal his amazing step-by-step progress to riches!

To begin with, Dan became completely convinced that buying **gold mine houses** in small groups was the path to wealth. He immediately took action and he's never looked back! Today, with more than 80 income-producing houses in California, it's clear Dan won't be needing his old computer job back! **How did he get so far so fast, you ask?** I'll tell ya how! I used to joke with Dan and I'd often tell him – *you attend more of my seminars than I do.* But like I tell all my students – **Dan got this far because he made it top priority to learn this business!** He understood the value of education and he never once looked for any magic shortcuts! Dan also knew he wouldn't end up a millionaire overnight, but he was always willing to do whatever it took! **I'd say Dan's 80 California houses prove the point!**

The following chart (Figure 17-1) shows the benefits Dan told me he was seeking when he decided to switch his investing plan to my kind of properties–small multiple-unit properties, or as I call them, **colonies**! Colonies can really make your fishing trip lots more fun. Folks often ask me–does the type of properties you're suggesting really make that much difference for building wealth? Dan says it does **and he oughta know**!

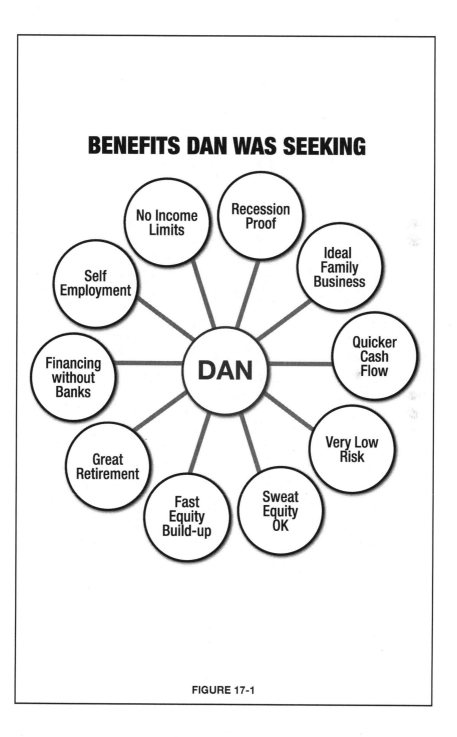

FIGURE 17-1

American Dream, Dead?

According to a nationwide survey conducted by Harvard University's Institute of Politics in Fall of 2015, when asked, "For you personally, is the idea of the American Dream alive or dead?" forty-eight percent of the 18-29 year old respondents said "dead."

Nearly half of the young adults in the US feel like the American Dream is dead for them personally. That's shocking!

For the real estate fishermen who refuse to accept this "sky is falling" nonsense, I can assure you, your Personal American Dream is alive and kickin'! Like I told you in the very first chapter, both Harvard Law students and high school dropouts can become successful fishermen with discipline, determination, and the willingness to learn.

CHAPTER 18

FINANCING YOUR
FISHIN' TRIP

The term creative financing in real estate can take on many different meanings, depending on who attempts to explain their own
version. Perhaps the best explanation in terms of real estate finance is
that it's one's ability to create a different way to pay for a property – the
emphasis being *something new and different,* created by the parties,
as opposed to some standard or "copy-cat" method of financing.
In my opinion, it almost always means *seller financing,* because I've
never once, after 50 years investing, had a mortgage from any bank or
financial institution that was very creative. Obviously, I don't consider
a variable rate loan or ARM mortgage as being creative! In general,
bank loans or mortgages are about as creative as a busted crutch, in
my opinion!

Any discussion about creative financing, which almost automatically involves the seller as far as I'm concerned, needs a bit more
clarification about what a mortgage is – *and what it's not.* To begin
with, the term seller financing is actually a *misnomer* – it's not really
a regular mortgage at all! It's an extension of credit, or terms granted
by the seller for the purchase of his property. In the typical financing
scenario, you have a buyer, seller, and a lender – usually, a bank or
private party who lends the money to purchase the property. Picture
an escrow closing if you will! You have a buyer who wishes to purchase
the property, but he doesn't have all the money. You have a seller who
wants to sell, but he wants all his money. You have a money lender

who is typically a bank or investor willing to loan the buyer money to close, in exchange for a promissory note – *or a mortgage*, secured by the real estate. The lender's only interest is to earn profits and income from his loan during the payback period. Common payback periods for bank loans or mortgages are generally 15 to 30 years with payments that will likely include both interest and the principal amount. Most likely they'll be amortized over the payback period!

CLOSING ESCROW WITHOUT A LENDER

Now picture, if you can, the same closing where the seller has agreed to carry back or provide the financing. Look hard, and tell me if you can see a lender anywhere! If your answer to me is there is none – give yourself a passing grade so far, but don't get too cocky 'cause we ain't done yet! If you can count, you'll notice the closing requires fewer people since we don't have a lender in the room! Only the **seller** and the **buyer** show up! Okay Jay, are you trying to tell me we can close this transaction without money for a new mortgage? The answer my friend, is **absolutely yes**, if the seller agrees that it's okay for me, *the buyer*, to have his property right now, so long as I promise to begin making installment payments on the price we've agreed on. Can you understand now, that seller financing is simply about the terms the seller is willing to give me so I'll be able to pay for his property over a period of time? Take notice that **the seller has not loaned me any money.** He simply agreed that I can purchase his property over a period of time – he's extending me credit!

Both definitions I used in the second paragraph to describe seller financing apply here! First, the seller has agreed to extend credit to the buyer – he will also allow the buyer some extra time (terms) to pay for his property. Quite often, sellers will agree to this with only a small down payment – *and sometimes*, without any down payment at all. Naturally, this depends largely on the seller's motivation to sell his property. **Terms of the sale or agreement** are about a seller helping the buyer close the deal. For example, the purchase agreement might say: the seller agrees to sell Jay his duplex for $100,000 full price, with terms as follows: $10,000 cash down payment at close of escrow – then monthly payments of $600 per month for 20 years, including interest and principal. Once again, it's the buyer and seller who create this deal. There is no loan or mortgage, and obviously no lender involved. The seller is simply extending me credit for a 20-year period. **He is not loaning me one thin dime.** Quite often, real estate agents will incorrectly characterize *seller financing* as a loan! They are seriously misleading their clients when they do this – but, what's even worse, they often lose the opportunity to close the sale by advising their client that *seller financing is simply too risky.*

When brand new investors read what I'm discussing here, they often find it very difficult to believe that ordinary sellers would take on the risk of extending *credit and terms* to someone they don't even know! First, let me define who an ordinary seller might be! My definition of an *ordinary seller* is someone selling his home! He's probably not an investor and his circumstances are likely to be much different than those of an investor. Also, his motivations are different, his reasons for selling are probably different, and he most likely knows that new mortgages are almost always available for financing regular home sales. *Ordinary sellers* are most likely advised by *ordinary real estate agents* that new mortgages are simply the way sales are done today – *and ya know what,* they're absolutely right!

It's for this reason that new investors, just starting out, who are looking to purchase single-family houses can honestly say – seller financing is very hard to get – and even harder to find. Most agents, *the listing types*, won't recommend it – and selling agents will seldom discuss the issue at all! It's always best to get all your money at closing with a brand new mortgage, *they advise.* Even if the issue of seller financing pops up, most agents will discourage the idea with their clients by saying something like this: Mr. Seller, the buyer's agent has asked me if you might consider financing your sale. The buyer has 10% for the down payment, but would like you to carry back the balance at 7% interest for 20 years.

AGENTS DON'T CARE MUCH
FOR SELLER FINANCING

Mr. Seller, I must strongly recommend you don't do this! *First of all*, you don't know the buyer or anything about him. You have no way of knowing if he pays his bills in a timely fashion or not! If he should suddenly stop paying, you'll be forever getting your house back – *and worse yet*, when people stop paying, they will likely stop taking care of your property too! You might end up spending a fortune redoing your whole house if something goes wrong! And finally they say – **you're not a bank**! Why should you loan your hard-earned dollars to a buyer so he can buy your house with your money? That's like loaning money to a broke poker player who's betting against you! *It's downright ridiculous!* Let's get the bank to take the risk, and you take your money! It's no wonder that single house investors often tell me: Jay, you're always preaching to us about asking sellers for financing – apparently you need to go out and try this for yourself! *Sellers simply won't do this anymore.* You must be smokin' them funny-smellin' cigarettes again!

Friends, sellers do offer credit and terms to sell their homes every now and then, but they're mostly the rundown junker-type properties – or the buyer is very persuasive. *Seldom will real estate agents make this happen on their own*, especially with their limited knowledge of what's good or not good for their clients. To begin with, analyzing their client's financial needs, such as tax status and personal skill level, is not part of the agent's job! Obviously, there are always a few agents who can do this, but I'm talking about realtors in general! Most sales agents don't seem to realize that *seller carryback paper* and *institutional loans* are not the same thing, although both are called mortgages. Banks issue fresh green dollars from their vault when they agree to provide a mortgage to the buyer. When I ask a seller to carry back the financing for me – **it's a whole lot different**! Even though a seller carryback is often called a mortgage, there's something extremely important that's missing! Can you make a wild guess what that might be? You're right on, **if you answered it's money**! How can there be a loan without any money? The answer, my friends – there can't be! Can you see now why seller financing is merely the seller granting credit to a buyer, and allowing him enough time (terms) to pay off the debt?

THERE'S SAFETY DEALING WITH SELLERS

Another extremely important issue is involved when a seller agrees to extend me credit and terms so I can purchase his property! Should I have tough luck renting out the property, or suffer some other financial setback making it impossible for me to continue the payments – *I can give the property back without further financial obligation.* Naturally, I'll lose my down payment, plus all the payments I've made, **but that's it!** Even if the property has lost value under my ownership – on the day I hand the keys back to the seller, my financial obligations are over!

With a bank loan or mortgage, **where actual green dollars have been disbursed**, your life could become much more complicated if you find yourself in a financial pickle. If the property loses value because you didn't have enough cash flow to provide for proper upkeep – and you eventually lose out to foreclosure – the bank who loaned the money might very well elect to have a judicial-type foreclosure, and obtain a **deficiency judgment** – then come after you for any losses they suffer. They can do this because it's written in their promissory note, which you signed, when you borrowed their money and promised to pay it back. This means other assets you own could be taken by the bank to satisfy their deficiency judgment. Naturally, the bank would be allowed to charge you their *padded attorney expenses* associated with foreclosure – *plus*, all the back interest payments you missed. This is yet another good reason to seek out seller financing and avoid this added risk of borrowing **real dollars** from **real lenders**.

FINANCING CAN MAKE YOU RICH – JUST LIKE EQUITY

Investors like me start out with very few dollars in our pockets. We struggle to build our fortunes using other people's money; commonly referred to as "OPM." The various ways in which we choose to finance or pay for our properties has as much to do with our success as the properties themselves. Let me say this another way so it's crystal-clear! A well-financed property that looks like crap is far more valuable to me than a super-lookin' property that has crappy financing. **The way a property is financed will directly determine its profitability**. If you have any doubts about this, you might wish to go back and re-read my Cherry Street transaction (Chapter 2) or "How to Make A $1,000,000 Working Smarter" in my book, *Investing in Fixer-Uppers*. Both of these real life examples were extremely profitable because I used seller financing to acquire them. The same financing allowed me to sell them by offering my buyers *excellent terms*, in exchange for **top market prices**.

Institutional financing, *banks and mortgage lenders*, will nearly always write a "Due on Sale" provision in their loan documents. Basically, this means you will need their permission to sell or alienate your property. Yes, I'm aware we all cheat a little bit with this – but banks still have the authority to "call the shots." *This is not good for us investors*. We need freedom to "wheel-n-deal" so we can maximize our profits. A good example where a due-on-sale provision could hurt is when a house has a low 4% institutional mortgage, and then the house is sold by the owner using *wrap-around financing* to bypass the due-on-sale provision – which would legally require a *formal assumption* or a full pay off! Chances are, the lender knows all about this shenanigan from the insurance company documents, but has chosen to do nothing, so long as he's receiving timely payments, *and* **the interest rates remain low**.

Then suddenly one day, interest rates shoot up to 10% or so! Now the bank (lender) will more than likely call their loan, *meaning* – demand the balance be paid in full! *The reason* – **with a payoff**, they can easily lend their money again for a much higher interest rate. The same thing could happen if you were doing lease-option deals, land contracts, or any other creative transactions where you most likely forgot to mention the deal to your bank (oops) and they decided to play hardball and call the loan! You might still be alright if your mortgage balance is small, or perhaps if you can hawk the family furniture to pay the bank off! Naturally, I'm only talkin' about this when you're caught – *otherwise*, just continue doing what you've been doing! **When you're caught – ask forgiveness!**

FOR BUYING AND SELLING – FINANCING IS IMPORTANT

As a buyer, I always want to assume *or take over* existing financing (subject to). **I want full control of the financing**! When I sell – **I still want full control**, so I use wrap-around financing in order to keep my existing low interest *long-term financing* in place. I will explain this further as we go along – also show you an example, but right now, let's explore some different ways to negotiate seller financing when the opportunity presents itself! First, let me repeat myself about **seller motivation**. If the seller has no motivation, you won't get diddly-squat! When you hear the seller or his agent make a comment like: Sure, I'd like to sell, but I'm really not in any big hurry – *but go ahead and make me an offer* and we'll see where it goes. That answer, my friend – **it's going nowhere**. Don't let out a peep – just nod your head, smile, pick up your saddlebags, and quietly leave. You'll only end up getting mad at yourself if you attempt to argue about a property that's not yet ripe for buying. **Motivation must be present** in some form in order to get the benefits you need – otherwise your efforts are just suckin' wind!

When you begin thinking about writing an offer – that's after you've done your Lieutenant Columbo research and developed the **$ numbers** using my INCOME PROPERTY ANALYSIS FORM (see Appendix C), *do not get hustled into offering more money than the property will support.* **And above all**, do not fall in love with the property no matter how wonderful you think it is, **or could be**! Stay true to your *discovery results,* the numbers on your **property analysis form**. Also, don't play solitaire with your offer. That's a little game you play by yourself, where you say – *I know he won't take that*, so I'll just increase my offer to what I think he might take. In this scenario, you've made yourself both the **executor** and the *stuckee*. **Don't do this**! Also, don't get overly concerned about what you think the interest and principal payments should be. The purchase amount and the payments you can afford to pay do not have to fit any particular rule or amortization schedule. **They can be whatever you say they are!** Quite often, I'm willing to overpay a little if the seller will give me *reduced payments*, so I can end up with cash flow.

Let's begin talking about terms without any preconceived notions that *there's a right way or wrong way to finance the property.* The only thing that matters is what the seller and buyer can agree to. Right about now is when folks will ask me – what's the legal interest rate for seller carryback notes (mortgages)? My personal answer is none, *like in zip!* Yes, I'm aware of something called *imputed interest.* The government (IRS) says you must charge interest on all mortgages. They use the mid-term bond or CD rate called the *applicable rate* as their measurement for the legal interest charge. Sellers who finance their property sales must charge interest the IRS claims or they will re-compute your sale transaction using the *applicable rate.* However, that's when they catch a no interest transaction on your taxes. Notice I said – *when they catch the transaction.* In 50 years, they've yet to discover a single one of mine. **Remember**, these are the same folks who moved like snails with Katrina and now they're bogged down with Obamacare and spying on the Tea Party! 50 years may not be enough time!

One of my favorite methods of buying junker houses is with *larger monthly payments* and zero interest – paid fully in 10 years. Example: **$100,000** property, **$10,000** down payment, **$90,000** divided by **120 months** = $750 month payments. Sellers get their money quickly – *in one-third the time* it would take to pay off the traditional 30-year home loan. For example, with a 30-year amortized loan with 6% interest, the seller would receive only $539.60 per month. The short-term higher payment appeals to older people who don't expect to be upright for 30 more years – **they want the higher income right now**. Don't forget, I'm dealing with *junker properties!* This stuff won't work worth a hoot on normal sellers with pride of ownership properties, so don't bother askin' if you don't like to hear cuss words!

With seller financing you must eventually get yourself **one-on-one** with the seller or you won't have much success making a deal. Sellers want to see you, smell you, and talk to you directly before they ever decide they trust you – *not too scientific perhaps*, but this is real world real estate dealing. Seldom have I ever negotiated a seller carryback transaction through a third party – i.e., real estate agent or the seller's mother-in-law. Sorry folks, ya gotta get to the couch or dining room table before the sellers will open up and start talkin' turkey!

For just a moment, let's pretend I've asked you to carry back financing for me! Let's assume I'm a perfect stranger to you – so you know nothing about me at all! In this example, I'd like to purchase your rundown rental property for $300,000, full price. I can pay you a $30,000 cash down payment – then I'll need you to trust me for the balance ($270,000). I propose to pay you $1500 per month for the next 20 years, if that's alright with you. Now, let me ask you – do you have any questions you'd like to ask me? **If you don't** – please allow me to rewrite my offer and trade you the Brooklyn Bridge for the down payment.

SELLERS WANT TO LOOK YOU IN THE EYE

Over the years, most sellers I've dealt with have lots of questions for me! The most obvious one of course is what assurance can you give me that you won't stop making payments if I agree to this contract? What happens to me if you can't manage tenants very well and they stop paying rent – or maybe they up 'n leave and there's not enough income? Worse yet, what happens if you don't take care of my property and can't make the payments, and I'm forced to repossess a big fat mess you've left behind? I think you would agree with me, these are very important issues for any owner. After all, you're asking the owners to sell their property to you without paying them most of their money upfront!

Here's the deal cadets: if you were asking me to sell my property to you and give you terms that allow you to pay me over time – I would certainly want to have a serious financial discussion with you! Even eHarmony.com runs you through 29 dimensions of compatibility before they turn you loose on a total stranger. To start with, I need to feel good about you. I need to look you in both eyes and judge for myself whether you look honest to me or not! At this early point – *it's all about the vibrations.* Do I feel at ease with you – and, in my judgment – **do I trust you?**

You might say to me – *Ya know Jay,* all this sounds a little bit silly to me, and certainly doesn't seem very professional! Why can't my real estate agent do this on a more *professional level*; after all, she's trained to deal with people and personalities? Friends, that idea is so stupid, I don't even have a good answer. If I'm the seller, I have no problem with a real estate agent sitting across the room listening – *and perhaps* even nodding, nudging, or twitching from time to time, but it's the buyer who needs to assure me that he can pay for my property over the next 20 years should we reach an agreement – **the agent can write up the contract**. Other than that, I respectfully suggest that she sit there quietly like a flowerpot!

SELLER FINANCING IS ALWAYS PERSONAL

Please don't interpret what I'm telling you here to mean any disrespect toward real estate agents. That's certainly not my intention here! I'm sure you can understand that agents could be running back and forth forever, trying to obtain what might seem like rather sensitive information requested by either the buyer or the seller! *Once again,* asking the seller for long-term financing becomes a very personal decision. *A rather common example*: many older sellers are planning retirement, and the safety of their money (mortgage payments) becomes a very important concern. A standard credit report can't possibly address all their questions about **a 20-year carryback payment plan**. Also, many times, sellers are planning to move away from the area when they retire. Naturally, they feel that having to take back their property should something go wrong would be physically more than they could handle. These are typical real-life issues that buyers must be prepared to address when asking the seller for carryback terms.

Obviously, my primary goal or strategy when buying properties from owners who are agreeable to carryback financing is to design a transaction that works best for me. Still, I must remain flexible enough to make the seller feel good about the deal; otherwise he'll never sign off! Once again, I remind you, **you'll never get to first base unless seller motivation is present**. Buying with good terms will never happen if you make up your mind that you must own the property. Sellers can quickly sense a developing romance between you and their property, and you'll end up paying the price. *No property is worth owning if it doesn't provide good opportunities for profits*! Don't ever forget this sentence when you're out there shopping! I think pop vocalist Neil Sedaka said it best in his number one hit song, "Breaking Up Is Hard To Do" – you must never fall in love with junky houses or you'll end up working your butt off for free! **Are we clear on this?**

The importance of your time on the couch with the property owner should not be taken lightly! It's the key to winning *concessions from the seller*. You gotta sit down together and talk things over to create the right feel! Think about this for a moment – don't we all loosen up a bit as we get to know each other a little better? Remember the first time you passed that scroungy-looking guy sitting near the supermarket door on your way to buy a few groceries? Remember how quickly you scampered on by? It's my guess, you didn't even think about dropping a quarter in his cardboard bucket in your haste to rush by him!

Then several days later on another trip, you accidently exchange a few words with the guy! You quickly learn that even though he looks awful and smells worse, he's actually a two-term disabled veteran! Now, every time you see him sittin' there by the door, you slip him a buck or two because you feel you've gotten to know him a little better. Obviously, you have more compassion and you now understand why he sits by the supermarket door.

Friends, this is exactly how things works with **seller financing**. You must **communicate** and **develop some understanding** with the property owner. People tend to give you a lot more when they feel they know you a little better and they understand your situation! This is why you can't do this by telephone, Twitter, Facebook, or fax – *and least of all*, by sending out your bewildered real estate agent. **It's personal stuff – ya got it!**

CREATIVE OFFERS MEAN YOU MUST CREATE THEM

Thorough preparation before you talk to anyone about the **price**, **terms**, and even a **tentative proposal** is your best guarantee against overpaying. I'm talking about *the purchase price* as well as *the monthly payments*, because they're both the most important parts of the deal. Quite often, sellers will get "hung up" on the purchase price they're asking, but will allow some wiggle room with monthly payments. Others seem to go the opposite direction! It's your responsibility to find out this information during your one-on-one visits with the seller. Do this before you ever begin formulating any dollar numbers. To me, the *monthly expenses* and *monthly debt service* are always my biggest concern. These fixed payouts are what it will cost me to operate the property every single month! You must get affordable terms or you'll go down the tubes quickly! With respect to the *selling price* – you can jack me around a little, *within reason of course* – because that's where I tend to be more flexible.

As an income property investor, it's my job to create a profitable purchase, and at the same time, *one that my tenants can afford to pay for!* Certainly you didn't think I intended to pay for their housing – **did you?** You might consider me the **arranger** or **negotiator** on a shopping mission for my tenants. As a general rule, my tenants and I cannot afford to pay any more than **50% of the actual rents** for debt service (the mortgage payments) no matter how much the property costs. We'll need the remaining rents (50%) to pay expenses like repairs, property insurance, taxes, utilities, and of course, my *tender-loving* management fees to keep my tenants happy. As you've already learned from my previous example, *a 10% down payment* is about all I ever expect to pay to purchase my kind of properties.

When negotiating with the seller, my real challenge comes when he sets his sights on too high of a selling price – this nearly always translates to higher mortgage payments as well! The problem gets worse if the seller insists on amortized payments even though his interest rate might still be reasonable. Naturally, it's my plan to stick with a 10% down payment, so a higher selling price would mean the seller must carry back a bigger mortgage. Assuming the price is a wee bit too high, yet still acceptable to me, I'm okay so long as the seller and I can figure a way to keep the *monthly mortgage payments affordable* (50% of gross income).

Using my example on page 301, I propose to purchase your rundown property for $300,000 and pay 10% down. This means I'm left with a $270,000 mortgage debt to be paid over time. My purchase price is eight times the gross annual income of $37,500, which is reasonable for my area! *The only fly in the ointment* – the seller is asking for 7% interest with a 20-year term and **amortized payments**. My offer is **5% interest, amortized over 30 years** – but, so far the 71-year-old seller has stood his ground.

A PROPERTY WITH ALL THE RIGHT THINGS WRONG

On the surface, the seller's proposal is not terribly unreasonable! The property consists of six older individual houses, somewhat rundown, but mostly suffering from a lack of routine maintenance. Rents are somewhat low because of the rundown condition. To me, the property looks old and tired, about like the seller. Still, this is exactly the kind of property I lust and crave for – **and in my opinion**, the price ($50,000) per house is an excellent bargain if I can just find a way for my tenants to afford the mortgage payments.

With only $3125 monthly rents, the seller's proposed mortgage payments of **$2093.31** are simply too high. It would take 67% of my total income to cover the mortgage payments. In this situation, I would agree to pay 7% **interest only** payments of $1575 per month – but the big stopper here is amortized payments for 20 years – they're about $500 too much! If the seller insists on a 20-year amortization schedule, the highest interest rate (amortized payments) I could pay would be 3.5% with payment of $1565.89 or, I could stay with the 7% interest, but lower the purchase price to $230,000 with $25,000 cash down. The amortized payments would then be $1589.36. Either of these choices would likely get me tossed out of the seller's living room with strict orders to go suck rocks – **and don't come back!**

With an *under-rented property*, I have a reasonable built-in safety valve because rents can be gradually increased as I begin making improvements to the property. With ugly and distressed-type properties, a 40-50% rent increase is quite possible; however, with that size of a rent increase, a complete switch of tenants would likely be necessary. As a general rule, tenants who are paying $500 per month rents cannot afford $750 even though it will take several years to complete the upgrading. Most likely I'll be renting to what I call "gypsy tenants" (the type who move around a lot) during my two- or three-year fix-up period. What all this boils down to is that even though I have an added money cushion (anticipated rent increases), that won't yet be a reality at the time of purchase. I expect gradual increases over a couple years! **It's also important to remember**, I'll be spending much of my rent money for upgrading long before I begin seeing any additional income.

BUYING PROPERTY BASED ON ITS CURRENT INCOME

Sellers – *and especially* their hired real estate agents, tend to rave on about the *future potential* of a property rather than talk about its current value based on the existing income. It's quite easy for new investors to become victims of this **B.S.**! If you do – you'll end up giving away your future profits by paying too much – *including* inflated mortgage payments. You should always design your transactions so the **dollar numbers** work with the current income (rents) on the day you become the new owner. **Don't structure your purchase on what the income could be**. Remember, what they could be or should be are your future profits.

I've found that sitting down with sellers (one-on-one) and discussing each of the separate expense items, and of course, the proposed mortgage payments, will produce the best results. My INCOME PROPERTY ANALYSIS FORM (see Appendix C) makes a perfect tool to begin your negotiations. Most income property owners know about how much it costs to operate their properties and more often than not, **their dismal earnings are the true reason they wish to sell**. Don't be a sucker and allow them to transfer their money problems to you!

In our example above, mortgage payments of $1600 are about as high as I would dare to go! That's why my original proposal was $1500 per month for 20 years. If the elderly seller won't agree to an extended 30-year amortized mortgage rather than 20 years, or lower his selling price, my only choices to make this deal work are to offer a variable rate monthly payment plan or pay lump sum principal payments over the 20-year mortgage term. My first choice would be to have mortgage payments of $1500 per month, with a full balloon payoff at the end of 20 years. Using a periodic payment plan, I could make lump sum principal payments during the 20 years – *say like five year intervals* – or perhaps at mutually agreed dates when the seller might need extra cash. Having *fixed monthly mortgage payments* is still a far superior payment plan in my judgment, because it allows me to enjoy a much safer "bottom line," meaning predictable *cash flow* every month. Stabilizing the monthly payments while receiving an increasing amount of "rental income" every month is far better than having variable rate mortgage payments that keep adjusting higher, sucking up all my increased rental income.

Naturally, every deal is different (that's the fun part), but as you become more skilled with **seller carryback financing**, you'll become quite good at assessing the *risk vs. reward factor* when you negotiate with the seller. You'll be able to make offers and design notes (mortgages) based on good sound probabilities – *or the likelihood* of what will happen in the future! In my offer above, it's not very likely a 71-year-old seller would ever wish to see his property again. In other words, I'm guessing it would take a serious breach of our contract before he would ever consider foreclosing. Should problems arise, he would most likely renegotiate. Just knowing this is quite comforting – *don't ya think*? Alright Jay, but what about his kids or the family, maybe they might want the property! True perhaps, but if the seller has kids, and if they showed any interest at all, *chances are*, he would have sold or given the property to them in the first place.

To further explain what I'm talking about here, let's suppose the seller agrees to a $20,000 principal payment to be paid five years from now! Five years pass and I only have $10,000 saved up! Can you guess what the 71-year-old seller (who's now 76) might do? Do you think he might just take my $10,000 and modify his note to accommodate me? While I can't offer you absolute certainty about the outcome, I can tell you that I'm in the same age range as the seller, and I would listen to just about any proposal that makes sense, rather than become a 76-year-old landlord again! **Been there, done that.**

Please don't interpret what I'm suggesting here as some *sinister rat-fink strategy* to cheat someone, or play "bait-n-switch" with a seller. Don't forget, he did you a big favor when he agreed to carry the financing for you. You have an obligation to make timely payments, as well as keep your promise to the seller. Doing otherwise, will give you a bad reputation, and as a businessperson, it would hurt you with future transactions. *That said*, if you agree to obligations you can't possibly keep – or you structure monthly mortgage payments that are unrealistic, *either intentionally* or because you didn't know any better – you'll likely crash and burn, hurting both yourself and the seller, regardless of whether you intended to or not! Work something out the best way you can!

In my purchase example, it's my responsibility to convince or educate the seller that if I agreed to pay him **more than 50% of the current income** – there's a much greater risk that he'll end up with his property back. *He has far less risk if he agrees to payments that are within my ability to pay them.* Wise investors (sellers) fully understand that if they design carryback terms so their new buyer can make a few bucks every month, **the chances of a default are greatly reduced**. Sellers will often exaggerate the income they actually receive by using the *gross scheduled rents*. They don't adjust their income for vacancies and uncollectable rents, which are almost always present in poorly maintained properties.

OVERESTIMATING YOUR ABILITY TO PAY MORTGAGE

One of the most valuable tools I recommend for every investor is a plain 'ol mortgage amortization book, which shows monthly amortized payments at various interest rates. For example, turning to the 7.5%

interest table, you'll find the monthly payment to amortize a $150,000 loan balance over 20 years (240 payments) is $1208.39. Some of you may be thinking – good grief! What century does Jay think we're livin' in? This advice sounds like Jay's still riding in a horse 'n buggy. Apparently he's not aware of that small plastic hand-held device called a calculator where you can quickly punch a few buttons – *and presto*, it shows you the payment amount!

Without trying to rain on your picnic – I'll try n' say this nice as I can! Yes, I do know about calculators and if you were to ever visit my home office, you'd find one on every table in my house. Still, a mortgage payment book never gives different answers like many calculator users seem to come up with. They're handy, fast and sure – and without weak batteries to worry about. My personal favorites are *Barron's Financial Tables for Better Management* and McGraw Hill's *Interest Amortization Tables*. Both are small books – they're light-weight, easy to carry – and I believe faster when comparing payments over a different number of years, especially when they're on the same page.

KEEP THE MORTGAGE PAYMENT
FIXED IN YOUR MIND

Whatever method you choose, you need to know roughly what you can afford to pay monthly for any serious proposal you're thinking about. My "quick-n-easy" calculation is to first make sure I know exactly what the property income is – then I simply divide it in half, and that's approximately the amount my mortgage payment should be. A fixed monthly mortgage payment is a cost you can't play around too much because it's calculated using the actual income generated by the property. Your negotiations should be about the price, down payment, and the *interest cost for mortgage* (payments). Where inexperienced buyers get themselves into serious trouble is agreeing to pay larger mortgage payments than the property can support. Considering any fixed monthly mortgage payment over 60% of the property income is flirting with disaster in my judgment. Even under the best conditions, you'll be working for free! Under the worst, **you'll go broke!**

Jumping back to my example with the $270,000 mortgage balance – you'll recall, the elderly seller was agreeable to financing the property for 20 years with amortized payments at 7% interest. To me, that seems fair enough, except the income is currently not enough to support $2093.31 mortgage payments. However, since the property is under-rented because the six junky houses are in need of work, I'll eventually be able to increase the rents – but you mustn't forget, **that's the future–this is now**! Don't lock in your monthly mortgage payments on future rents – the future ain't here yet!

This is where your creativity comes into play. Think about this for a moment! How can I satisfy the aging seller (71 years old) who insists on a 20-year mortgage term with what I would call a reasonable interest rate – *and also satisfy myself*? I need a plan that gives the seller what he wants – along with mortgage payments I can afford to pay starting the day I close the sale. The financing I propose is a **graduated payment plan** that meets these requirements. You'll recall my start-out rents are only $3125 per month.

SELLER CARRYBACK MORTGAGE PROPOSAL
GRADUATED PAYMENTS

	ANNUAL INCOME	MO. RENT	AMORT.MORT PAYMENT	PROPOSED PAYMENT	SHORTAGE/ PLUS AMT.
Yr. 1	$37,500	$3125	$2093.31	$1600	-$493.31
Yr. 2	$37,500	$3125	$2093.31	$1600	-$493.31
Yr. 3	$43,500	$3625	$2093.31	$1650	-$443.31
Yr. 4	$49,700	$4142	$2093.31	$1650	-$443.31
Yr. 5	$56,250	$4687	$2093.31	$1700	-$393.31
Yr. 6	$56,250	$4687	$2093.31	$1775	-$318.31
Yr. 7	$57,000	$4750	$2093.31	$1850	-$243.31
Yr. 8	$58,200	$4850	$2093.31	$1926	-$168.31
Yr. 9	$58,200	$4850	$2093.31	$2000	-$ 93.31
Yr.10	$59,000	$4916	$2093.31	$2093.31	-0-
Yr.11	$61,080	$5090	$2093.31	$2093.31	-0-
Yr.12	$62,000	$5167	$2093.31	$2186.62	+$ 93.31
Yr.13	$63,400	$5283	$2093.31	$2261.62	+$168.31
Yr.14	$65,000	$5416	$2093.31	$2336.62	+$243.31
Yr.15	$66,900	$5575	$2093.31	$2411.62	+$318.31
Yr.16	$71,900	$5992	$2093.31	$2486.62	+$393.31
Yr.17	$72,200	$6017	$2093.31	$2536.62	+$443.31
Yr.18	$73,200	$6100	$2093.31	$2536.62	+$443.31
Yr.19	$74,200	$6183	$2093.31	$2586.62	+$493.31
Yr.20	$75,000	$6250	$2093.31	$2586.62	+$493.31

This carryback mortgage proposal I've designed stands a very good chance of being accepted by the elderly seller because it contains almost everything he is asking for – the mortgage payments have been rearranged giving me the extra time to improve the property and increase the monthly rents. The seller gets a 20-year mortgage term, fully paid off with 7% interest on his $270,000 principal balance. I'm asking that he accept my variable payment schedule, which gives me time to upgrade the property and increase my rental income over the 20-year payback period. I have not asked the seller to take one penny less than he asked for – **only to allow me to rearrange how I pay the mortgage debt**!

When you multiply 240 months (20 years) of payments amortized at 7% over 20 years ($2093.31 x 240 = $502,394.40), you have the total payback amount. The interest charges are $232,394.40 and of course, the principal amount of the seller's carryback mortgage was $270,000. When you add up all the monthly payments for my proposed "graduated payment plan" above, you'll discover they add up to the very same amount over 20 years ($502,394.40). The only difference is **how much** and **when I pay** during the 20-year payback period.

With the straight amortized payback plan, the property will not earn enough money from rents during the first five-year period. With my graduated payment plan, the rents will cover the mortgage payments. For example, in year number one, my rents are scheduled to be $3125, which is about twice the amount of my proposed mortgage payment ($1600). That's consistent with my 50% mortgage to income rule. You'll notice my mortgage payment to income ratio improves as I begin to upgrade the property and increase my rents as I go along. For example, you'll notice that in payback **year number five**, my rents have risen to $4687 per month, while my mortgage payments are only $1700. This means I'll be paying only 36% of my income to service the mortgage debt. **By year number 10**, the debt to income ratio has grown to 42%.

WHEN AND HOW MUCH

The message here is to design a mortgage payback plan that will meet most of the seller's objectives, as well as one that works for the buyer too. Underline what I'm about to tell you next – **it's very important**. When designing seller carryback mortgages, **when** and **how much** are more important to a buyer than the interest rate, or even the amount of the mortgage (within reason of course). Say for example, using my $270,000 carryback mortgage, if the amount were changed to $300,000 with 8% interest, I could still do the deal and make money if the seller would allow me to choose **when** and **how much** the payments will be.

You might be thinking: as the seller, wouldn't it be a lot safer for me to get as much money as I can right from the very beginning – *meaning bigger mortgage payments* right from the start? That way, should something go wrong, at least I will have collected more money before it happened! The answer my friends is no! In fact, just the opposite is probably true! Let's say you convince some "barnyard dummy" into paying elephant-size mortgage payments when you carry back the financing! That's the best way I know of to get your property back! When the buyer eventually discovers he's losing real foldin' money every month because the mortgage payments and operating expenses add up to more money than his income, chances are, you'll become the new owner once again – *and generally*, it's not a pretty sight when you're forced to take a property back!

All too often, angry buyers who finally realize they've been duped, become very poor losers. They file bankruptcy; they strip all the appliances from the property. They let the grass die and the fences fall down, then finally – when they realize they've lost their entire investment, *in desperation*, they rent the property to the town's highest paying tenants, "the dope dealers"! Now they can collect some fast pocket money before mailing you the keys. Here's my message: design your mortgage payments to work for both sides, *the buyer and the seller*. If a compromise cannot be reached – walk away and don't look back!

ACHIEVING POSITIVE LEVERAGE – A MUST

Positive leverage means you're earning more money from the property than the cost to finance it. It's a simple concept, but you'd be surprised just how many folks who call themselves investors violate this rule! When they do, it's called *negative leverage*, and needless to say, that's the quickest path for going broke! Some folks may say – Jay, everyone knows negative cash flow properties are bad – how elementary can you be? You must be the top graduate from "financing for dummies" school to even bring this up!

Friends, all kinds of *so-called investors* do this every day. Allow me to show you an example of what I mean. Take a typical "run of the mill" property that cost $120,000. It has a 7.5% 30-year amortized mortgage and rents for $900 per month – let's assume there was a $20,000 down payment, so the amount financed is $100,000. The mortgage payments are only $699.21 per month – so what's the big problem? Take your pick – **too much financing or not enough income**! Here's why!

Expenses to operate this property will be at least $360 per month (40%). That leaves only $540 to pay the $699.21 mortgage payment! In this example there's a $159.21 shortage – or *negative leverage*! Obviously to fix this problem, assuming the rent is already at the market rate, I'll need a $540 mortgage payment. A 30-year mortgage amortized at 5% interest with payments of $536.82 will do the trick. 7.5% is way too much in this example.

NEGOTIATING INTEREST RATE OFTEN BETTER THAN FIGHTING OVER PRICE

As a general rule, sellers who are willing to carry the financing are more reluctant to reduce their selling price than about lowering the interest rate on their carryback mortgage. In other words, the interest rate is less important to them than giving ground on the price. For long-term hold investors like myself, I've always felt it's better to negotiate an interest rate reduction rather than "beat up" the seller over his price. You might say it's like losing a battle but winning the war! Allow me to explain! Let's suppose the seller is asking $110,000 for his property and has indicated he'll accept my offer for that amount with $10,000 down. He's also offering seller financing for 30 years with amortized payments at 7.5% interest. My initial offer of $100,000 was **just flat rejected**. In fact, he got so upset he wouldn't even write a counter offer! By all indications, this seller is a very stubborn man. Still, in my opinion, the property would be a very good deal for me, so I'll try again!

My second offer was for the full price, $110,000, with the same down payment, same seller carryback mortgage – *only at 6.5% interest* (reduced 1.0%). This time around, the seller signed the deal without batting an eye! Sometimes, your initial offer will allow you to discover what's most important to the seller. My ill-fated offer had proposed $10,000 off the asking price. That's roughly a 9% reduction ($9900). The seller went ballistic stomping up and down on my offer – plus he got so worked up he wouldn't even respond. My second offer was apparently much more soothing! Obviously, receiving full price meant a great deal to him because reducing the interest rate to 6.5% on his carryback financing sailed right through without even a cuss word! Emotions will sometimes have more to do with making a deal than you might suspect. By giving up one percentage point of interest, 6.5% instead of 7.5% on the carryback financing, the seller actually sold me the property **$24,000 cheaper** than my first offer. The difference between paying back $100,000 at 7.5% interest versus 6.5% is $24,170.40 – or nearly two and a half times the $10,000 price reduction I had asked for initially.

You might be thinking – sure it's cheaper with less interest to pay, but you still must wait a long time to realize the savings. True enough, but remember I'm a long-term hold kinda guy! Much like the most desirable wines, true real estate wealth will take you a little more time! I will tell you this much – patient real estate investors always end up a whole lot richer than the "quick turn, flip 'n flop" bunch. If you need any further proof – read *The Millionaire Next Door* by Thomas J. Stanley. He explains how the rich get rich in America!

HOW AGENTS CAN HELP YOU WITH SELLERS

The majority of all real estate transactions are done by licensed agents, so don't even think about cutting them out of the pie! You'll need them if you plan on convincing sellers about the benefits of seller financing on properties they have listed! Seller financing is worth millions of dollars to me, but to most agents it don't mean "diddle squat"! To be successful, however, you'll need to work with your own agent, as well as listing agents involved, assisting them any way you can! Let me give you an idea about how I work with my agent Fred!

To start with, most real estate agents, including Fred, have been taught to keep the buyer and seller apart! When principles get together, things get screwed up and deals fall apart! Whether that's true or not, it's certainly what most agents believe so there's not much use arguing about it! Still, we investors don't stand much of a chance of negotiating seller financing unless we can personally meet with the sellers. Here's how I've learned to explain the situation to Fred when I need his help:

"Fred, I'd like for you to get permission from the seller's agent so I can meet with the sellers. We can all sit down together and discuss some advantages of seller financing! I'm sure it would be most helpful for the seller to meet me so I can answer questions about myself, my credit worthiness, and of course, the terms of the *financing I'm proposing.* I promise not to discuss anything else about the deal that doesn't pertain to the financing. Once I've made my financing pitch, I'll excuse myself and leave the room! If there's anything you guys wish to discuss, I'll wait outside. By the way, soon as we get this financing issue cleared up – **we're ready to close and everybody gets paid!**"

For just a moment, picture yourself as my agent Fred! Ask yourself, am I being sensitive to your concerns? The answer is yes! I've asked for permission to meet with the seller and I've agreed not to start blabbing about anything other than the financing terms. I've also let it be known that after we clear up the financing, *we're ready to close and everyone gets paid.* These are important matters to any real estate agent and *the mention of closing and getting paid* is like yelling "strike" in a gold mine. I think it's well worth repeating here that sellers who are even thinking about providing financing will nearly always want to meet personally with the buyer. They want to talk with him or her, *look 'em in the eye*, and generally make their own personal judgment about whether or not the person is of good character or not. I've found that sellers need to feel good vibes about the person they'll be trusting to mail in their payments every month.

SELLERS MUST FEEL COMFORTABLE WITH YOU

In my experience, I've found that most sellers will "open up" a little bit if they like me! Obviously, that's one reason I insist on meeting them in the first place so I can present myself! I've found that when sellers like me, and judge me to be a decent person, they'll also tell me many things about themselves. Sellers will most likely inform me about their future plans and what they intend to do with the money from the sale. When I'm able to acquire properties from older sellers who are retiring – I can almost guess their situation every time! The payments they'll be receiving from me will be part of their retirement income. Most likely they'll deposit their payments in a bank account and use it to supplement their retirement income. That's pretty much what we all do when we sell out – **wouldn't you agree?**

Many of these retirement-minded folks are not terribly well educated when it comes to financing their properties. They need a little coaching! This takes patience and understanding because it's difficult to change how people feel about their money and its use. For example, my Mom and Pop both thought saving money was how you end up wealthy. It was their opinion that investing like I do is far too risky! I doubt seriously if they ever changed their views even after they watched my success. Mom thought I was just lucky – and Dad never really figured out what I was doing!

YOU MUST THOROUGHLY EXPLAIN
FINANCING TO SELLER

As I mentioned earlier, most sellers don't ever hear about any other plan for financing except what their real estate agent tells them – "get the cash," take your money, and run, they advise! Why should you loan money to Jay so he can purchase your property? Let Jay go to the bank and get all your money so you make sure nothing goes wrong! When you finance your own property, there's just too much risk involved – sell for cash, put your money in the bank and now you're totally safe! That's normal real estate agent advice!

I've found there's a much better way for me – **and quite often, much better for the sellers when it's properly explained to them**! To begin with, Mr. Seller, we're not talking about a loan here. **I'm asking you to give me terms instead**! I'll pay you the full $120,000 price you're asking for your property – however, I'd like to pay you a $20,000 cash down payment right now – then pay you the balance of your money in payments of $700 *or more per month* until it's all paid off. I'm willing to pay you 7% interest on the unpaid balance.

UNDERSTANDING THE SELLER'S PLANS

It's my understanding, Mr. Seller, that you need **$700 each month** to supplement your retirement income so you can travel and spend time with your grandkids. I'm also aware that your real estate agent has suggested that you sell for all cash – he has advised you to put your money in a bank account where you can draw out $700 payments every month. I'm here to show you an **alternative plan** that might just work to your advantage. To begin with, I'm willing to pay your full **asking price**! Most often, cash buyers will be looking for a sizable discount when they agree to pay you all cash!

I'm not exactly sure if your agent explained how these checking and withdrawal accounts work at the bank – or if he told you how long your $100,000 will last! While it's true, these drawing accounts will pay you a small amount of interest annually based on your year-end balance, it's a very piddly amount – it's currently less than a quarter percent! Frankly folks, their interest rate sucks! You should also know how long your money will last. *In other words*, how many $700 monthly payments do you expect to receive before your money runs out? That answer, Mr. Seller, I can tell you, is roughly 13 years, give or take a few months! That's how long it will take to use up your total $100,000 deposit, including the small amount of interest the bank will pay you.

JAY'S ALTERNATE FINANCING PLAN

On the other hand, Mr. Seller, if you would allow me to pay you **$20,000 cash down now** – *then begin making payments* of **$706.78 per month** along with 7% interest, your money's gonna last you a whole lot longer! Would you care to take a guess? **The answer, Mr. Seller, is 25 years**! Now let me ask you – *which plan do you like the best?* Sellers always ask me the obvious question – why is there such a big difference in the number of monthly payments? It's because of the 7% interest I'll be paying – you'll actually receive an additional **$112,000** interest income from me! That's in addition to your original **$100,000** principal amount! The bottom line is, **you'll be earning more than twice as much from my seller financing** – and perhaps even more important for you, your retirement checks will keep arriving in your mailbox for almost twice as long!

CHAPTER 19

EASY TERMS CATCH BIG FISH

*F*inancing is the absolute heart 'n soul of building wealth with real estate – beginning from the time you purchase your first property till the time you cash in your chips (sell out). In the early years, most Mom and Pop investors (the folks I associate with) simply don't have enough knowledge to understand that financing will have a great deal to do with their success or failure in this business! Like most investors starting out, I had no idea that financing would eventually involve almost everything I've been able to accomplish with my properties!

The way you finance your properties when you acquire them will greatly influence future sales, trades, lease options, and seller financing when you decide to call it quits. To say this another way, the financing you negotiate or place on your property will have a great deal to do with when and how you can retire ("smell the roses") and more importantly, your profits. In most institutional mortgages today, banks and mortgage companies automatically write due-on-sale clauses in their mortgages or deeds of trust. This single clause prohibits any sale or transfer without their written consent. Rarely will they waive this restrictive clause without jacking up the interest rate or requiring a brand new mortgage.

CONTROL DETERMINES WINNERS AND LOSERS

Underline this next sentence and don't ever forget it! **By far the biggest profits in real estate are earned by investors who control**

all the moving parts. Control over financing is more profitable than neighborhoods, quality of the buildings, timing, negotiating skills, and whatever else you can think of. Please don't misinterpret what I'm saying here by thinking these things I've mentioned are not important! Location and quality of the real estate are always important. All I'm saying is control over financing trumps them all!

Creative financing is a term most generally associated with acquiring real estate directly from the seller, as opposed to third party financing, such as a loan or mortgage from the bank. Seldom are banks very creative! If you as the borrower don't fit their so-called lending programs, *as they like to call them*, you can pretty much go suck rocks! Obviously, banks must have a more conservative approach to lending along with much stricter mortgage rules because they're loaning out bank depositor's money. With bank mortgages (loans) we're talkin' about green dollar bills loaned directly from their safe deposit vault to pre-qualified borrowers. Most new homes are purchased using this type of financing – but not all types of real estate.

SELLERS ALWAYS MAKE THE BEST LENDERS

The big dividing line that determines whether banks will finance real estate or not, for most regular Mom and Pop investors is drawn between four and five living units. For purposes of real estate financing, one to four units are considered to be a residential mortgage or loan, whereas, five units or more are considered a commercial mortgage. For Donald Trump, getting commercial loans are easier than a one foot putt; but if you're not Donald Trump and you plan to purchase the kind of units I buy, *five units or more*, you may as well kiss your banker farewell! Even if you're golf buddies or you try to bribe him with lunch – forget it! He's bound by strict banking rules and your application will probably be treated like chopped liver!

The late Warren Harding, long-time real estate investor and trainer, used to always tell his students:, "You don't dance with the real estate – **you dance with the people.**" In my opinion, the wisdom of that statement has no equal, and nowhere does it apply more than with seller financing! Seller financing with customized terms is the Cadillac of financing for buying investment real estate using an installment plan!

Some may argue that price (what you pay) for investment real estate is the key to profitability! In my view, the amount one pays for an income property pales in comparison to how it's financed. In fact, in almost all my transactions over the past 40 years, I've given in on the price in order to get good financing terms. **Terms control the cash flow**, which most every investor lusts and craves for.

The *constant*, the amount you must pay every month to service the debt, must be kept low enough so it don't gobble up all the income! Otherwise, you could end up having to reach in your wallet every month to make up for operating shortages. This situation is often called an *alligator property*. The constant can be kept lower when amortization can be avoided. This will never happen with bank mortgages – but your chances with the seller improve dramatically. In fact, many sellers even prefer interest only mortgages when they carry back financing. I'm in that group myself!

The transfer or sale of almost any investment property you can think of can be made more attractive for both parties, the buyer and seller, with **creative financial terms** and some **imagination**! For small-time investors like myself and those who are hoping to be, regular bank mortgages or financing will greatly limit the kind of properties you'll be able to acquire. Generally speaking, banks will finance or provide their standard mortgages for **one- to four-unit properties** in good condition in decent areas – but **creativity** is a foreign concept to most banks. They're about as creative as prunes for breakfast! If you should happen to request financing for five or more units – you're in for a very special treat! It's called commercial lending!

SELLER FINANCING IS NEVER OUT OF STYLE

McGraw Hill, my giant New York book publisher, called me before the last housing meltdown when banks were trying to outdo each other by dishing out money to any applicant who could fog a mirror! *Liar loans or no doc mortgages*, they called them! McGraw's senior real estate editor was baffled by several chapters I had submitted about seller financing. He nearly dropped the phone when I told him that more than 80% of all my deals had involved seller financing! His response to me – our local brokers are telling us that seller financing is not done anymore because it's so easy to get bank mortgages. Obviously, he was talkin' about people's homes! Still, I informed him that I've kept every escrow file since I began investing and invited him to fly out for a visit if he needed more proof! Several days later he called back to say his brokers had found several local seller financed deals – so he approved my chapters and stopped calling me!

With seller financing, you can buy or sell properties that wouldn't otherwise be very attractive if they were dependent on a new bank mortgage or refi! A seemingly poor investment can be turned into a winner based on the terms that people (the buyer and seller) can agree to. Much of the investment risk can also be eliminated by terms of financing. As a general rule, the longer the payback period and the smaller the monthly constant (payment), the safer the deal is for both parties.

Creative financing is not simply a seller carryback arrangement that both parties say yes to! It goes much deeper than that because it can solve almost any financing problem for buyers and sellers alike! For example, I have intentionally overpaid for properties because the seller agreed to give me monthly payments I could easily pay from the rents – even with my small 10% down payment. Paying a 90% mortgage payment on a typical transaction under average circumstances is difficult to do without having negative cash flow. **Structuring the payments to fit the available income is more important to me than paying a higher price** (within reason of course). Besides, I also get more generous depreciation deductions because my basis is higher.

CONTROL THE FINANCING IMPORTANT

Bank financing is a lot like *dancing with a gorilla* – the dance is never over till the gorilla says so! That's giving up way too much control to suit me. Legally, when you have a bank mortgage on the property, you need permission to do almost anything that sounds creative! For example, selling with a lease/option agreement would not be permitted if you asked! "Subject to" or taking over loans with due-on-sale clauses only work when the bank looks the other way. From a legal standpoint, however, banks could call the loan making it fully payable anytime they choose. Most wrap-around or all-inclusive type financing is not permitted by banks if you ask for their permission!

Had I been dealing with banks rather than individual sellers for the majority of my property financing, I'd be roughly a million dollars worse off today. Seller financed notes (mortgages), both the ones I structured or created when I purchased my properties, and also those I took over or assumed on properties I've acquired, have given back to me generously over the years! **How do they give back, you ask?** It's called discounting! The owners or holders of notes (mortgages) payable by me with a total face value of 3.3 million have graciously accepted discounts from me averaging nearly 28% because I paid them off early and gave them cash. This very lucrative profit center comes from **dancing with people**, like Warren Harding so eloquently put it.

BENEFITS HAVE DIFFERENT VALUES

There are many parts or benefits to real estate investing. These parts or benefits all have different values to different people. Financing is quite subjective – some folks value how much, others want yield or income. This is why zero interest mortgages can be negotiated with some sellers while the next guy throws you out for asking! Discounting private financing (notes) like I mentioned above is strictly a people business. If the beneficiary needs money (which most people do), it works slick as a whistle! I've negotiated 70% discounts and I've had the note holders sic their dogs on me for even asking. There is no right or wrong way to ask for a discount – it's entirely your own creativity! The following hypothetical purchase will give some pretty good ideas about how you can set the stage!

Let's say I purchase a rundown property for $400,000 with a cash down payment of $40,000. I successfully negotiate seller carryback financing in the amount of **$360,000**, with monthly payments of **$1950, interest only**, at 6.5% interest for 20 years. The financing or *promissory note balance* is all due in 20 years. Once again, I want you to think about the rundown property and what we might assume about the seller and his financial situation. I'm only speculating, but by the looks of the property and the seller's lack of management skills, he's likely about the same way with his financial affairs. Can you possibly guess what the seller would have much rather had instead of a $40,000 down payment? **The answer my friends**–he would much rather have had **all of his money**, or at least a lot more cash than he got when the sale closed.

If there's anything worse than waiting for time to pass when you're broke – then it's got to be waiting for 20 years to go by when you know you've got a pot full of money coming **someday**! Waiting 20 long years for most of your money has got to be extremely painful for financially strapped sellers! I think I've painted you a somewhat accurate picture of our seller in this hypothetical purchase, considering the condition of his property and his willingness to agree to a 20-year installment plan – wouldn't you guess he's in poor financial shape? It's very likely this seller really wants or needs more money, but he simply couldn't get any more than 10% down because of the condition of his property! I'm also guessing it's the same reason he was forced to settle for long-term interest only payments or risk losing the deal altogether!

NOTE: I have used the terms mortgage, note and loan throughout this chapter – for the purpose of understanding. They basically mean the same thing – a debt instrument secured by the property.

HIGH PROBABILITY OF BUYING BACK MY DEBT

Unless a seller calls me, I will seldom make any further contact with him or her for at least a couple years after we've closed escrow. Generally, I will have religiously mailed him payments for at least two years. By now I figure he's gotten adjusted to the money coming in every month from my mortgage payments – also, I'm guessing he spends every nickel I send. I've found the type of seller we're discussing here spends more money than he takes in. Whatever he earns he spends, because he manages money about the same way he manages his property. For whatever reason, this type of seller will always need more money!

Reaching out to my seller is my term for making him an offer he most likely won't refuse. I call this technique **buying back my own mortgage debt**! I don't mind telling you right upfront; *this is a very profitable business*, but it can only happen when sellers finance their properties rather than banks. When it comes to buying back your mortgage debt, you can be as creative as your mind permits. Also, you can do it without showing your teeth like many so-called professional note buyers. Those guys purchase notes using only their cold-blooded calculator! To some degree, we can use our heart!

My million dollar plus **mortgage buy-backs** range from 30 to 70% discounts. In our hypothetical purchase above, using the $360,000 carryback note as our example – I could buy it back in chunks, rather than all at once. Chunks are very effective because you can solve what I call **continuing money problems** for the mortgage holder over the entire term of his debt. That is, every time the mortgage holder has a new financial crisis in his life – **you're right there like his dealer!**

In many ways, I like **chunk discounting** better than buying back the total debt because in most cases I'm able to negotiate a few extra years on the term of the mortgage in the same transaction! For example, let's say the mortgage holder wants or needs **$50,000** of his $360,000 note. I'll ask him for a double reduction in my mortgage balance ($360,000 less **$100,000** = $260,000), plus, I'll ask him to extend the 20-year mortgage three or four more years. This is very acceptable to most note holders who need quick cash and don't wish to sell or assign their note to a cold-hearted money broker (hypothecate).

If you had asked me about this part of my business when I first started investing, I would have not known or understood what you were even talkin' about! Why would anyone give up (sell) all or part of their carryback note and give all sorts of other concessions for a far less amount of cash than their note balance? The answer, my friends, **is so they can have their money right now**! In case you're still wondering why – just take a look around your local neighborhood and observe the rapid expansion of title loan operators (car titles). Their 20% monthly fee equals 240% annually! People will do anything for money and for their own reasons, and no price seems too high when they want the cash now!

WHY TERMS ARE MORE IMPORTANT THAN PRICE

Owing 3-5 million dollars to private note holders (beneficiaries) when you can successfully negotiate an average discount rate of almost 30% is nothing to sneeze about. In our hypotetical example of a $400,000 purchase, it would mean the actual price paid would be less than **$300,000** for the property after the 30% discount. At the beginning of this chapter I told you seller financing is not the best because I said so! It's best because it made me **$1,000,000** richer.

The quicker you can start thinking about **real estate investing as a business** with many various ways to make money besides simply selling for a profit or renting, the faster your bank account will grow. It takes a while to get the hang of this stuff, but the best way to start is with the right vehicle capable of taking you to the Promise Land. In order to become a lot richer and faster, which has always been my goal, you must change your thinking about investing to **multiple profit opportunities** rather than what the real estate looks like or where you think it should be located. Signing private notes with people (sellers) rather than banks is the best way to begin!

CREATIVITY FLOURISHES WITH PEOPLE

Several paragraphs above, I mentioned other concessions besides discounting the mortgage and I meant every word. **Creativity knows no bounds**! At my seminars I'm often asked – Okay Jay, I agree with you, this discounting sounds great, but where do I get the money to pay the note holder his cash? Here's one of my favorite methods, which I call "the switcheroo" or *walkin' the mortgage*. Let's say for example, Mr. Jones holds my note for $200,000. He wants or needs

$50,000 fast. I say fine Mr. Jones, I can do it, but you'll need to reduce our note balance by $100,000 (double the amount you're asking for), plus, you'll need to transfer the note balance to my property on West Street. Once he agrees to my offer, that frees up the property his note was on so it's now free and clear without debt. I'm now able to borrow $50,000 on that property and give the money to Jones. The formal term for what I've just accomplished is **"substitution of collateral"** and it's done every day with the note holder's permission. See how simple this stuff is! It's also lots more fun when you can create your own profits outta thin air!

Over the years I've intentionally sought out multiple-unit properties with **multiple seller carryback notes** secured by the property. It's my dream to find these kinds of properties and buy them subject to three or four (even more) seller financed notes. By now you should begin to see why I'm trolling for these kinds of opportunities! It's my intention to contact each of the note holders after **I'm the new owner** and advise them I've got a pocket full of cash while it lasts, if they are willing to settle for less than their current note balances! Whoever gets here first with the best offer gets my money, *I tell them*! See my Christmas letter (Appendix G).

When you begin to realize that people have ups and downs, good times and bad as they bounce along living their daily lives, it's not too difficult to imagine they'll run out of money from time to time! Doesn't everyone? Here's what I want you to underline and never forget. When people are experiencing serious money problems and you've got a few bucks laying around, *or you can get it*, you can ask for some pretty big favors (like mortgage discounts) and likely have great success so long as you can provide **fast cash relief**! You'll find my 28% average is probably nowhere near the record. During my apprenticeship I was much too timid with my discount requests!

LEASING WITH OPTION IS BACK DOOR FINANCING

Leasing with an **option to purchase** is financing by another name, and you can pull off some super cost saving advantages when you acquire properties by putting this technique to use! First of all, most sellers do not think of a lease option the same way as a sale, and will not ask for the customary down payment because they're leasing! After all, they will still own the property until you exercise the option to purchase! Let's say for example, the seller is having difficulty finding a buyer because his rundown property looks butt ugly. With no reputable buyer in sight, the owner has become somewhat desperate! Suddenly, out of the blue, you show up. The price is $300,000 with 10% down; however, you just happen to be $30,000 light!

The current rental income is $45,000 annually, so you propose leasing the property with an option to purchase 15 months from now. You explain to the seller who wants out right now that you don't have the down payment just yet, but you are willing to **take over immediately by leasing the property** till the down payment gets paid. You offer to lease the property for $2,000 per month, with full credit for lease payments going toward the $30,000 down payment. After 15 months with credit for 15 lease payments, you now exercise your purchase option with a balance owing of **$270,000**. You can now convert your $2,000 monthly payments to pay off the $270,000 mortgage balance. If you're successful, you've acquired the property with **no down payment** – plus you've made principal reduction payments without paying one dime's worth of interest for 15 months. You couldn't do much better with hamburger helper!

Obviously, the key to making this transaction work has mostly to do with solving the seller's problem and having knowledge about the various remedies available – *in this case*, the lease/option arrangement! The seller wanted out for sure, but he also wanted $30,000 down before he would even talk about financing the sale. In the end, he financed it anyway! We just called it another name!

Thinking outside the box and being creative earns the biggest paydays in the real estate business. There are more ways to profit than I ever imagined when I first started out. Like I told you about discounting notes or mortgages – *in the beginning*, I only looked for discounts on the mortgages sellers carried back for me when I purchased their properties. Later on, I discovered that when buying *multiple-unit properties* and small apartments – the deals often came with a whole new assortment of private notes. Seems that each time these small income properties were sold, the sellers would carry back a large share of their equity. I have purchased these small colonies (multi-unit properties) with as many as four or five private mortgages attached, *which of course*, I would assume or take over with the purchase! When I learned about this "mother lode" of private party mortgages, I began to hunt for them in earnest. This is when my discounting reached an exciting new level!

EDUCATION IS THE KEY TO CREATIVITY

Creativity, I've found, comes with education. You can't expect to be in the driver's seat or do much creative financing if you don't understand numbers or what different terms mean! I talk with beginners all the time who don't know a *trust deed* from a *grant deed* or *general grant*. I'm a strong believer in "on-the-job training" – but please don't neglect the home study part of learning this business. With creative financing, you must learn the jargon and what the numbers and values mean in order to make deals and prepare your own contracts to benefit yourself.

Many newbies stumble over *interest rates, yields*, and *compounding*. Does the seller need to have amortized payments or not? Above, I introduced the word **constant** – it's the total mortgage payment you must pay every month on your loan. It's not the stated interest rate on the mortgage – it's higher because it also includes amortization or principal pay down! *Simple interest* and *compounding interest* are completely different birds! Simple interest is the annual interest rate on the loan amount times the term or *number of years* on the note. Thus a $10,000 note with a 10-year term written at 15% interest would require a $25,000 payoff in 10 years when the loan matures–$10,000 principal + 10 periods of $1500 = $15,000 = $25,000. The same $10,000 loan compounded annually at 15% would require a $40,450 payoff in 10 years. The higher payoff is because compounding *applies the 15% rate* to both principal and the accumulating interest added on annually for the term of the loan. When you borrow money, ask for simple interest!

Learning to draft your notes or mortgages the way you want them is well worth your time and effort, a simple error or even a *single word* in your note can make a serious difference in the payoff or your profits if you own the note. You need to understand the difference between **including** or **plus** interest. If your note receivable reads $10,000, including 15% interest due in 10 years – you'll be very disappointed when you receive just **$10,000** ten years from now. Had you typed in – *plus 15% interest* instead, you'd receive **$40,450** if your note had compounding interest. Learning this kinda stuff will make the cost of a **good financing seminar** seem cheap – **say Amen**!

TRADITIONAL FINANCING LIMITS OPPORTUNITY

Creative financing can be whatever **the buyer** and **seller** agree to. When you begin searching for some magic method to help you find sellers willing to carry financing and give you the kind of terms you need – you'll find there is only one major ingredient you need to be concerned about! It's called **seller motivation**. Motivated sellers are the ones who can help you design mortgages that will allow you to have cash flow when you close escrow. If you think banks are even slightly concerned about this, I've got this great lookin' bridge I'll sell ya!

With bank mortgages, **both the borrower and the property must qualify**. Any blemishes on your credit report will pretty much send you packing – assuming you're able to pass muster, your next big hurdle is called the property appraisal. This process is sometimes more insulting than all the bank's paperwork, but assuming you pass, you're still far from being done! The bank's underwriter says you now need a home inspection report – water heater straps, termite report, verification of smoke and gas detectors, and copies of all the leases if you have renters. And if just one shingle turns up missing off the roof – you'll need a roof inspection report too!

In my business, I rarely wish to put up more than 10% of the purchase price for my down payment. This is very difficult on cash flow because you still must finance the remaining 90% balance! With almost any kind of regular mortgage, financing 90% of the debt makes it nearly impossible to end up with cash flow after paying all the expenses. This won't work for me, so is there anything else I can do?

You must never forget – **creative financing** must work for both sides or you'll never get your deal approved! This is why you must sit down with the other party and determine what he or she really values – and of course, what they might be willing to give up. **Remember, there must be motivation here or don't bother wasting your time**. I know of no way to purchase anyone's property if they are unwilling to sell! Many beginners try, and if they succeed, they usually end up with an alligator, which eats them alive!

Shelving Equity Technique

Mr.Seller: I like your property and I agree with you – it's probably worth $500,000 like you say; however, the income seems a bit low! The seller usually answers by saying – that's why it's worth the price because you can immediately increase the income! This exchange is very common and often ends with no further action – or some "low ball" offer, which the seller quickly rejects. In some situations, the seller is correct! There is a great potential! Still, you mustn't ignore the current income that not up to snuff. There are also situations for whatever reason – the seller is zeroed in on his price but might be open to other **creative arrangements**. This is why you must sit down with the seller and figure out his weak spot. This might be a situation where a somewhat over-priced deal can work if the seller will allow me a **creative payback arrangement** using two separate seller carryback notes or mortgages. I call this **shelving equity** and it works like this:

PURCHASE PRICE	$500,000	Full Asking Price
DOWN PAYMENT	$ 50,000	Jay's Typical 10% Down
AMOUNT FINANCED	$450,000	2 Separate Notes or Mortgages

Gross Income $5,000 per Month
Note No. 1 $350,000 with payments of $2500 per month – starts now
Note No. 2 $100,000 with payments of $750 per month – deferred

Mr. Seller, I like your property even though it may be a bit over-priced! You're probably right – I think it has good potential – still, the income is weak! Here's what I'm willing to do. I will pay you **full price $500,000** for your property. I can pay you **$50,000** cash down like I've already told you; however, you'll need to help me with the financing! There's not enough income to make payments on the entire unpaid balance of $450,000. I propose to split up the financing into two separate notes or mortgages. The first will be for **$350,000** with payments of **$2500** per month, and I will begin making payments immediately. The second mortgage will be for **$100,000** with monthly payments of **$750**. I will begin payments 10 years from now. This allows me time to build up the income and gives me the extra safety I need – *and you*, Mr. Seller, will receive your full asking price!

As a rule, I consider paying more than 50% of the current income to be somewhat risky. Generally speaking, operating expenses and vacancies will consume 40-45% of the gross income over time. Also, I'd like to receive a token return on my $50,000 down payment. In some cases where I haven't quite convinced the seller on my split mortgage concept, I'll toss in a couple additional provisions!

Mr. Seller, I can see you're a bit skeptical about deferring $100,000 worth of debt for 10 years – so here's what I'm willing to do so you're protected. I'll add the following terms or conditions that apply to mortgage No. 2 as follows:

Term #1: Should the income increase to $6000 per month, I'll begin making payments on mortgage no. 2 as agreed – $750 per month.

Term #2: Mortgage no. 2 shall be paid in full if property is sold any time before 10 years.

These two clauses or terms are generally enough to clinch the deal if the seller is truly motivated to sell.

PREPARATION REQUIRED TO MAKE GOOD DEALS

You should understand that good deals are not found lying around waiting for you. I'm sorry, but **you'll need to create them yourself**!

When I negotiate with sellers to purchase their real estate, I spend countless hours doing "Columbo style" detective work. I talk with them, and I study their surroundings. I meet with the kids, I drink coffee with the grown-ups, and I try very hard to keep my mouth shut – at least as much as I can for a blabbermouth with a large ego. I have practiced very hard to do this and after 50 years I've made some progress.

Webster tells us negotiating means to *arrive at a settlement*! No one can settle anything unless both sides get what they want. I don't need to spend much time figuring out what I want – I already know what I want when I arrive at the seller's house. The time-consuming part is my effort to find out what the seller wants so we can arrive at a settlement. I have never met a seller who asked me what I wanted! The truth is, most couldn't give a tinker's damn about me. Sellers are tuned into one radio frequency only when I arrive. **It's called Station W I F M.** It means *WHAT'S IN IT FOR ME*? Don't waste your time trying to move their dial. Instead, prepare yourself to listen and mostly keep your mouth shut!

Sellers are interested in what they can get – or what you are willing to give them for their property – **that's it**! If you understand this, and you can accept it, you've won yourself a big fat "A" in my classroom. Down payments, *subject to mortgages*, interest rates, and seller financing can all be negotiated in many different ways – **with different outcomes**, and with different sellers, because they're all different people. As you know, people have different wants and needs. **One size never fits all.** There are no "cookie cutter" negotiating solutions. You as a dashing wanta-bee real estate tycoon must find out what each individual seller needs and/or wants, then determine what you're willing to give up to get it.

PROPERTY SELECTION IS THE KEY

Before you explain to me that you've tried to find seller financing opportunities, but you can't seem to get past first base – let me interrupt and say this: negotiating with sellers who own nicer-looking, sweet-smelling properties, probably won't give you diddly squat! *Their properties look good, and that gives them too much control.* They don't have to give you any concessions! They don't even need to be fair-minded about selling because there's a lot of dummy buyers willing to pay anything they ask for their property – *and of course,* **sellers know that!** Just remember, it shouldn't be you! Naturally, the control transfers to my side with rundown property (my specialty) because potential rundown property buyers are a lot more scarce. Once again, I'll repeat, **I'm in the investing business for the money,** *not just to own the property.* Years ago, I owned nice looking houses filled with sweet smelling tenants. Everything was beautiful! The only thing ugly back then was my bank account.

Power is always in the hands of those who have the most. *In the real estate business this means the owners who have the nicest looking properties.* However, this power rapidly fades for owners of rundown buildings and "ugly dumps." This huge power shift is what earns the big bucks for investors who choose to turn the underperforming properties into cash producing winners. My main message here is **never fear negotiating one-on-one with seller.** If they truly wish to sell, they couldn't care less about how new you are or your experience level. Frankly, they don't give a rat's hoot so long as they can get something they want.

The number one reason why sellers object to *carryback financing* is safety – **their safety.** When banks finance their deals, they get the money soon as escrow closes – it's done. When they carry back financing for the buyer – *it's not done!* They may have to wait 15 or 20 years before it's done! This is where the seller's safety comes in. Their big concern is **will they get their money as promised?** That's the big question you'll need to answer to their satisfaction if you intend to do much seller financing business. Simply telling the seller that you're an honest, upstanding person won't likely cut the mustard!

Sellers will want a bit more assurance that they'll get their money as promised. One of my favorite techniques is to offer what I call **double protection** in the form of additional collateral. I'll pledge equity in another property that I already own, in addition to the security of the property I'm buying. In other words, *I'll explain to the seller* – if I should default on my *carryback financing* with you, you will be in position to not only take back the property you're selling me – **but also**, you can take the additional property I'm pledging as well! This gives you the extra assurance that I'll keep my promise to pay you! This additional collateral method works well with many sellers and it saves me down payment money without costing me a dime.

MULTIPLE UNITS AND SELLER FINANCING GO TOGETHER

New investors constantly ask me – how do you get so many seller financing deals (roughly 81%)? The answer, my friends, **is buying the right kind of properties**. Single house buyers rarely find sellers who will agree to carry long-term financing because they don't have to! It's that simple! Investing my way, you'll find the right vehicle makes all the difference in the world when it comes to seller financing. Multiple-unit investing almost drives you to negotiate financing with sellers instead of relying on third party lenders. Even if banks would agree to offer mortgages, an investor like me would have to jump through all kinds of hoops to qualify! If you think securing a regular home mortgage is tough – just try qualifying to get a commercial mortgage on what the banks call *non-conforming properties*. Six rundown rental houses on a residential lot, is *non-conforming* and unless zoning is changed – forget bank financing!

Depending on the financing terms, it's possible to transfer both **immediate cash flow** and/or **sizable profits** from the seller to the buyer. For example, I've used *variable payment mortgages* to purchase properties that otherwise wouldn't work or "pencil out" (see Chapter 18). I needed smaller payments for the first few years when my income was low, in exchange for higher payments over the last few years when I expect much higher rents. The price of any investment or income property can be raised or lowered by terms of the financing. As a rule, I'm always willing to pay a higher price for your property if you'll provide long-term financing with payments that allow me to have an immediate cash flow. Price to me is not nearly as important as my monthly payment. If you have experience with negative cash flow – **raise your hand and say Amen!**

Amortized mortgages will almost always suck all the cash flow out of leveraged real estate transactions. Amortization or principal reduction mortgages are common everyday stuff when you're acquiring single-family houses with typical bank financing. *In my business, amortization is not everyday stuff.* In fact, I generally don't want amortized financing – here's why! Suppose I'm trying to purchase a $350,000 property with #35,000 down and the seller says he's willing to carry financing for 20 years at a 6% interest rate! I will always negotiate very hard to get interest-only payments. I might even offer higher interest if the seller plays tough! If the 6% mortgage were amortized, my payments would be $2257 per month! Interest-only payments would reduce my mortgage cost to **$1575 per month.** The difference to me is **almost $700 per month additional cash flow** – starting the day I close escrow!

CHAPTER 20

CRUISE'N IN YOUR SUNSET YEARS

*P*erhaps the mother of all rewards for the do-it-yourself investor is to end up someday with a pocket full of money, substantial cash flow, and no more tenants or toilets to worry about! Finally the end of day-to-day management hassles! Now it's time to start living off the fruits of accumulated wealth. Some investors have a pretty good idea about when they can do this because they've planned it well. Others will eventually make it, even though they're not exactly sure when it will happen. What starts out as a dream will take a little planning to maximize your ultimate rewards.

One of my most prized accomplishments during the rough and tumble years of buying and fixing up houses has been the **carryback notes** I've created along the way from selling my fixed-up properties. My *note receivables* come from the carryback financing I've designed and made available to the buyers who've purchased my properties over the years. Today, these notes provide a substantial monthly income for me regardless of whether I get outta bed in the morning or not. It's a great feeling to know that I'll never have to interview another tenant or approve his rental application in order to reap the benefits from the paper profits I've created. My biggest carryback note to date pays me $6000 per month – the smallest is $427. But, when you start adding them altogether after buying and selling for many years, they add up to a respectable monthly income. Remember, these notes are passive income! That means you receive the payments rain or shine without lifting a finger!

ARRANGING YOUR FINANCIAL AFFAIRS

Living off **note receivable income** – *or as I like to call it*, "pajama money," gives you an incredible feeling of security when retirement finally rolls around! I wouldn't rush this event; however, it seems to get here much quicker than we all expect! When the time finally arrives, hopefully you'll look back as I often do, and thank your lucky stars that someone taught you how to set the stage for **the world's best retirement plan**. For me, it started with an early dream, and today, I'm living proof of how well it works! Friends, I gotta tell ya, it's even better than I ever imagined!

Commonly known as **seller carryback financing**, it's one of the most valuable benefits when you invest in the kind of properties I recommend! In fact, learning about **financial benefits** should be one of your first steps before you ever spend a dime to acquire a property. You must learn to become what I call the **arranger of your financial affairs** beginning with your very next purchase. Buying right will guarantee your "pajama money" when it comes your turn to call it quits! I often refer to this as "womb to tomb" investing, and every investor needs to begin planning each financial step as he goes along.

When I write about this subject, I use terms like *trust deeds*, *promissory notes*, and *beneficiaries* 'cause I live in California! However, mortgages work exactly the same way in non-trust deed states. The beneficiary is the person who receives the payments, *meaning he or she benefits* – and it's those payments coming to me every single month from the sale of my properties that I sometimes refer to as *pajama money*. The reason I call note payments pajama money is because I can jog down to my mailbox once a month in my pajamas to fetch my checks. Nothing could be easier, and nothing in the real estate business is quite so much fun.

A friend of mine, named Sidney, bought houses while he worked for a chemical company. Sidney recently sold his last eight-unit apartment. He retired almost two years ago. His retirement check from the chemical plant is $1900 per month. His carryback notes from investing are $11,500. Sidney will be the first to agree – note payments coming in every month are what allow him to have a lifestyle that many can only dream about. Sidney worked nearly 34 years to earn $1900 per month – but it took him only half that long to **add on $11,500**. The bad news about selling all your properties with carryback financing is that you might not be in a position to pay all cash to buy a new Mercedes, *but the good news is* – it won't matter too much because they'll sell it to you anyway – **exactly the same way you sold your houses**!

CASH SALES DON'T NET HIGHEST PROFITS

If you happen to be a new investor, say you're just starting out, you've probably never thought very much about playing the role of banker someday when it's time to sell your properties. Pay close attention here because I'm about to show you how to make some **very serious profits** you've probably never even heard about! In my opinion, every Mom and Pop investor should learn how to take full advantage of this lucrative opportunity! Obviously, it's one of my favorite strategies, and by the time you finish reading about it – I'm guessing it'll become one of yours too!

There are some who say – you really haven't made a legitimate sale of your property unless you have all your money! They're talkin' about an all cash sale. Obviously, everyone's entitled to their own opinion – but selling for all cash will not come anywhere close to the **financial rewards** of substituting yourself for a banker! That means *financing the property for your buyer*. Folks who recommend all cash sales are always quick to point out that *you lose the value of money over time if you wait to get paid*. They also like to bring up the **missed opportunity argument** – meaning, the dollars you don't have in your hand to immediately re-invest after the sale. To be fair, there's a bit of truth in both these arguments, but as is so often the case, **truth** and **profits** seldom line up on the same side in the real world.

INSTALLMENT SALES FETCH HIGHER PRICES

Selling income properties with **seller financing** and **good terms** opens the door to some powerful profit opportunities that would not be available with all cash sales. One of the more obvious benefits is the fact that you can sell a property for top dollar (**the highest price**). This happens for exactly the same reason that almost anything will sell for more money if the buyer is allowed the **extra time** to pay for it (*as in making monthly payments*).

A *second major reason* is because **seller financing seldom involves an appraiser**, which is always the case with a regular bank mortgage. Even though income properties are generally appraised using the **income stream method of value**, hired bank appraisers are still very conservative. This is especially true for the older properties like I've owned. I have sold properties for thousands of dollars more than what they would have been appraised for by offering my buyers' **easy terms and seller financing**!

Very much like boats, cars, and even the houses we live in, price becomes a whole lot less important if we're allowed to pay the cost over a longer period of time. What's most important to investors – *how much are my monthly payments*? This is pretty much how most people think – and of course, people are mostly who I sell to. One other issue (my personal view) concerning *appraisals* – I do not consider appraisals beneficial to me unless the purpose is for borrowing hard money on my property. **Appraisals for the purpose of selling can be a very restrictive document to have lying around**. Let's say your first sales attempt falls through and you move on to another potential buyer, but hold on a minute – *you now have knowledge about the appraisal* and a duty to disclose whatever you know! Chances are, you'll need to 'fess up" if you're asked about it! I'm certain that *disclosure issues* would likely pop up if the appraisal suddenly shows up after you've accepted a new offer for $100,000 more than what the appraisal says! **Can you see the dorsal fin coming through the waves here?** If you don't, just keep reading 'till you do!

SELLING FOR TOP PRICE AND INTEREST INCOME

When I add value to properties, *I not only increase the rents, but my gross rent multiplier number goes up* as well. **My goal is a two-point increase in the gross rent multiplier.** For example, if I purchase a property for six times gross rents of $20,000 annually or $120,000 – *then after two years of fixing* and gradually increasing my rents by at least 50% ($30,000), my new gross rent multiplier number now moves up to eight, because I've increased the value with additional income. Therefore, 8 x $30,000 equals my new property value of **$240,000.** No formal appraisal would likely be needed because I'm basically selling *a $30,000 annual income stream!* In other words, investors in my town will pay **8 x gross income** to acquire a property that earns **$30,000 annually.**

Let's say I accept an offer for my full asking price of **$240,000.** I usually accept full price offers. *That's a weakness I have!* The sale terms I'm offering are **$40,000 cash down to me** – then I'll carry the balance of **$200,000 for 20 years**, at 7% interest with amortized payments of $1550.60 per month. Some may ask – is 7% interest enough today? **Interest rates are sensitive to the times.** Right now 7% interest is more than three or four times what banks are paying on certificates. I've had higher interest *carrybacks* in the past – but remember, **rates have a lot to do with the current market**. Besides, there's no need to "belly up" to the "hog line" in this business. It's *highly profitable* without gouging your customers.

By accepting my payments over time (240 months), *I'll take in nearly twice the amount of my note's face value* **($372,144).** The interest alone adds up to **$172,000,** or roughly $717 per month for each one of those 240 monthly payments. *I don't know about you,* but earning $717 every month without lifting my little finger works alright for me. *Pajama money,* I call it, and even after you deduct my cost for new pajamas every few years or so, I'm still a long ways ahead. **Don't you agree?**

Interest income is very powerful stuff! It's what makes small buildings grow to big ones! When I was a very small boy, my dad took my sister and me on a trip to San Francisco. While we were downtown walking, he showed us the stately Wells Fargo bank building in the heart of the city. "Just look up there," he said, "That building is 18 stories high." It wasn't too many years later as a young man, I had occasion to visit San Francisco again. By now the Wells Fargo had grown to 36 stories! *How did it grow so high, so fast, you ask?* The answer, my friend, is **interest income**! Right then and there I decided that if interest earnings can add 18 stories to the Wells Fargo Bank building – it can certainly add to my bank account as well!

SELLING REQUIRES SMART PLANNING

New investors, and even some who are not so new, often disagree with my advice about hanging on to good income-producing properties. Once again I'll point out – after doing this stuff for over 50 years, I'm hard pressed to think of anyone who has become a millionaire from simply buying and selling properties. I have several friends who are *on again off again millionaires*, but they always seem to give it all back during tough times. Their lifestyle is something like a yo-yo. The truth is, my friends, **you must keep your assets earning and compounding if you wish to make it to the big leagues**. In short, you must keep your name on the deed as long as you can! Do that and you'll end up a whole lot richer someday – **I'll give ya my word on that**!

With that said, all investors must eventually consider how they wish to live (lifestyle) during their sunset years. In case you're wondering what a "**sunset investor**" looks like – take a quick peek at my books or brochures with my picture on the front. That should give you a pretty good idea! I'm definitely aware of the shadows creeping up around my worn-out straw hat! I'm also aware that when I leave, *my real estate must stay* – thus spending a good share of my equity before the sun finally sets has always been a major part of my overall master plan.

Installment selling is the tax term! When I sell, I'll ask for a small down payment (10-15%) and allow my buyer to pay me the balance of the selling price over a period of time. Other than tax deferred exchanging under revenue code 1031, you'll find **installment sales are the next best strategy for holding off the tax man**. With installment sales, you're allowed to pay taxes as you receive payments from your buyer. With *wrap-around financing*, which is the way you should sell your properties that have existing mortgage debt, you'll benefit even more. With wrap-around financing, you can avoid paying taxes that would be required if the existing mortgages were assumed or *taken over* by your buyer. *They call this debt relief!* If you don't understand what I'm saying here, check it out with your tax advisor. Above all, do this before you finalize any deal!

WRAP-AROUNDS PROVIDE SAFETY AND PROFITS

Wrap-around financing has several other major advantages besides the tax savings! First of all, you, *the seller*, who carries back a promissory note (or mortgage), *will receive just one single payment every month* even when there are several unpaid mortgages on the property at the time you sell. They're called **underlying mortgages** and the unpaid balance of each one will be included or made part of the **new wrap-around mortgage** you *carry back* for your buyer. That's **what wrap-around means**! Whatever debt (notes or mortgages) are owed on the property when you make a sale will all be wrapped inside one single mortgage with one single payment. When you receive your payment each month, you must first send out payments to the underlying mortgages. **Then you can keep what's left for yourself!**

For example, suppose I sell my property for **$400,000**. At the time of sale, I'm making payments of $800 per month on the first mortgage with a balance of $100,000. I also make $600 payments on a second mortgage, with a balance of $60,000. Obviously, my equity is **$240,000** ($400,000 less $160,000 = $240,000). After receiving $50,000 cash down payment – I agree to carry back a **new wrap-around note** (or mortgage) for the balance of ($350,000) with payments to me of $3000 per month. Each month when I receive **my $3000 payment** – *I'll send payments to both underlying mortgages* ($800 and $600), leaving me a balance of **$1600** to keep for myself.

A big safety feature of *wrap-around financing* is that I'm *dead-bang* certain the underlying mortgages will get paid. Why, 'cause I'm the one who will pay them! If my two existing mortgages had been assumed or taken over by the new buyer, I might not know right away if my buyer was making those payments as agreed – especially if I was receiving my payments on time. There are several other ways you can protect yourself, but none better than **controlling all the money** with a wrap-around mortgage. **Better to be payee than stuckee!** Wouldn't you agree?

Earning bonus profits with *wrap-around financing* is another juicy little moneymaker with wrap-around mortgages. Here I'll introduce the term *spread*. No, this has nothing to do with peanut butter and jelly sandwiches. It has to do with the difference between *the mortgage interest paid out* and the *mortgage interest received* when you use wrap-around financing. The difference can substantially increase the profits you'll earn.

In my $400,000 sale above, I agreed to accept $50,000 down and wrap or include the existing mortgages (two) in my new **$350,000** wrap-around mortgage. The payments to me are **$3,000 per month at 8% interest**. On the $100,000 first mortgage, called underlying because it's part of the new wrap-around, the interest rate is 6.5% and on the $60,000 second mortgage, the rate is 7%. **The interest rate differences** between these two underlying mortgages and my new wrap-around mortgage rate of 8% interest is called **the spread!**

With **wrap-around financing**, I'll continue making payments on the first mortgage ($100,000) at 6.5% interest. Thus, my interest payout will be $541.66. However, the amount of interest I'll be earning on the same $100,000, which is part of my $350,000 wrap-around mortgage, is $666.66. **The difference or the spread equals $125, which is pure gravy for me.** The bottom line is, I earn 8%, but I only pay out 6.5% interest on money ($100,000) that doesn't even belong to me. It's not part of my equity, which is really all I had to sell. Spread earnings are sometimes called phantom income. Take it from me, *phantom income* is a whole lot more fun than sitting through the opera with the same name!

Obviously, the spread works the same way with the second mortgage ($60,000). I'll earn 8% interest, but pay out only 7%. In this case, *my bonus profit will be the 1% spread!* Thus, my extra earnings are $50 per month. In this example, my extra earnings are **$175 per month** because I used wrap-around financing.

RETIRING SELLERS MUST BE CONCERNED WITH SAFETY

The number one reason investors like me should be extremely cautious when selling properties with low down payments is because **WE DON'T WANT THE PROPERTY BACK**! Obviously, this could be even more crucial for sellers who retire and decide to travel around the world on their mortgage income. **What's the big problem, you ask?** Suppose you sell your older fixed-up apartment building to someone without a whole lot of landlording experience, *and further,* suppose the buyer informs you that his "hippie tweaker" brother-in-law who lives nearby will manage the property and look after things.

You must always remember that older properties, *more so than newer units,* require the tender loving care of an owner who will keep his eye on his property and perform the necessary upkeep. When I decide to sell and carry back the financing, I always spend considerable time checking out the buyer. I design my carryback note mortgage payments to maximize the buyer's cash flow, (*within reason of course*). **The point is that I want my buyer to succeed**. If he doesn't, he'll likely default, and I'll end up with the whole stinkin' mess back in my lap! You should **always run credit checks** on every buyer you intend to carry financing for! Mostly to see how they pay, and how much consumer debt they have.

SLEEP BETTER WITH ADDITIONAL COLLATERAL

As an added safety precaution, I'll often ask for **additional collateral** with low down payment sales. Many income property buyers already own their own homes, and quite often they'll own other income properties. Suppose I'm negotiating the $400,000 sale above where I accepted the $50,000 down payment. **Under different circumstances** I might just balk at $50,000 down. In fact, I might tell the buyer something like this: Mr. Buyer, I'd really like to have a 25% cash down payment so I feel a little more secure. Since I've already discovered the buyer owns a home worth $200,000 with an existing mortgage of only $100,000, I will probably say something like the following:

Mr. Buyer, I can work with your small down payment of just $50,000. I don't mind being a bit flexible, but here's my real concern – **I need a little more security**. After all, $50,000 is only 12.5% down and I generally like to get at least **25% down**! The reason I want 25% down is because I'm concerned about my safety! In my opinion, $50,000 wouldn't be enough in case I ever had to take the property back! Still, I believe we can make this work. You can easily eliminate my **safety concerns** and it won't cost you one thin dime. The equity in your home can help you out here! I'll draw up a second mortgage on your home ($50,000 limit) as **additional collateral** to secure my $350,000 carryback mortgage. This means I'll have **two properties** as security for my mortgage – the property I'm selling to you, plus your home ($50,000 worth). Should you ever quit paying me, and I'm forced to take my property back, I could also take $50,000 worth of equity in your home as well!

USING WHAT YOU HAVE TO GET WHAT YOU WANT

On the positive side, Mr. Buyer, you're using equity you already own. This will allow you to purchase my property with **only $50,000 down**, just like you've requested, and it won't cost you one extra penny so long as you keep your promise and make your mortgage payments. You're simply using an asset you already own (your home) instead of paying me an additional $50,000 down payment! Using what you already own to help you acquire **more income properties** is an excellent wealth building strategy! Here's what I tell the buyer:

After we close and you begin establishing a good payment record with me, *we'll say 60 months' worth of payments*, I will agree to remove the additional security (your house) from the trust deed or mortgage. It's called a *reconveyance* or release of collateral. After five years' worth of timely payments, I feel that's enough evidence concerning my buyer's ability to pay and successfully operate the property. **Additional collateral**, with my five-year reconveyance provision, will create a win-win proposition for both parties.

IMPORTANT REASONS
TO USE WRAP-AROUNDS

1. Does not usually trigger due-on-sale clause
2. Avoid big tax bill from debt relief
3. Retain the opportunity to buy back debt (underlying mortgages) at a discount sometime in the future
4. Control – make sure all underlying mortgages continue to be paid (you pay them)
5. Enjoy extra profits from interest spread; it's the difference between the interest you earn and the interest paid out on the underlying mortgages
6. Provides flexibility, which allows the seller to customize the monthly payments for the buyer so the numbers will work. In the following example, **as a seller**, I have the flexibility to set payments for any amount above **$1675.00**. This is the amount I must pay out to service debt on the three existing (underlying) mortgages. Any amount above **$1675.00** is my money to keep or spend as I see fit.

The following example shows you how a hypothetical wrap-around transaction works.

EXAMPLE OF HOW WRAP-AROUND
FINANCING WORKS

JAY'S SELLING PRICE	$500,000
CASH DOWN PAYMENT RECEIVED	$ 50,000
SELLER FINACING (NEW WRAP-AROUND)	**$450,000**
MONTHLY PAYMENT: $3301.95 P and I	
($3302 ROUNDED)	
TERM: 30 YEARS AMORTIZED	
RATE: 8% INTEREST	

NEW WRAP-AROUND MORTGAGE TO INCLUDE THE EXISTING MORTGAGES (CALLED UNDERLYING MORTGAGES)

First Mortgage (Balance at Sale) $101,500
Monthly Payments $725 P and I
Rate: 6% Interest
(22 Years Remaining)

Second Mortgage (Balance at Sale) $ 59,300
Monthly Payments $500 P and I
Rate: 6.5% Interest
17 Years Remaining)

Third Mortgage (Balance at Sale) $ 39,200
Monthly Payments $450 P and I
Rate: 7% Interest
(12 Years Remaining)

HERE'S HOW PAYMENTS ARE DISTRIBUTED

JAY HOLDS A MORTGAGE (NOTE)
RECEIVABLE FOR: $450,000
   When the buyer sends Jay his monthly payment of $3302 (rounded)
   Jay must send payments to existing underlying mortgages
   as follows:
EXISTING FIRST MORTGAGE: $101,500 (Balance at Sale)
   Jay sends mortgage holder payment of: $ 725.00
EXISTING SECOND MORTGAGE: $ 59,300 (Balance at Sale)
   Jay sends mortgage holder payment of: $ 500.00
EXISTING THIRD MORTGAGE: $ 39,200 (Balance at Sale)
   Jay sends mortgage holder payment of: $ 450.00
TOTAL PAYMENTS JAY SENDS OUT $1675.00
TOTAL BALANCE JAY GETS TO KEEP   **$1627.00**

On the following page (Figure 20-1), the annual mortgage payment chart shows how annual mortgage payments are received by Jay (Col. 1) and how payments are distributed to the three underlying mortgages (Col's 2, 3 and 4).

Earlier, I told you that cash sales don't always provide the biggest profits, and that allowing the buyer to pay over time can add substantially to your retirement fund. The chart clearly shows the installment sale advantage. Using my **$500,000** sale and wrap-around financing, you'll see the total payback equals **$50,000** cash down payment – plus annual payments of **$863,607**. The total amount received is **$913,607**. It shouldn't take too many sales like this to give you that extra glow to go with your sunset years. **Can ya dig it?**

ANNUAL MORTGAGE PAYMENTS
Act. Payment $3,301.95 Rounded $3,302

	COL. 1	COL. 2	COL. 3	COL. 4	COL. 5	COL. 6
BALANCES	$450,000	$101,500	$59,300	$39,200		JAY'S EQUITY
YEAR	Jay Receives $	Mortgage 1	Mortgage 2	Mortgage 3	Mortgage 4	Jay's Net $
1	3,302	725	500	450	——	1,627
2	39,624	8,700	6,000	6,000	——	19,524
3	39,624	8,700	6,000	6,000	——	19,524
4	39,624	8,700	6,000	6,000	——	19,524
5	39,624	8,700	6,000	6,000	——	19,524
6	39,624	8,700	6,000	6,000	——	19,524
7	39,624	8,700	6,000	6,000	——	19,524
8	39,624	8,700	6,000	6,000		19,524
9	39,624	8,700	6,000	6,000	——	19,524
10	39,624	8,700	6,000	6,000	——	19,524
11	39,624	8,700	6,000	6,000	——	19,524
12	39,624	8,700	6,000	6,000	——	24,477
13	39,624	8,700	6,000	6,000	——	24,924
14	39,624	8,700	6,000	3,500	——	24,924
15	39,624	8,700	6,000	——	——	24,924
16	39,624	8,700	6,000	——	——	24,924
17	39,624	8,700	4,684	——	——	26,240
18	39,624	8,700	——	——	——	30,924
19	39,624	8,700	——	——	——	30,924
20	39,624	8,700	——	——	——	30,924
21	39,624	8,700	——	——	——	30,924
22	39,624	285	——	——	——	39,339
23	39,624	——	——	——	——	39,624
24	39,624	——	——	——	——	39,624
25	39,624	——	——	——	——	39,624
26	39,624	——	——	——	——	39,624
27	39,624	——	——	——	——	39,624
28	39,624	——	——	——	——	39,624
29	39,624	——	——	——	——	39,624
30	39,624	——	——	——	——	39,624
31	36,300	——	——	——	——	36,300
TOTALS	$1,188,698	$175,000	$95,184	$54,897		$863,607

FIGURE 20-1

CLOSING THOUGHTS FROM JAY

Perhaps you're thinkin' to yourself – wow, Jay's Fisherman Strategy sounds great to me! I can't wait to start, but I'm just wondering – what if I don't acquire all six properties like Jay's example; will I still be okay? Would just one or two properties be worth my efforts?

For heaven's sake, yes – just one property like Jay's **Cherry Street houses** (Chapter 2) will earn you more money than most wage earners make during their entire working lives. As you may recall, Jay's annual earnings for the time he operated the property and then financed the sale, averaged more than **$53,000**. Granted, we're talkin' gross income, but do the math! Even if you only got to keep half of $4400 per month for a long-long time, would that work? Would that be a decent return on your $20,000 down payment? **Think about that for a moment!**

Lots of folks don't earn that much money from Social Security, so in terms of planning for your future, just one **Cherry Street property** could well become your guaranteed retirement plan! Don't forget, after Jay sold out and no longer had anything to do with managing the property or the tenants – the income from his **carryback financing** was **$3250** every single month for 20 years. I can't speak for other property owners, but receiving **$780,000** in financing fees works quite well for me! Besides, all I had to do was boogie down to the mailbox every month in my pajamas to pick up my check!

DREAM A LITTLE BIGGER

I want you to close your eyes and dream with me for a minute! Let's assume you fall headlong in love with **Jay's six-colony investment model** and you begin to wonder —- Just how far can I go with this? How much money could I make?

To begin with, the sky's your only limit! Even though Jay's six-property model with 40 rental units has a beginning and end, the truth is, **there is no limit**! Jay has owned and operated many more than 40 units during his 50 year career – yet 40 units is enough to make you a millionaire several times over. Also, 40 units is a very reasonable goal! I think we can all agree – six properties with 40 units is also very achievable!

Okay, since we're only dreaming here – let's pretend you've owned and operated Jay's six colony properties with 40 rentals for the past several years! **How successful would you be today financially?**

To start with, you'd have a great income! By simply using Jay's modest hometown rents of $695 per unit – your gross income would be almost **$28,000** per month! **Roughly one-third, or $9300, would be yours to keep.** By the way, very few people in my town earn that much, so you'd be very popular and on all the local mailing lists. Obviously, you would have created yourself a **"full-time"** career along the way!

RENTS GO UP WITH INFLATION

A loaf of bread, pork 'n beans, and toilet paper all go up with the times – **so will your rents**! Let's assume your rents go up to $825 per month! Who gets to keep the extra money? The answer, my friend, is you do – **it's yours to keep**! You'll immediately start hearing from all your long-lost relatives. They'll begin showing up outta nowhere! I don't know how they do it, but they seem to smell **your money** from miles away!

Finally, the time comes to cash in your chips. **What happens now?** If you've been following my teachings, you'll carefully begin selling off properties to the next generation of fishermen. The time has now come to let them start baitin' the hook for you. You've already caught your limit for a lifetime! I've specifically written Chapter 20 to show you how your continuing earnings will allow you to enjoy "full course" fish dinners for the rest of your days on the planet! And, you'll never need to go near your tenants again – *unless of course, you miss 'em!*

FINALLY YOUR DREAMS COME TRUE

If you're like me, you'll be a whole lot richer than you ever dreamed – you can take my word on that! Let's say you sell six colony properties and provide the financing just like Jay's plan! **Is there any way of knowing how rich you might be?** Not exactly, but we can look back to my **Cherry Street Property** for some guidance (Chapter 2). You may recall; I owned the property for 26 years, and the value increased nearly four and a half times. That's just a smidgen over $19,000 per year. When I bought the property, I could have never guessed; but an up and down economy always favors real estate. It's hard to look forward and imagine prices going up so much – yet, looking back at history, they always do!

For the sake of comparing, let's use **Cherry Street** to calculate just how rich you might end up. Today, Cherry Street properties will cost a skilled buyer in my town between $350,000 and $400,000. Even if we estimate values will be three times higher when you decide to sell and retire – that would add up to **six to seven million dollars**!

I'll assume you'll follow my advice and sell for about 10% down and carry back at least **$5,000,000** or so in private mortgages! Financing at **6% interest only** on the unpaid mortgage debt will allow you to live quite happily with a monthly income of **$25,000**. Unlike rents, your mortgage payments won't go up! But by now I'm assuming, you'll be old and wrinkled like me, and you'll easily adjust to **$25,000 per month**! Regarding the principal when it finally comes due! Let the kids have it – they'll know exactly what to do with it – **agreed**!

Allow me to conclude by presenting you with a "snap shot," *or my personal view*, about what you might expect if you decide to follow my fisherman strategies. On the following page you'll find what I call **"The Three Stages of Investing."** These are the stages every investor must pass through on his way to the Promise Land. As you read about these various stages, keep in mind you may well be reading about your own future! For me, however, these three stages have been part of my history. It's been a very rewarding career I might add! In closing, **I'm wishing the same fishin' career for you**! Happy fishing!

THE THREE STAGES OF INVESTING

Stage One: learning how to buy the right kind of properties that produce cash flow the quickest. This will be your most challenging and exciting learning period. You should expect to attend as many training seminars as needed and purchase educational products to develop your investment skills. This is also the stage where you make your mistakes and work out the bugs as you fine-tune your craft. Money will always be *tight* – and there is no cure till you get it *right*.

Stage Two: should find you a much more sophisticated "deal maker." It's also the weeding out and *trading up* stage. Dump poor performers, trade for cash flow and higher potential properties. By now your skills should be good enough to attract passive investors with cash if you wish. With equity financing available from an angel, the sky's the limit; *bigger deals – more profits* – life is good!

Stage Three: reaping the harvest. By now you're living well – and "cashing out" will put you on **Easy Street**. Sell properties on good terms, take back installment notes for more monthly income, and from here on out, you can pretty much do as you please, so long as you manage your portfolio well.

APPENDIXES

A. GROSS RENT MULTIPLIER CHART (JAY'S AREA)

B. VILLA APARTMENT DIAGRAM (SKETCH)

C. INCOME PROPERTY ANALYSIS FORM
   INSTRUCTIONS FOR USE - ANALYSIS FORM

D. PROPERTY INSPECTION SHEET (CHECKLIST)

E. FIVE (5) INVESTMENT LOCATIONS

F. JAY'S CO-OWNERSHIP AGREEMENT

G. JAY'S CHRISTMAS LETTER

H. RESOURCES FOR PROPERTY INVESTORS
   BOOK, NEWSLETTERS AND EDUCATIONAL
   SEMINARS

GRM CHART

(Gross Rent Multiplier)

JAY'S INVESTMENT AREA

GRM	Description	Rent	6 Units	Annual	Value
13x	Snob Hill	$900	$5,400	$64,800	$842,400
12x	Premo	$875	$5,250	$63,000	$756,000
11x	Deluxe	$825	$4,950	$59,400	$653,400
10x	Nicer	$795	$4,770	$57,240	$572,400
9x	Average	$725	$4,350	$52,200	$469,800
8x	Economy	$635	$3,810	$45,720	$365,760
7x	Butt Ugly	$540	$3,240	$38,880	$272,160
6x	Pigstye	$425	$2,550	$30,600	$183,600

MULTIPLE

**TYPICAL UNITS — HOUSES/DUPLEXES
2 BR — 1 BATH — 750 SQ. FT. (APPROX.)**

NOTE: My investment goal is to purchase a butt-ugly property for 7 X Gross ‒ or approximately $272,000 Improve property to average condition (9 X Gross) New Value ‒ $469,800 new rents $725 per unit.

TO MAIN STREET ---->

43RD AVENUE

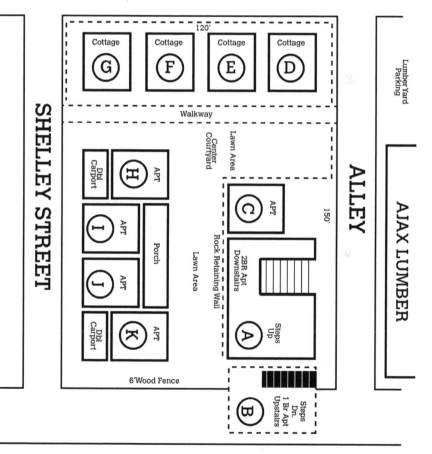

VIOLA APARTMENTS
11 UNITS

INCOME PROPERTY ANALYSIS FORM

Property Name___**EASY STREET**_____ Date _____

LINE NO.	INCOME DATA (MONTHLY)	PER MONTH	
1	Total Gross Income (Present)	$ 3610	100%
2	Vacancy Allowance Min. 5% LN-1 Attach copy of 1040 Schedule E or provide past 12 months income statement for verification	$ 180	05
3	Uncollectable or Credit Losses (rents due but not collected)	$ 180	05
4	GROSS OPERATING INCOME	$ 3250	

EXPENSE DATA (MONTHLY)

5	Taxes, Real Property	$ 315	08
6	Insurance	$ 250	06
7	Management, Allow Min. 05%	$ 360	10
8	Maintenance	$ 360	10
9	Repairs	$ 180	05
10	Utilities Paid by Owner (Monthly)	$ 350	09

} 48%

Elec	$ _____
Water	$ 240
Sewer	$ _____
Gas	$ _____
Garbage	$ 110
Cable TV	$ _____
Totals =	($ 350)

11	Total Expenses	$ 1815	48%
12	NET OPERATING INCOME (LN 4 - LN 11)	$ 1435	

Existing Mortgage Debt	(Monthly)	Due Mo/Yr
1st Bal Due 315000 Payments $ 1400		20 Years Ask For
2nd Bal Due _____ Payments $ _____		_____
3rd Bal Due _____ Payments $ _____		_____
4th Bal Due _____ Payments $ _____		_____
5th Bal Due _____ Payments $ _____		_____

13	Totals _____ (13A) $ _____		
14	MONTHLY CASH FLOW AVAILABLE (LN - 12 - 13A) (Pos or Neg)	35	

NOTE: Line 14 shows available funds to service new mortgage debt from operation of property.

REMARKS: All lines must be completed for proper analysis. Enter the actual amount on each line or 0.

INSTRUCTIONS
(Income Property Analysis Form)

LINE 1   TOTAL GROSS INCOME – All Rents available this number assumes all units are rented.

LINE 2   VACANCY ALLOWANCE – All multiple unit properties will have vacancies over any period of time. I allow a minimum of 05% - sometimes 10% for rundown properties with existing vacancies.

LINE 3   CREDIT LOSSES – Tenants who skip out owing rents, which become uncollectable – allow 05%.

LINE 4   GROSS OPERATING INCOME – This is the amount left after vacancy allowance and credit losses are deducted – what's left to operate the property.

MONTHLY OPERATING EXPENSES

LINE 5   REAL ESTATE TAXES – aka (advalorem taxes) for this line, use the new tax amount at close of escrow. For example; in California the new tax value after sale will be approximately 1.1% of the selling price. The new monthly tax would be figured as follows: $300,000 sale x 1.1% = $3300. $3300 divided by 12 months = $275 (amount on Line 5).

LINE 6   INSURANCE – Fire and liability on property. This means fire insurance for value after purchase. – also for liability $ amount that's appropriate. **Caution:** Often a long time owner will have a low cost policy (minimum liability coverage) and fire insurance so low it would not cover today's fire lost.

LINE 7   MANAGEMENT – I charge 10% management fee when managing for others. This line is very controversial when buying small multiple unit properties from Mom & Pop operators. They argue; we manage ourselves, there is no additional cost! This argument doesn't fly when I ask them to continue managing for me, for the same amount, after I become the owner. I will often us 05% on this line to make the deal more acceptable to the sellers – I compromise.

LINE 8   MAINTENANCE – Use 10% on this line. There is no way to do maintenance for less, especially with older rundown properties. Maintenance is an on-going expense to keep the property competitive in the rental marketplace.

LINE 9   REPAIRS – I use 05% for this line! Repairs are expenses for things that break or quit working. When an older roof leaks, immediate repairs are needed. Broken windows are not maintenance – they are repairs. The cooling stops working, repairs are needed, etc.

LINE 10   UTILITIES PAID BY THE OWNER – Check these expenses very closely! Most multiple listing sheets furnished by agents are not accurate. Sellers are also prone to minimize these costs. Most utility companies will provide annual usage data with the seller's permission. The yearly summary will give you the average costs.

LINE 11   TOTAL EXPENSES – on this line. Obviously the age and condition of the property will make these expenses somewhat variable, however; I've found the following percentages are a good guideline for estimating.

Very Good condition (new)   33-40%

Average Condition (older)   36-45%

Below Average (fixer-uppers)   45-55%

Remember: Expenses are not capital items, such as new roofs, new systems, etc. Expenses are those costs required to keep the property "up & running" in order to continue earning competitive rents.

LINE 12   NET OPERATING INCOME – What's left over when all expenses are paid. This is all the money left for debt service (mortgage payments) and the owners draw, otherwise known as **CASH FLOW.**

LINE 13   TOTAL OF EXISTING MORTGAGE DEBT – and monthly payments. Fill in all mortgage payment amounts and when they are due or paid in full.

LINE 14   MONTHLY CASH FLOW AVAILABLE – This line can be a positive amount – *or negative.* Note: This line includes what's left after paying existing mortgage debt assumed or taken over "subject to" at time of purchase. Stated another way – this amount is all the property can afford to pay the seller for any new mortgage debt he carries back as part of the selling price, commonly known as seller carry back financing.

PROPERTY INSPECTION SHEET

1. Estimate overall condition of property (10 is high)   1 to 10 _____

2. Based on surrounding neighborhood, rate location   1 to 10 _____

3. Full concrete foundations, all living, houses/apts.   Yes/No _____

4. Roofs – Are they flat or pitched, or both   Yes/No _____

5. Type of siding on building, <u>wood</u> or <u>stucco</u> or <u>brick</u>   _____

6. Do houses/apts. have individual electric service meters   Yes/No _____

7. Rate or estimate condition of painting <u>overall</u>   1 to 10 _____

8. Do houses/apts. have individual gas meters   Yes/No _____

9. Find out; determine if units have city/county sewers   Yes/No _____

10. Find out; determine if units served by city water service   Yes/No _____

11. Are houses/apts. served by private septic system   Yes/No _____

12. Are houses/apts. served by private water well   Yes/No _____

13. How many water meters are serving property   (how many) ____

14. Are all units being lived in at this time   Yes/No _____

15. Are any units classified as non-livable   (how many) ____

16. What is roof material - comp shingles(cs), wood(w), metal(m) _____

17. Does property appear to have adequate parking   Yes/No _____

18. Do units – or most units have individual yard space   Yes/No _____

19. Do all units appear to have renters at this time   Yes/No _____

20. Does property sit low or have drainage problems   Yes/No _____

21. Look at property – separation from neighborhood ok   Yes/No _____

22. Rate property overall for rundown and/or trashy   1 to 10 _____

23. Your personal opinion – is neighborhood a safe area   1 to 10 _____

24. Would you personally be ok working on/around prop.   Yes/No _____

5 Investment Locations

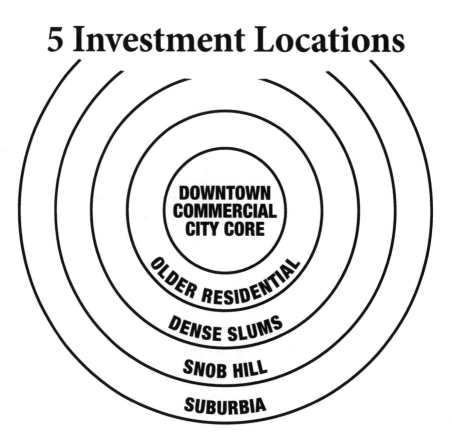

DOWNTOWN COMMERCIAL CITY CORE

OLDER RESIDENTIAL

DENSE SLUMS

SNOB HILL

SUBURBIA

SNOB HILL
This is where the wealthy folks live

DOWNTOWN – COMMERCIAL
Mostly Businesses — Acres of Concrete Blacktop

OLDER RESIDENTIAL
Surrounding Downtown Area
Likely 50 Years or More Older

DENSE SLUMS
Downtown or Pocket Areas
Often Older Houses — Duplexes

SUBURBIA
Sprawling Subdivisions — Tract
Houses. Mostly Owner Occupied

Most duplexes and multi unit properties recommended in this book
can be found in almost any sizable town or city in 2 locations.
DOWNTOWN COMMERCIAL & OLDER RESIDENTIAL

CO-OWNERSHIP AGREEMENT
1234 EASY STREET
UGLYVILLE, CA 96001

THIS AGREEMENT is made effective as of the 23rd of March, 1997 between Jay P. Decima dba Fixer Jay and Ivan M. Smith dba, Investor Ivan.

1. **Transaction**: Investor Ivan (Ivan) and Fixer Jay (Jay) will join together as co-owners for the purpose of owning and operating that certain real estate located at 1234 Easy Street, Uglyville, CA. herein called (the "Property") for the mutual benefit and profit of each. Each party agrees to perform fully under this Agreement for the success of both parties herein.

2. **Acquisition of Property**: Ivan and Jay have purchased the Property for a purchase price of Three Hundred Fifty Thousand Dollars ($350,000) pursuant to Escrow Instructions dated February 25, 1997 to North State Title, a copy of which is attached hereto as Exhibit "A". The cash down payment of Fifty Thousand Dollars ($50,000) was paid equally.

3. **Cash Distributions from Rental**: All excess cash derived from rental of the Property, after payment of all expenses and debt service, shall be divided fifty percent (50%) to Ivan and fifty percent (50%) to Jay.

4. **Cash Proceeds From Sale or Refinancing of the Property**: Net cash proceeds derived from sale or refinancing of the Property shall be shared as follows: First each party shall receive back all of his capital invested in the Property by way of initial down payment, fix-up expenditures and operating expenses made pursuant to paragraphs 2, 11 and 12 hereof. Thereafter, all remaining proceeds derived from sale or refinancing shall be shared fifty percent (50%) Ivan and fifty (50%) Jay.

5. **Management**: All decisions regarding the management of the Property shall be made upon the joint approval of both Ivan and Jay; provided, however, it is agreed that Jay will have primary responsibility for the day-to-day management operations, such as rent-ups, property maintenance, repairs, cleaning and the like in order to conduct an efficient rental business. Jay shall receive a management fee of ten (10%) of the gross rents collected from the Property for management of the Property and shall be reimbursed for his actual out-of-pocket costs and expenses incurred in connection with such management.

6. **Books & Records**: All books and records will be kept at the office of Jay. A statement of operations will be provided to Ivan on a monthly basis. This statement will be prepared by Jay as part of his management duties.

7. **Bank Accounts**: Jay shall maintain a commercial checking account at North Valley Bank, 2930 Bechelli Lane, Redding, California or at such other banking institution that shall be approved by Ivan, for the purpose for operating the Property.

8. **Indemnification**: Each party shall indemnify and hold harmless the other party and the Property from and against all separate debts, claims, and demands of said party.

9. **Termination**: This Agreement shall terminate upon sale of the Property or by mutual consent of Ivan and Jay. Ivan shall have the sole right to determine when the Property is to be sold; provided, however, that Ivan shall first offer Jay the right to purchase the Property for the same amount and upon the same terms and conditions as Ivan is willing to sell the Property pursuant to a bona fide offer received from any third party. Jay shall consummate the transaction within ninety (90) days after exercise of his right of first refusal.

10. **Death of Parties**: Upon the death of Ivan, Jay shall have the right to either purchase Ivan's interest in the property in the manner described in Paragraph 9 hereof based upon a bona fide offer received by Ivan's estate or, in the absence of such an offer, Jay shall have the right to cause the Property to be sold and the proceeds divided in accordance with Paragraph 4 of this Agreement. In the event liquidation is elected, Jay shall proceed with reasonable diligence to liquidate the Property within six (6) months after Ivan's death.

11. **Initial Fix-up Expenditures**: Initial fix-up funds for rehabilitation of the Property will be contributed equally. All work will be performed by employees of Jay, ONE STOP HOME RENTAL COMPANY.

12. **Operating Funds**: All expenses, improvements, taxes, insurance, maintenance and other operating expenses deemed necessary for the operation of the Property shall be paid first from rental income derived from the Property and thereafter from additional funds to be contributed equally.

13. **Business Address**: The official management office for the Property will be ONE STOP HOME RENTAL COMPANY, located at 2551 Park Marina Drive, Redding. California 96001 . Mailing address is c/o JMK Traders, P.O. Box 493039, Redding, California 96049-3039.

14. **No Partnership or Joint Venture**: The relationship between Ivan and Jay under this Agreement shall be solely that of co-owners of real estate and under no circumstance shall said relationship constitute a partnership or joint venture.

IN WITNESS WHEREOF, the Parties have executed this Agreement as of the day and year first above written.

By _____   By _____
                    Investor Ivan   Investor Jay

Location:_____ Date: _____

"JAY'S CHRISTMAS LETTER"

Dear Mortgage Holder:

My, how time flies! Only six more weeks till **Christmas again!** As you know, I've been sending you monthly payments since I bought the property on Easy Street over two years ago. Today, I just received word that I'll be getting a substantial cash distribution from my late Aunt Lucy's estate. It's not quite as much as the balance I owe you $227,571 as of now, however; I'm writing to everyone I send monthly mortgage payments to in order to find out who might need cash right now! According to the terms of our mortgage note, we still have about 15 more years of payments till it's finally paid off.

In the past, several folks I send mortgage payments to have asked me if I could pay them cash instead of monthly payments. Naturally, they are willing to reduce the amount I owe them in exchange for cash now! Since my income is mostly from rents, I seldom have enough cash at one time to take advantage of their very generous offers. Still, I do appreciate them asking and I will certainly pay them cash when I have it.

I should be able to have my money **before Christmas**, which is always extra special, but certainly no later than January 1st, I'm told. If you have a need for cash before Christmas or perhaps you need money for your son Dave's college fees this coming spring, now's the time to let me know while I still have the money. Also, if you could give me some idea about how much discount you would give me, I'd appreciate it very much.

Two years ago when I sold my apartment building, one of my mortgage holders is still raving about the 12 day cruise she took her whole family on. Naturally, I sent her the money from my sale – still, she gave me a very good discount! It was the best Christmas we both had that year. At any rate, I've got the money if you need it!

If you wish to find out the value of your mortgage, you can visit almost any professional note buyer. Most are listed in the yellow pages. They will calculate the value for you free of charge. I assure you that I will nearly always be willing to pay you more than what the pros will give you. Also, I never charge anything extra for handling all the paperwork and we always use a professional title company to keep the money safe till we close escrow! Please call me if you're interested, (500) 123-4567.

Yours Truly

FAIR TRADER JAY

RESOURCES FOR
REAL ESTATE INVESTORS

BOOKS

Brangham, Suzanne, "Housewise", (Clarkson Potter)
Butler, Mike, "Landlording on Auto-Pilot", John Wiley and Sons, Inc.
DeCima, Jay P., "Investing In Fixer-Uppers", (McGraw Hill)
DeCima, Jay P., "Smart Small Profit Big In Real Estate", (McGraw Hill)
DeCima, Jay P., "Investing In Gold Mine Houses", (McGraw Hill)
Kroc, Ray, "Grinding It Out, The Making of McDonald's", (St. Martin Press)
Nickerson, William, "How I Turned $1000 into Five Million in Real Estate", (Simon and Schuster)
Reed, John T., "Aggressive Tax Avoidance for Real Estate Investors", (Reed Publishing)
Robinson, Leigh, "Landlording: A Handy Manual for Scrupulous Landlords", (Express Publishing)
Schaub, John W., "Building Wealth One House at A Time", (McGraw Hill)

NEWSLETTERS   FREE COPY BY WRITTEN REQUEST

Trade Secrets Newsletter (monthly)
Jay P. DeCima
KJay Publishing
P.O. Box 491779, Ste. D
Redding CA 96049-1779
1-800-722-2550

Strategies and Solutions (6 issues annually)
John Schaub
2677 S. Tamiami Trail, Suite 4
Sarasota, FL 34239
1-800-237-9222

SEMINARS & WORKSHOPS

Jay P. Decima	Real Estate Investor's Training Seminar
1-800-722-2559	Managing Tenants & Toilets
www.fixerjay.com	One-On-One Counseling
	2 days private training
Peter Fortunato	Acquisition Techniques
1-727-397-1906	
www.peterfortunato.com	
John Schaub	Making it Big On Little Deals
1-800-237-9222	
www.johnschaub.com	

INDEX

ABOUT THE AUTHOR

"Fixer Jay" DeCima is a seasoned real estate investor-landlord with over 50 years' experience and 200 rental houses to show for his effort. Jay is also a successful career-changer having worked more than 20 years for the telephone company.

Thirty years ago, Jay began teaching others his high profit *fixing and adding value techniques*. Jay's popular real estate Investor Training Seminars are taught each year in Sacramento, California, in addition to his Landlording Seminar, Managing Tenants and Toilets. Jay is widely regarded as the undisputed king of fixer-uppers on the national teaching circuit!

TRADE SECRETS, Jay's monthly **how-to newsletter**, is the only national newsletter written specifically for the do-it-yourself investors, landlords and career-changers. Jay writes about practical techniques and strategies with special emphasis on creating a lifelong income, financial independence and a worry-free retirement.

Write for a free copy to: Fixer Jay, KJAY Co., Box 491779, Ste. D, Redding, CA 96049. Valuable investment tips can be found on Jay's weekly (Monday morning) blog, "MOM & POP MILLIONAIRE". **www.fixerjay.com**

THE NEXT STEP – LET'S "TURBO CHARGE" YOUR EDUCATION

I will assume, by the time you've finished reading this book – you're rarin' to get started or at least "fine tune" your investing strategy a bit. If you're like most folks who contact me, you're probably wondering where or how you can attend my next live training seminar to learn more details about starting out now and finding the most profitable kind of properties.

Readers of "FISHERMAN" are in for a special treat to speed up their education. For the first time in more than 30 years of teaching students about my high profit techniques, I have totally revised and upgraded my 3 **day training manual**. The newly revised course is even bigger (564 pages) and now comes with 10 new, 60 minute studio recorded CD's. This revision converts the entire training manual and 3 day seminar into an easy to follow, step-by-step home study course. Best of all, students can now save a bucket full of money and here's why! Besides the basic seminar fee ($995), former students often had to pay an additional $1500-$2000 for hotels, meals and pricy airline tickets. <u>Now you can learn at home using the same training course for just a fraction of the cost.</u>

Besides getting older with fewer seminars in the picture, it became clear to both Jay and his helpers, the best way to offer **financial freedom** to a whole new generation of serious minded investors was to make Jay's training available when and where students need it! Real estate investing, Jay's way, never goes stale, it never goes out of date and it's truly one of the last ways for average working folks to start from scratch and become **financially independent**. I'm assuming of course, you're willing to work hard and keep learning as you go. I'm only guessing, but if you've read my book from start to finish and you like my easy to follow investment strategies, this could well be the biggest opportunity of your lifetime! I've helped create many successful investors with some millionaires sprinkled in the mix – and if you're ready to go right now, I'll help you do the same.

On the following pages you'll find the order form to purchase my seminar training manual I've recently converted for home study use. I'll guarantee, with what you already know, this course will give you enough detailed "how to" knowledge to get you started quickly. When you purchase my home study training course within 30 days after you acquired my book (send copy of book receipt), I'll send you my monthly newsletter, TRADE SECRETS, **ABSOLUTELY FREE** for one year (12 issues).

Also, assuming you like my book and you purchase my training course, I want to make sure you stay on target. Send me a hand written testimonial (25 words or less) about what you thought of my "Fisherman" book! If you'll do that, I'll give you absolutely free, **one full hour** (just you and me) of telephone mentoring or personal counseling, at your convenience any time after I receive your testimonial. Kathy will send you my personal telephone mentoring phone number. Mail your testimonial to Fixer Jay, P.O. Box 491779, Redding, CA 96049-1779, attention Kathy. **Together, we can start building you a more prosperous future.**

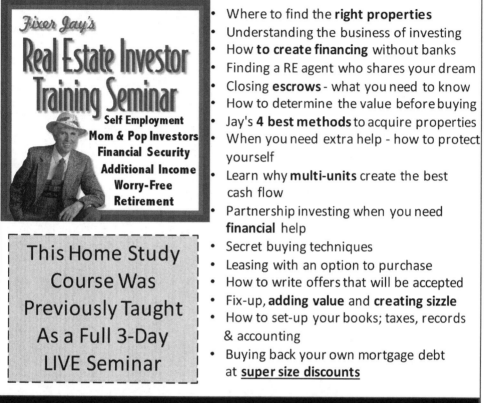

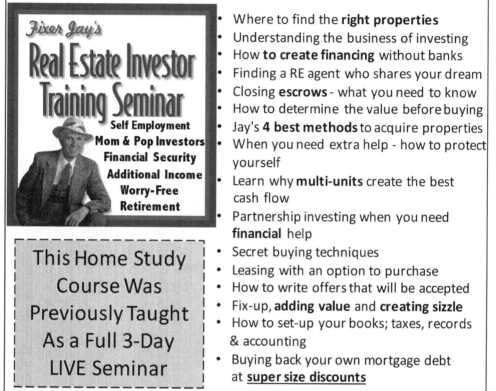

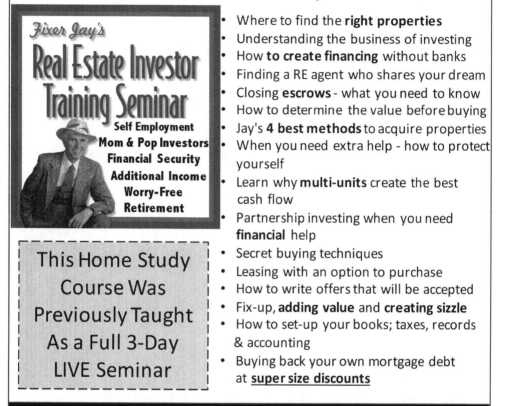

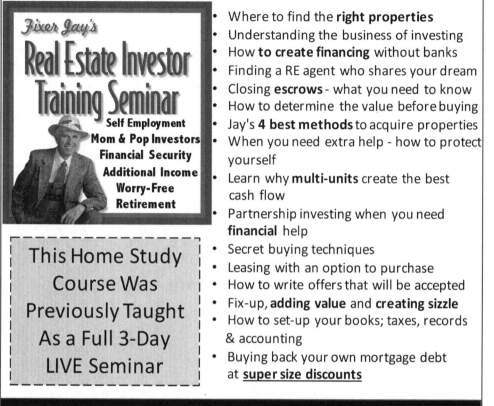